Ernst Hirsch Ballin · Emina Ćerimović ·
Huub Dijstelbloem · Mathieu Segers

European Variations as a Key to Cooperation

Ernst Hirsch Ballin
Tilburg University
Tilburg, Noord-Brabant
The Netherlands

Emina Ćerimović
Netherlands Scientific Council
for Government Policy
The Hague, The Netherlands

Huub Dijstelbloem
Netherlands Scientific Council
for Government Policy
The Hague, The Netherlands

Mathieu Segers
Netherlands Scientific Council
for Government Policy
The Hague, The Netherlands

https://doi.org/10.1007/978-3-030-32893-1

Preface

This book is a translation and adaption of the Dutch report 'Europese variaties', published by the Netherlands Scientific Council for Government Policy (WRR) and presented to the Dutch government in 2018.[1] In this study, the WRR advises the Dutch government to readdress the fundamental question of uniformity and diversity in the Union. The government gave its formal response in a Memorandum to Parliament, in which it embraced the perspective of variation. More information is available on the WRR website: www.wrr.nl/en.

This publication was written by Ernst Hirsch Ballin, Emina Ćerimović, Huub Dijstelbloem and Mathieu Segers. Together they formed a project group, chaired by member of the Council Ernst Hirsch Ballin and coordinated by Huub Dijstelbloem. Previous members of the project included André Knottnerus, Henk Griffioen and Eva Hendricks. The group was assisted by interns Roel van Oosten and Neha Bagga.

Prof. Dr. Linda Senden, Dr. Ton van den Brink and Prof. Dr. Sybe de Vries of Utrecht University deserve special mentioning as they conducted the analysis of the Internal Market on which Chap. 6 is based.

The book is the product of an extensive process of research, consultation and analysis. In addition to studying the academic literature, we conducted numerous interviews with experts, policy makers and stakeholders. We are very grateful for their time and effort. Their names are listed at the end of the book. Special thanks go to the experts who were prepared to read and comment at length on an earlier

[1]The original Dutch publication (2018) has been adapted for an international audience, but not updated.

version of this book: Ir. Jeroen Dijsselbloem (former Minister of Finance and Chairman of the Eurogroup), Prof. Dr. Ben Smulders (European Commission and Free University of Brussels), Dr. Mendeltje van Keulen (Lector Haagse Hogeschool) and Prof. Dr. Jan Rood (Clingendael and Leiden University).

Tilburg, The Netherlands — Ernst Hirsch Ballin
The Hague, The Netherlands — Emina Ćerimović
The Hague, The Netherlands — Huub Dijstelbloem
The Hague, The Netherlands — Mathieu Segers

This Is What We Have Agreed In Europe

Politicians and journalists often use these seemingly transparent words to refer to the legislation and policy of the European Union, but their precise meaning is somewhat obscure. In many cases, they refer to the outcome of rather complex decision-making processes, unfamiliar to many of us.

Still, we can begin our brief explanation of how the EU operates by observing that what matters, in the end, is what we *have* agreed in Europe: the agreements laid down in the Treaty on European Union (TEU), based on the Maastricht Treaty of 1992, and the agreements laid down in the Treaty on the Functioning of the European Union (TFEU), based on the Treaty establishing the European Economic Community, concluded in Rome in 1957 by six Member States (including the Netherlands). These Treaties are indeed agreements, binding under international law, concluded by the Member States and ratified by their individual parliaments. Beyond these two Treaties, the third foundation of the European Union is the Charter of Fundamental Rights, which enshrines certain long-standing basic civil rights. Under Article 6 TEU, the Charter has had the same legal status as the Treaties since 2009, but the method by which it was drafted in 2000 was entirely different: the national parliaments were directly involved and it was solemnly proclaimed at the end of that year.

In essence, the role of the European Union is to apply this trio, i.e. the two Treaties and the Charter. In their entirety, they underpin the rights and obligations of the Member States, citizens and their enterprises and other organisations. The 'principle of conferral' (Article 5 TEU) is essential in this system. What this means is that the EU's institutions may act only within the limits of the competences conferred on them by the Member States in the Treaties. This differs fundamentally from a state, which can, after all, decide on its own authority to address a new subject of legislation or governance.

The much-discussed expansion in the scope of the EU regulation is the result of two processes: the process of amending the Treaties, in which the Member States have added new subjects; and the process of working with policy objectives that have already been adopted, leading to the realisation that additional competences are needed. The 'flexibility clause' (Article 352 TFEU, based on Article 235 of the

1957 Treaty) allows additional competences to be granted to the Union upon a unanimous decision of the Council of the European Union (sometimes referred to simply as the Council)—in other words, only if all the Member States agree—concerning a proposal submitted to it by the European Commission after consulting the European Parliament. This provision cannot be used as a basis for the approximation of laws between the Member States.

The European Union's competences are divided into exclusive competences, competences shared with the Member States, and supporting, complementary and coordinating competences. The Treaties stipulate which competences apply in many specific tasks and procedures. The exercise of non-exclusive competences is subject to the principle of 'subsidiarity'. This means that the Union may act only in so far as the Member States are unable to attain a certain objective at the national, regional or local level. All competences are also subject to the principle of 'proportionality', which means that the Union may not take action beyond what is necessary to achieve the objectives of the Treaties. The national parliaments are involved in scrutinising adherence to these principles, with detailed substantiation being required.[2]

Since the establishment of the European Union, its main socio-economic objective has been to operate an internal market permitting the free movement of goods, capital, services and persons, to ensure equal rights for men and women, to guarantee adequate social protection, to combat social exclusion and discrimination and to protect consumers. These were joined in the final decade of the twentieth century by the demands of sustainable development, along with new main objectives, in particular regarding the 'area of freedom, security and justice' and the Common Foreign and Security Policy.

The most important part of the European Union's work is its legislation, which takes precedence over national legislation. Among other things, its laws set uniform requirements for products that may be freely traded in the internal market. If these requirements were not harmonised, the internal market would not be able to function. Other European Union legislation concerns environmental requirements, asylum procedures and mutual recognition of judicial and administrative measures in the Member States.

European legislation consists of regulations, directives and—as in the case of national legislation—delegated and implementing acts. Regulations are European

[2]See Article 5, Protocol No 2 to the Lisbon Treaty: 'Draft legislative acts shall be justified with regard to the principles of subsidiarity and proportionality. Any draft legislative act should contain a detailed statement making it possible to appraise compliance with the principles of subsidiarity and proportionality. This statement should contain some assessment of the proposal's financial impact and, in the case of a directive, of its implications for the rules to be put in place by Member States, including, where necessary, the regional legislation. The reasons for concluding that a Union objective can be better achieved at Union level shall be substantiated by qualitative and, wherever possible, quantitative indicators. Draft legislative acts shall take account of the need for any burden, whether financial or administrative, falling upon the Union, national governments, regional or local authorities, economic operators and citizens, to be minimised and commensurate with the objective to be achieved'.

laws that are directly enforceable throughout the Union; all individuals and legal persons, including enterprises, are bound by them and can invoke them, even against their own public authorities. Directives, on the other hand, are European laws that must be transposed into national laws to be binding on individuals. When we say that we have 'agreed' something in Europe, we are often referring to EU regulations and directives. However, these laws do not constitute actual 'agreements' that can be revoked, although all EU laws are based on agreements, i.e. the Treaties.

Unlike a state, the European Union is not responsible for implementing its own legislation in most policy domains; implementation is largely the task of bodies and organisations run by the Member States, with the important exceptions of competition policy, agricultural and other subsidies, the European Central Bank and, increasingly, the surveillance of external borders.

Any initiative to introduce new legislation or to amend existing legislation must be taken by the European Commission. As noted above, such initiatives may only concern matters which, according to the Treaties, fall within the competence of the Union. From the outset, the Commission was intended to be the driving force behind the process of European integration, but it can only do so to the extent permitted by the Treaties (over which the Member States reign supreme). Although it initiates European legislation and is involved in the legislative process (regulated by Article 294 TFEU), the Commission does not control the outcome of that process. That is because, with a few exceptions, the adoption of regulations and directives is the responsibility of the European Parliament and the European Council (Scheme 1).

The legislative process aims to achieve legislative convergence, harmonisation or even uniformity under the guidance of the Commission but with the direct involvement of the Member States, both in prior consultation and through the intermediary of the Council. The aim is to create a single market in the European Union as a whole without distortionary differences in legislation and policies. New Member States are expected to adopt these attainments of European economic integration, the *acquis communautaire*, in their entirety.

By its very nature, then, this legislation is geared towards uniformity. The policy domains in which the European Union has been active since the 1990s have been subject to the same Community legislative system,[3] with the same implicit focus on uniformity, even though life in all its diversity has often proved to be more powerful than doctrine.[4]

[3]The third pillar of the Maastricht Treaty had a predominantly intergovernmental model of decision-making for cooperation in the area of justice and home affairs, but the Amsterdam (1999), Nice (2000) and Lisbon (2007) Treaties gradually replaced the Community model of decision-making by sub-area.

[4]According to the judgment of the Court of Justice of 5 February 1962, Case 26–62, ECLI:EU: C:1963:1 (Van Gend & Loos v. Netherlands Inland Revenue Administration), in which it considered that '[t]he Community constitutes a new legal order of international law for the benefit of which the states have limited their sovereign rights, albeit within limited fields and the subjects of which comprise not only member states but also their nationals. Independently of the legislation of member states, community law therefore not only imposes obligations on individuals but is also intended to confer upon them rights which become part of their legal heritage'.

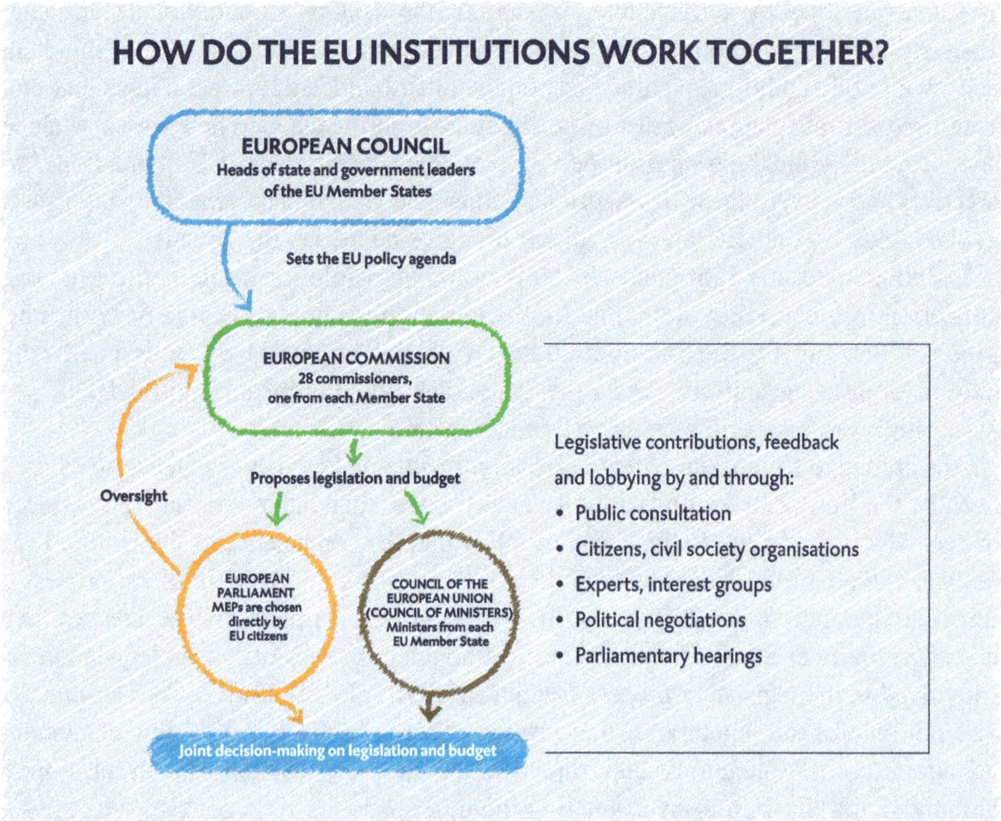

Scheme 1 How do the institutions work together?

Because the crux of the European Union's functioning lies in its legislation—in particular as a way of eliminating unwelcome disparities between the Member States when allowing the free movement of capital, goods, services and persons—the Union is, in its origins and despite all the changes, first and foremost a legal order. It is a political order, with institutions reminiscent of state institutions, only *as a function* of that legal order. The Commission must focus on the general interest of the Union; its members must not take instructions from a national government or any other body. The Council is composed of national ministerial representatives; in the exercise of the tasks conferred upon it by the Treaties, it decides, in most cases, by a qualified majority corresponding to the number of Member States and the populations they represent. However, in the case of sensitive issues as defined in the Treaties, additional tasks or new subjects, unanimity is required. The Parliament is elected directly by EU citizens according to a system of electoral regions in which voters in relatively small populations exercise relatively more influence. The Court of Justice of the European Union ensures the uniform interpretation of EU law by ruling on points of law brought before it by the national courts; it also settles disputes between the Member States and between the Member States and the EU institutions. The Union's institutional framework also includes the Court of Auditors and the European Central Bank, the European Ombudsman (elected by the

Parliament), as well as Europol, Eurojust and other specialised bodies and organisations.

The rise of the European Council—not to be confused with the Council (of Ministers) of the European Union—shows that controversial political issues are coming to play a greater role alongside the legislative competences of the European Union. The European Council consists of the heads of state (insofar as they exercise political leadership) and government leaders of the Member States, together with its President and the President of the Commission. The High Representative of the Union for Foreign Affairs and Security Policy also takes part in the European Council's work. The European Council has no legislative authority and virtually no administrative competences, but instead sets the political agenda; according to Article 15 TEU, it 'shall provide the Union with the necessary impetus for its development and shall define its general political directions and priorities thereof'. It was born out of an initially informal political deliberation by the heads of state and government leaders, was incorporated into the EC Treaty in 1987 and became an official European Union institution in 2009. The agreements reached by the European Council, known as 'Conclusions', set the political agenda but are not legally binding; they are often amended or watered down in the course of further negotiations. The European Council is a significant political arena; when it comes to binding decisions, it is most effective in those cases where a decision needs to be taken on an issue about which Ministers failed to reach agreement in the Council and as a framework for final negotiations on structural changes such as Treaty amendments (Scheme 2).

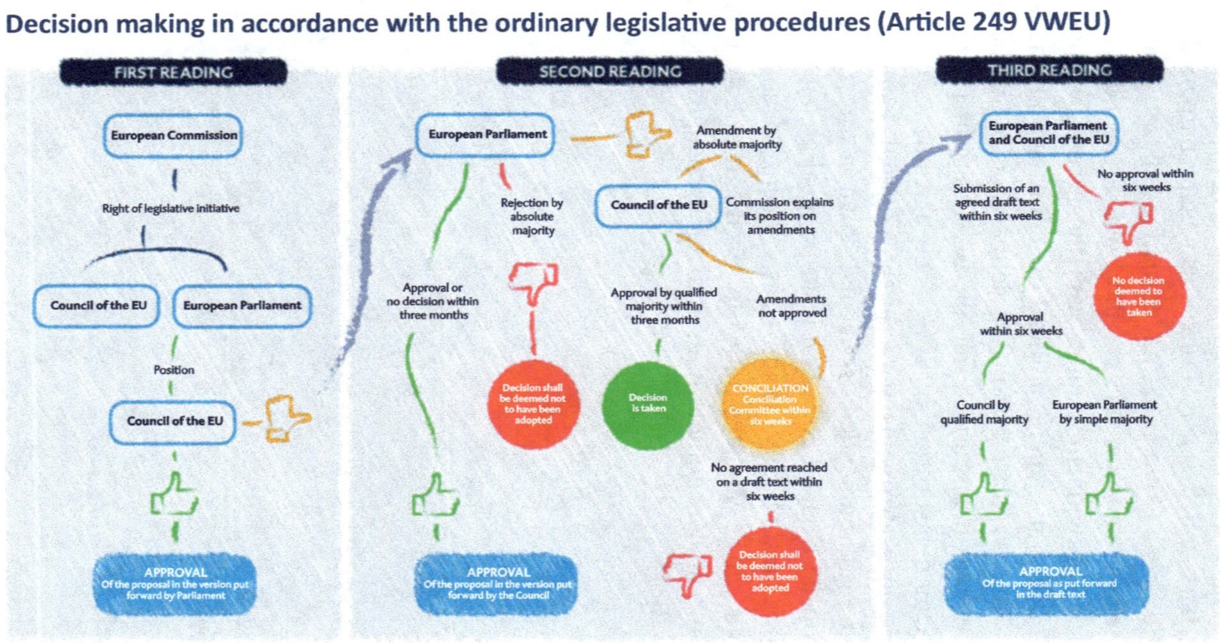

Scheme 2 Decision making in accordance with the ordinary legislative procedures (Article 249 VWEU)

Contents

About the Editors

Ernst Hirsch Ballin is Distinguished University Professor at Tilburg University and, as Professor of Human Rights Law at the University of Amsterdam, President of the Asser Institute for International and European Law in The Hague. He was a member of the Scientific Council for Government Policy (WRR, 2014–2019) and was subsequently appointed as a consultative member of the council. He is also a member of the Royal Netherlands Academy of Arts and Sciences (KNAW) and of the Advisory Council on International Affairs (AIV). Ernst Hirsch Ballin was the Netherlands Minister of Justice (1989–1994, 2006–2010) and represented as such the Netherlands in the Council of the European Union for Justice and Home Affairs. He was also a member of Parliament (1994–1995 Lower House, 1995–2000 Upper House), followed by his appointment to the Council of State (2000–2006). In 1999/2000 he was a member of the Convention charged with drawing up the EU Charter of Fundamental Rights.

Emina Ćerimović was affiliated to the WRR from 2016 until 2018. She holds a bachelor's degree in European Studies and a master's degree in European Policy from the University of Amsterdam. Inspired by the discrepancy between the conflicts that resulted from the disintegration of her birth country Yugoslavia and the 'never again' slogan embodied by the European Union, she developed an interest in the soft power of the EU. Her master thesis investigates the post-war education system in Bosnia and Herzegovina and its obstruction to interethnic reconciliation and lasting peace, specifically shedding light on the (lack of) efforts by the international community regarding policy reforms in this field. She conducted internships at the Europe Department of the Ministry of Foreign Affairs and the NGO Women to Women in Sarajevo. Currently, Emina works as a policy officer at the Ministry of Social Affairs and Employment on subjects that relate to migration, integration and resilient society. She is a board member of the Hartman Young Professionals for Europe network.

Huub Dijstelbloem is Professor of Philosophy of Science and Politics at the University of Amsterdam (UVA) and Senior Researcher and Project Leader at the Scientific Council for Government Policy in The Hague (WRR). As a visiting scholar, he was affiliated to the University of California San Diego (2014) and to the University of Mapoto's Center for Policy Analysis (2010). He is involved in public debates about science, technology and democracy and is one of the initiators of *Science in Transition* (www.scienceintransition.nl). His research is concerned with border control technologies, security policies and migration issues and has been published in various books, edited volumes and journals including *Security Dialogue*, the *Journal of Borderland Studies* and the *European Journal of Social Theory*.

Mathieu Segers is a professor of Contemporary European History and European Integration at Maastricht University and Dean of University College Maastricht. From 2008–2016, he was Senior Lecturer in European Integration and International Relations in the Department of History and Art History in the Faculty of Humanities at Utrecht University (UU). He has been a Fulbright-Schuman fellow at the Center for European Studies of Harvard University and Senior Research Fellow at the Department of Politics and IR at the University of Oxford. A political scientist by training, he obtained his doctorate as a historian. His academic work is multidisciplinary and situated at the interface of the social sciences and humanities. He has published in journals of different disciplines, including The International History Review, *Journal of European Integration History*, Contemporary European History, *Journal of Cold War Studies*, and *Journal of Common Market Studies*. He is a member of the European Affairs Committee (CEI) of the Advisory Council on International Affairs (AIV).

Acronyms and Abbreviations

AIV	Adviesraad Internationale Vraagstukken (Advisory Council on International Affairs)
CEAS	Common European Asylum System
CFSP	Common Foreign and Security Policy
DNB	De Nederlandsche Bank (Netherlands Central Bank)
EC	European Commission
EC	European Communities
ECB	European Central Bank
ECHR	European Convention on Human Rights and Fundamental Freedoms
ECJ	Court of Justice of the European Union
ECOFIN	Economic and Financial Affairs Council
ECSC	European Coal and Steel Community
EEA	European Economic Area
EEC	European Economic Community
EFSF	European Financial Stability Facility
EMF	European Monetary Fund
EMU	Economic and Monetary Union
EP	European Parliament
EPU	European Political Union
ESM	European Stability Mechanism
EU	European Union
GDP	Gross domestic product
GDPR	General Data Protection Regulation
IMF	International Monetary Fund
OMC	Open method of coordination
OMT	Outright monetary transactions
SER	Sociaal-Economische Raad (Social and Economic Council of the Netherlands)

SGP	Stability and Growth Pact
TEU	Treaty on European Union
TFEU	Treaty on the Functioning of the European Union
WTO	World Trade Organisation

Chapter 1
Introduction

1.1 Room for Variation in the European Union

The European Union will have to offer more room for variation. That is the main thrust of this book, which we are presenting at a time when the European Union is under pressure, both internally and externally. Two decades of growth, both in the number of Member States and in its tasks, have placed so great a strain on the Union's internal resilience that cracks have begun to appear in its basis of support and even in respect for its democratic foundations under law. Both the current policy of the President of the United States and Russia's policy respond to trends that are weakening the position of the European Union, such as Brexit, internal political controversies concerning migration and economic policy, and external trade conflicts. In this book, we argue that more flexibility is needed in the Union's structure to bolster it in its critical tasks, including the internal market and protection against crime and social injustice. This is the lesson that we should be drawing from the experiences of the past 25 years, since the Maastricht Treaty took effect on 1 November 1993.

The Maastricht Treaty followed the upheaval in Central and Eastern Europe, which had changed the balance of power dramatically on the continent. At that time, few questioned that the process of European integration should continue. The Treaty integrated the European Communities and the new domains ('pillars') of European policy—law enforcement, migration, and foreign and security policy—into a broad new framework: the European Union (EU). Much has changed since then, not only because 16 new Member States have acceded but also because the content of its policy has 'deepened', for example the introduction of the euro and a common asylum system. In virtually every domain, the European Parliament, which is elected directly by the people, is now a co-legislator, together with the Council, composed of ministers representing the Member States. Moreover, since the entry into force of the Treaty of Lisbon on 1 December 2009, the institutional structure

E. Hirsch Ballin et al., *European Variations as a Key to Cooperation*, Research for Policy, https://doi.org/10.1007/978-3-030-32893-1_1

has been simplified by merging the three pillars into one revitalised European Union.

The European Union must overcome the conflicts about its future that have arisen ever since. To be persuasive, changes must be driven by a realistic view of the European Union, which, despite Brexit, has almost 30 Member States. The Netherlands' position and the contribution it makes to the inevitable changes in the EU's functioning matter.

Uncertainty about the future of the European Union has arisen in a changed political environment. Today, European integration no longer goes without saying. The relief with which Europe welcomed the creation of a common market with free movement of persons, goods, capital and services—not least in Central Europe, with its recent history of closely guarded borders—has given way to a desire for greater protection of the individuality of the Member States. The introduction of rules and authorities to guarantee the functioning of the market is viewed on the one hand as interference and on the other as the dismantling of existing protective institutions such as state-owned companies and the ban on dismissals. Faltering 'Europeanisation', for example an asylum policy that is only partially harmonised, or the rather noncommittal coordination of foreign policy, has made the EU's institutions responsible for their own weakness. That weakness was laid bare by a series of dramatic events, from the repercussions of the Yugoslav Civil War (already raging at the time of the Maastricht Treaty), through the deep divisions over the Iraq War and the financial crises, to the current Syrian catastrophe and its consequences for migration.

And yet the institutions of the European Union perform vital tasks, day in, day out, to organise economic life and guarantee an area of freedom, security and justice for people and businesses. The fact that many are now questioning and have lost confidence in the EU shows that a Union of so many and such different Member States as the current 28 cannot be built on the idea that all of them, even after their transitional periods, will be integrated on an equal footing. Despite the aforementioned tensions, however, the enlargement of the Union to include Member States with disparate economies, histories, and legal and administrative cultures has given many people a more solid economic and social basis. The Union has shown itself capable of rebalancing after crises. That has had consequences, how-ever. Often, and perhaps increasingly, it has had to accept the withdrawal of some Member States from certain aspects of EU legislation and policies. With regard to the Schengen Agreement, the euro, migration and asylum policy, and even the enforcement of fundamental rights and freedoms, it has, more or less reluctantly, accepted differences between Member States or conceded during tough negotiations. These are powerful indications that there is a need for variation between Member States. That is true not only of the new Member States, moreover. Differences of opinion that have arisen between the initial six Member States in new policy domains, such as monetary union and migration policy, also indicate a need for variation.

1.2 Opening Positions in the Debate on the Future of European Integration

The time when the process of European integration was clearly charged to the positive side of the political balance sheet is over. But the direction in which changes are to be made—less integration, transformation, deepening or variation—is controversial. The reasons for criticising the current state of affairs vary. Some emphasise the restrictions placed on national policymaking, others the lack of solidarity on the most pressing issues, and yet others the absence of democratic foundations or the inability of the Union to stop democracy from declining into authoritarianism in some Member States.

Relinquishing an all-too-common fixation on uniformity opens up new opportunities for a debate on the future of European integration. A 'freer' perspective that allows for more variation can foster a more realistic debate. The perspective proposed in this book makes it possible to move beyond the over-simplified debate that pits nation state against federation. While the contrast seems clarifying, it does not do justice to the multifaceted nature of reality. Many European citizens, politicians and policy-makers concerned about dichotomous thinking are extremely sensitive.

Variation in European integration is not a sign of weakness. European integration seems to have reached a point where solidarity, resolve and national engagement will in fact benefit from specific forms of cooperation. Variation supports the provision of public goods such as security, stability, prosperity and social protection. Accepting it can thus be a proactive means of revitalising the relationship between internal and external, between institutions and citizens, and between public tasks and perceived needs.

The trio consisting of the Treaty on European Union, the Treaty on the Functioning of the European Union, and the Charter of Fundamental Rights of the European Union provide the constitutional basis for the relationship between its own institutions, between those institutions and the Member States, and between those institutions and the citizens of those Member States. Although there are only minor differences between this trio and the unsuccessful Treaty establishing a Constitution for Europe with regard to their legal implications, the system that has been accepted is more open in purpose and therefore less specific and unequivocal. Continuing to see the European Union as a set of institutions serving a non-exclusive European legal order has given rise to openness as a principle. That is what we wish to elaborate on in this book.

The guiding principles enshrined in Articles 1–6 of the Treaty on European Union have been respected and put into practise: the European Union is a union among peoples—note the plural—based on common values such as respect for human dignity, democracy and the rule of law, but also characterised by pluralism and respect for equality between the Member States and their national identities. The constitutional principles governing the Union's competences (Articles 4–6) mean that the Union has no more power than that which the Member States have conferred on it by treaty, that the Member States are expected to be loyal to one another, and that the Union must adhere to the principles of subsidiarity and proportionality in its actions.

These principles must do more than merely pay lip service to national diversity. With the European Union now encompassing a wide variety of Member States, tasks, and therefore societal problems—the result of the changes that occurred in the 1990s and 2000s—the need for variation must be acknowledged. This book considers the notion that, if these constitutional principles are taken seriously, then the process of European integration might not only mean entrusting more competences to the Union and increasing the level of uniformity, but also giving the Member States scope to take responsibility for themselves and therefore allowing for pluralism within the Union.

It is not only jurists trained in a single legal system but also many others who are inclined to see legal and political orders as pyramids: the top is more important than the base, and the intermediate levels carry the weight of the top and pass on the instructions issued from there. Regardless of whether this image was ever completely accurate, it is in any case not up to date. International, supra-state, national and regional decision-making influence one another. The standards established in a broader context can only work if they are interpreted in smaller circles and are tailored to the situation in which they are applied—i.e. in different ways. Multi-level governance of this kind is the actual but also necessary form of governance and administration in the European Union.[1] Our view of this reality becomes blurred because we see the European Union as a kind of state, but also because we deny what has been the case since 1957, namely that the sovereignty of the Member States is limited because they have transferred legislative, executive and judicial competences to EU institutions. It is important to note that even when competences are transferred in this manner, the Member States exercise considerable influence on the drafting of legislation and the resolutions adopted within the Council of Ministers.

1.3 Democracy in Plural

Variation will not always be the outcome, not even when Member States express a wish for it. The nature of the tasks involved or the level of solidarity required may prevent it from being accepted. Nor is variation an end in itself, and there must always be solid common ground between all the Union's Member States, particularly regarding the founding values of democracy and the rule of law, the common market, and solidarity in the defence of freedom and security. Last but not least, allowing scope for variation addresses the desire to give the European Union more credible democratic foundations. The European Union has a relationship not only with its citizens, who are represented as a whole by the European Parliament, but also with the citizens of the individual Member States, who are represented by their national parliaments. While is true that the European Parliament has become a co-legislative body, it is precisely the other 'leg' of the Union's legislature, namely the Council (in which ministers represent their Member States and usually decide by qualified majority), that is too far removed from the democratic process in the Member States that it represents. As a 'demoicracy'—*demoi* is the plural of the Greek root *demos* in 'democracy'—the European Union must continue to align itself with the ideas and interests of its Member States.[2] The Council of Ministers is still too much of a negotiating platform to fulfil its representative role properly. There is room for improvement, even without amending the Treaties.

The notion of 'demoicracy' put forward in this book is based on the assumption that the 'demoi', the *political* peoples of Europe, should be regarded in plural. This would, for example, be possible if national parliaments not only had negative powers, such as the yellow card procedure, but also the right to initiate European policy and legislation, including variations in that policy. What we are emphasising here is that there are no hierarchical but rather cooperative relationships between EU and national institutions. The EU's current system is in fact not modelled on the structure of the national state, in which legislative, policy-making, administrative and judicial competences are derived from the power structure shaped by history. The exact opposite is true in the European Communities and now in the European Union: the need for a partly common legal order led to the creation of institutions by treaty.

What this implies is that, at European level, the principle of democracy takes on a different meaning. The European order is a legal order, an economic order and, in a certain sense, a political order, but it is not a democracy in the same manner as a state. The EU provides a structure for cooperation, to offer protection and build a future lived in freedom; based on those goals and the common values in which they are rooted, however, it is also a structure for taking and overseeing joint decisions. In this European context, citizens exercise their influence primarily through their national elections, and it is there that the EU must seek its basis of national support.

Ultimately, proposals for the reform of the European Union are judged in terms of what is required to tackle common and cross-border problems and how such public goods as freedom, security, stability, prosperity and social protection can be provided. Reasoned choices will have to be made about the intensity of cooperation and the method of decision-making used for the tasks that must be performed, and those choices *may* vary from one Member State to the next. When it comes to the free movement of goods and other issues, full cooperation is required, and the Community method is the most appropriate. In this book, the Community method refers to joint decision-making by supranational institutions and representatives of the Member States. At the moment, the most important example is the ordinary legislative procedure set out in Article 294 TFEU: EU legislation (regulations and directives) is adopted by the Parliament (acting as a supranational representative assembly) and the Council (of Ministers, representing the Member States) acting jointly on a proposal from the Commission. In this procedure, the Council decides by qualified majority.

1.4 Variation Is More Than Differentiation

Variation is not an end in and of itself, but it certainly should be considered as a general solution for the major problems that beset the EU today, both internally and externally. Accepting variation does not, after all, mean that uniformity and like-mindedness are lacking, but rather that real differences in Member States' needs, views and modes of action are recognised.

Accepting variation as a distinctive feature of the European Union's future means keying into existing differences within the EU that the Netherlands' Adviesraad Internationale Vraagstukken (Advisory Council on International Affairs) (AIV) described in its advisory report of 2015 as 'differentiated integration'. The report claims that the EU's existing differentiation is the result of political impasses in negotiations on the preferred aim, namely the uniform integration of each and every Member State. When this could not be achieved, differentiated integration was accepted. The AIV cites the following as the most significant features of differentiated integration:

- enhanced cooperation: a formal EU instrument introduced in the Treaty of Amsterdam enabling a lead group of at least nine Member States to take the initiative to further integrate a specific policy domain, with the possibility of other Member States joining later (Article 20 TEU, 326–334 TFEU). This requires a (qualified) majority decision by the Council;
- temporary or permanent opt-out and opt-in (i.e. exemption) clauses;
- temporary or permanent intergovernmental cooperation, on the basis of agreements under international law; recent examples include the Treaty Establishing the European Stability Mechanism (2 February 2012) and the Treaty on Stability, Coordination and Governance in the Economic and Monetary Union (2 March 2012);
- transitional provisions for parts of the acquis in the event of enlargement of the Union.[3]

In some instances, differentiation has been incorporated into the Treaties them-selves, resulting in key policy domains in which not all Member States participate. Not all Member States participate in the euro area and the Schengen Agreement, whereas some non-Member States do (e.g. Montenegro and Kosovo are not EU Member States but do have the euro as their currency; Liechtenstein, Norway, Iceland and Switzerland are not EU Member States but do participate in the Schengen Agreement). There are also associations with non-EU Member States that conform to EU internal market rules and legislation to varying degrees, in particular the European Economic Area (EEA) and Switzerland. There are, moreover, many forms of integration in which *all* the Member States participate but which leave scope for individual states to fulfil their public tasks as they see fit. That is the nature of directives as a category of EU legislation, as opposed to regulations, which are directly applicable. The 'open method of coordination' leaves further scope for differentiation. The Member States then coordinate their policy by formulating joint policy objectives and monitoring the results; in this case, however, there is no EU legislation.

The concept of variation described in this book includes forms of differentiated integration, but goes beyond differentiated integration as we know it today. It is not a derogation accepted after negotiation, but a desirable feature of the EU of the future, given the large number of Member States, each one very different from the next. Variation is not regarded as a failure of European integration, but rather as another, and in certain situations better, way of ensuring its success. The reasons for variation and its impact on citizens must be both acceptable and convincing. Variation thus builds on the principle of subsidiarity and, as a matter of principle, leaves room for the democratic functioning of each of the Member States: the EU as a 'demoicracy', in which each *demoi*[4] is part of its own state *and* part of the European Union.

Our proposal regarding a future European Union with well-considered variations also makes clear that the aim is not (or no longer) to form a European federal state. In a federal state, the relationship between the members and the federal authority is, in principle, symmetrical; asymmetry only occurs in exceptional cases.[5] Allowing variation is an asymmetric structuring principle. Even so, it does not imply a general aversion to the supranational competences of EU institutions. Where the nature of the tasks (for example organising the common market) so requires, Community integration and the participation of all Member States remains a possible outcome. In this book, the we propose a method of assessment in each individual case.

In the line of thinking outlined above, the question is not so much *whether* varied cooperation should be permitted to ensure that the European project can continue successfully, but rather *how* variation can best take shape. The book will explore this and outline various possible considerations.

European variation offers a continuum of options in this way. By deliberately accepting scope for variation, it becomes possible to break through long-standing deadlocks and to maintain sufficient cooperation, despite the differences. The analytical approach outlined in this book can be used to address the many issues facing the EU and its Member States, both in existing policy domains, whenever uniformity appears to be generating too much tension, and in new areas of European cooperation. This book explores the option of variation in greater detail in three domains: (1) the internal market, (2) the euro area, and (3) asylum, migration and border control. The main purpose of these chapters is to clarify the many ways that variation in cooperation can take shape. Although we have limited the discussion in this way, it should be noted that the variation perspective elaborated here will also be effective in other policy domains.

Accepting variation in the number of participating Member States may, in certain contexts, resemble the 'two-speed' Europe, consisting of a 'Core Europe' and the remaining Member States. What we envisage may go even further than that, however. The circle of participating Member States may vary; indeed, it is conceivable that two or three circles could arise simultaneously, if this would provide the most meaningful pooling of forces. Instead of a 'hard core', there would be a flexible core (or cores).[6]

1.5 The Netherlands in the European Union

The founding of the European Communities gave the Netherlands a say in the law and policy of its neighbouring countries for the very first time,[7] on a *collective* basis. It marked another stage in the history of Dutch-European relations. The Dutch state is not only the result of national self-awareness and a desire for liberty, but also of coordination with other European states, first through the series of treaties known as the Peace of Westphalia (1648) and then within the framework of the Congress of Vienna (1815). *Shared* control became acceptable once it was realised that some interests should preferably not be surrendered to the dominance of one state over another. It is here that the organisation of common European interests by legal remedy has its origins.

How this works out in practice can be problematical, however. In this book, we address the 'why' and 'how', the reasons for the European Union, its purpose, its form, and how all these things relate to one another. This approach entails consideration of the following issues:

1. What do we want from European integration? (tasks)
2. Why do we want it? (values, goals and public interests)
3. How do we organise it? (institutions and standards).

The overriding principle is that form follows content. The form that cooperation takes can only emerge after the goals of that cooperation have been determined. For a comprehensive consideration of such questions about European cooperation, we first need to know why things have gone as they have during the various episodes of European integration.

The first step is to understand the results of European integration in the context in which they arose. Present-day discussions about the future of Europe generally assume, without further explanation, that the EU is a new public law entity with a territory, a population and a centrally organised authority. But the EU is not a state. Many even consider it to be unique ('*sui generis*'). Nevertheless, the EU is usually compared to a state as an organising structure. Both proponents and opponents use this image and then either argue that the EU should develop into a federal state or are terrorised by the prospect. Presenting things in this way obscures the reality of the EU's history and hinders its further progress. The Communities from which the EU stems and the Union itself are the outcomes of a desire to arrive at a *common legal order* and *common policy* on certain issues. This is precisely how the Communities were described in the early case-law of the Court of Justice of the European Union (in short, the Court of Justice). In the Van Gend en Loos ruling of

5 February 1963,[8] the Court of Justice found that 'the Community constitutes a new legal order of international law for the benefit of which the States have limited their sovereign rights, albeit within limited fields, and the subjects of which comprise not only Member States but also their nationals.'[9]

The EU's institutions were created precisely to construct this common legal order and to implement this common policy. Together, they form the institutional structure that should enable the EU to translate the objectives linked to a common legal order and a common policy into the fulfilment of European public tasks. In this book, we do not focus on this institutional structure but on what is required of the EU: the fulfilment of European public tasks. 'Public tasks' is not an administrative concept but a political and constitutional one. Public tasks concern matters that enable citizens to live freely and to take responsibility for their lives, such as market regulation, education, health care and infrastructure. Essentially, these tasks can be derived from the definitions of fundamental rights, including economic, social and cultural rights, and everything that relates to peace and security. The Charter of Fundamental Rights of the European Union basically provides a legal guarantee of these public tasks. This naturally makes demands on implementation by the Member States, but it does not exclude variation (as noted in research on the open method of coordination.[10]

European integration has its origins in the hope that cooperation will provide a lasting counterweight to the dynamic forces of nationalism in international politics. After all, those forces lead to conflicts or to trade-offs, in both cases amounting to the view that 'your profit is my loss' and 'your security is my threat'. The European integration process put an end to this zero-sum-game thinking. From the outset, the aim was for the 'union among peoples' to focus on shared values. Public tasks in the EU are therefore more than just a matter of common interest. They are a shared actualisation of the values that guide European integration. Respect for human dignity, and therefore for human rights, is decisive in this. However, how these and other values of the Union are defined in Article 2 TEU leaves room for a wide range of national interpretations. For this reason alone, the institutionalisation of European cooperation requires constant reflection on Europe's tasks and functions.

1.6 Europe in the World

The process of European integration always takes place in dialogue with changes occurring in the world that surrounds Europe. That is and will remain true both of the widening and of the deepening of integration. Within the framework of the European integration process, the aim from the outset has been an ever-closer 'union among peoples'. But reinforcing that union economically, socially and culturally is more than just an inward-looking European affair. European cooperation aims to combine globalisation in economic and interpersonal contacts with socially embedded economic freedom and a common 'area of freedom, security and justice'.[11] In so doing, it has given substance to the task of attaining the closely interrelated aims of peace, socio-economic stability, security, and international trade and mobility.

The European Union is meant to be an international force that increasingly acts in unison; in 2009, it also gained full recognition as a legal entity. But every era has different challenges and sees different demands and desires being expressed by the participating Member States and peoples. Something fundamental has also changed. The dissolution of the Warsaw Pact and the break-up of the Soviet Union have altered entirely the context in which European integration is taking place. The old negative reference point has disappeared. For more than two decades now, the Union has no longer been able to base its identity on being 'different'—i.e. freer, more trustworthy and more economically efficient—from its counterparts in Eastern Europe, and China seems too far away to serve as its new opposite number. Time and again, the Union will have to determine how European integration stands in relation to such geopolitical challenges as economic globalisation, migration, security, global warming, financial stability and social protection. The fulfilment of 'public tasks' to produce the public goods demanded of it must be understood within that relationship. The demand for public goods by European societies may differ from one era to the next and it may also differ between Member States and within them.

In the same way that the Netherlands is 'attached to other countries', as the WRR put it in 2010, the EU is inextricably linked to global politics and the world economy. That link is a two-way street. One the one hand, it forces the EU, time after time, to accept its share of responsibility in international affairs, not only in trade policy and development cooperation but also in foreign, security and climate policy. On the other hand, being more relevant on the international stage may help to reduce scepticism about European integration. European integration was originally driven, at least in part, by the ideal of lasting peace among peoples: the nations of Europe were no longer prepared to submit to the 'us-against-them' forces of nationalism and instead wanted to ensure the collective protection of rights and interests for future generations. It is extremely important to emphasise in politics and governance that security, stability and human rights come at a certain cost. It takes sustained, collective effort and dedication to guarantee these public goods, time after time.

1.7 Structuring Principles of the European Union

Many authors reflecting on the nature and future of the European Union assume that the EU 'overarches' the national legal orders, as it were, in the form of an extra tier on top of the Member States. However, this notion does no justice to the particular way in which the European Union is structured. That structure is difficult to compare with such familiar patterns as federal states or confederacies.

Although EU law is binding on the Member States and has its own institutions, these only fulfil public tasks with respect to specifically designated issues. The EU is primarily a legal order that regulates the rights and obligations of citizens and their organisations and enterprises through the incorporation of its law into the national law of the Member States, as indicated in the rulings of the Court of Justice in the early years of the European Communities. For the most part, the EU's legal order is shaped by the interaction between its institutions and its Member States. People must be able to rely on this common legal order and that is why institutions and procedures are necessary. However, these institutions and procedures are not some mandatory template for resolving differences between the Member States or issues that affect the populations.

The EU is not finished, and it never will be. Removing the pressure to achieve uniformity offers scope for a discussion on the future of European integration that does more justice to reality. The notion that all the Member States must cooperate in every policy domain, resulting in ever more harmonised standards, is unrealistic. We advocate taking a more proactive approach to the concept of variation and considering it in a broader context. This does not mean that the EU should be regarded as a kind of à la carte menu. There are downsides to variation as well. But thinking only in terms of uniformity means disregarding all kinds of variations that already exist, or that could be developed further. In addition, it is important to recognise variations in cooperation for what they truly are: a fully-fledged method of European cooperation. In the real world of European integration, variation in cooperation is neither 'second best' nor merely opportune in times of crisis, when nothing else helps.

Variation does not weaken the relationships that in fact shape Europe and the Netherlands. Since the founding of the European Communities, the Netherlands too has had a say in the law and policy of its neighbouring countries. *Shared* control became acceptable once it was realised that some interests should preferably not be surrendered to one state's dominance over another.

This book recommends first introducing this approach as a political concept and mode of action regarding the future of the European Union before proposing any Treaty amendments. A thorough overhaul of the Treaties is a politically complicated process that also involves complex constitutional procedures in several Member States. In many instances, variation can be achieved by having the participating Member States conclude their own treaties, as was the case with the Schengen Agreement and emu, for example. In addition, variation can be applied more often by using open standards and minimum harmonisation, and by making more deliberate trade-offs within and between policy fields.

1.8 Structure of the Book

Chapter 2 starts with an analysis of European integration after the fall of the Berlin Wall in 1989. At that time, the integration process faced numerous political challenges that proved difficult to cover in the Treaties. The core elements of the integration process remained in place, such as reciprocity and harmonisation as a basis for mutual market access, convergence driven by market integration, and the Community method as an institutional decision-making process. There are, however, growing reservations about the triad of (1) the unique and intensifying momentum of market integration, (2) spill-overs between sectors, i.e. the 'dissemination' of integration practices from one policy domain to another, and (3) their consolidation by supranational institutions that uphold the rule of law in both the theoretical and practical sense.

Chapter 3 describes how the pursuit of social protection has been pushed into the background in recent decades by a focus on market liberalisation, and how that has affected democratic trust in the EU's institutions and the evolution of human rights within the European legal order.

Chapter 4 applies the theory of motivations for collective action to create an analysis matrix that aims to provide a better understanding of the discussions concerning some of the EU's most sensitive issues. The matrix is constructed along two axes: 'motivations for collective action' and 'institutional order'.

Chapter 5 describes the different forms of variation that already exist within the internal market and that may therefore exist in other policy fields.

Chapter 6 analyses what variation can and cannot achieve. Here, variation in cooperation is deliberately viewed on a continuum. The EU's current situation calls for a new, more conscious and proactive form of reflection on the potential of variation. Variation can help get a better grip and a stronger sense of control; it is an alternative to relying on a future 'binding effect' of convergence.

Chapters 7 and 8 explore the potential of variation in Economic and Monetary Union (EMU) and in migration, asylum and border control. They do not contain specific recommendations concerning these policy areas; it is beyond the scope of a single chapter in this book to make such recommendations anyway. What these chapters do instead is broaden our understanding of the existing variation and suggest various methods for identifying suitable forms of cooperation.

Finally, Chap. 9 will present the main conclusions with regard to an EU that allows for variation. In particular, it examines what this approach means for the Netherlands and its position in the EU.

Notes

1. Piatonni (2010: 247, 260).
2. Nicolaïdis (2003, 2012).
3. AIV (2015: 8).
4. Peoples in the constitutional sense, as opposed to ethnically identified 'nations'.

5. For example the position of the District of Columbia in the federal system of the United States.
6. Cf. Schmidt (2016: 10).
7. Leaving aside the Central Commission for the Navigation of the Rhine (CCNR), which was granted supranational powers as long ago as 1815.
8. ECLI:EU:C:1963:1.
9. The concept of the European Community as politically neutral, a technocratic 'community based on the rule of law' in that sense, has evolved into that of a legal area with a much more pronounced political complexion. See Von Bogdandy 2017.
10. Armstrong (2016: 15).
11. Article 3(2) TEU and Part Three, Title V TFEU.

Chapter 2
The Tension Between Image and Reality

2.1 Introduction

Security, freedom, stability and prosperity create the conditions for people to maintain economic and personal relationships with one another, to express themselves freely and to profess their beliefs, to be free from violence and to be protected from disproportionate risk. That is, in brief, the meaning of a democratic and social legal state.[1] The societies of Europe are in urgent need of these public goods, which can no longer be provided by individual states acting on their own. However, there is considerable debate about the way in which European cooperation furnishes these public goods.

There is nothing new about the force field in which the relevant decisions must be taken. This book begins its analysis by considering the historic changes that followed the fall of the Berlin Wall in 1989 and that are associated with the Maastricht Treaty (1991–1993). The Maastricht Treaty marked a turning-point in the pattern of European integration initiated by the Single European Act of 1986 by triggering a process of fundamental change. It was followed by further significant changes, most recently the Treaty of Lisbon (2007), which taken together determine the nature of European integration today. In the remainder of this book, we stress the significance of the Maastricht Treaty in that regard by referring to it as the 'Maastricht Gateway'—a gateway to a long road—through which European integration passed upon the signing of that Treaty and the creation of the European Union.

What *is* new about these problems is the incisive way in which they are being addressed. That incisiveness creates scope for a debate on new directions for European cooperation, one in which change and diversity are viewed as a realistic starting point rather than as an obstacle.[2] A similar approach can be found in the White Paper presented in 2017, in which the European Commission (EC) attempts to force a discussion between supranational institutions, Member States and EU citizens.[3] The White Paper spurs the search for new forms of integration. It should

E. Hirsch Ballin et al., *European Variations as a Key to Cooperation*,
Research for Policy, https://doi.org/10.1007/978-3-030-32893-1_2

be noted, however, that that search remains doggedly focused on the 'how' of European integration. We believe that this scope is too limited. After all, appeals for greater diversity should also consider the 'why' of integration.

Any form of cooperation within 'Europe'—if it is to be stable—must be a sufficiently credible and therefore visible reflection of real needs and requirements. Acknowledging that reality starts by admitting that, in many respects, we already have the answer to the question 'What kind of Europe do we *want* to live in'. After all, we cannot alter history and geography. Geography alone has condemned Europe to work constantly at maintaining its internal relationships. Indeed, it is unique in the deeply penetrating, finely meshed, and multifaceted nature of those relationships, and that colours European reality.

Cooperation as a credible reflection of real needs and requirements also means that the EU's 'inner' and 'outer' spaces must always be closely connected. Reality does not cease at the external border, after all. It is in the relationship between internal and external that international cooperation takes shape and values can be fulfilled.[4] That is why the system of internal organisation applied in the context of European integration must respond to the external challenges facing European societies, such as the arrival of refugees, security issues, and climate and environmental matters.

Under the Maastricht Treaty, the EU consisted of the European Communities and two other, new 'pillars'; sixteen years later, the Union absorbed these pillars under the Treaty of Lisbon. After 'Maastricht', the EU moved beyond the broadly accepted realm of administrative tasks regulating a common European market. European integration thus ventured into more controversial and political arenas, and the number of Member States grew considerably. Accompanying these events were new and more diverse forms of integration, the most striking examples of which were the Schengen Agreement and the euro area. Despite these profound changes, the integration process remained focused on further economic and social convergence based on institutionally regulated reciprocity, rooted in a common market.[5] In other words, while the reality of European integration after 'Maastricht' required more and more institutional adjustments and political change, the dominant approach to European integration remained roughly the same. That has caused problems, with significant examples of divergence emerging in the euro area and Member States such as Poland and Hungary falling out of step in terms of the basic conditions guaranteeing the rule of law.

As the pressure of circumstances mounted, other forms of institutional integration have proved possible, both within and outside the framework of existing EU Treaties. The crux of the credibility problems now challenging European integration is that diversity has been an increasingly important factor ever since the Maastricht Treaty, but so far has not been acknowledged and defined, or only to a limited extent and in any event not as an independent pathway to achieving integration.

2.2 The 'Maastricht Gateway'

After the fall of the Berlin Wall in November 1989, European integration abruptly found itself in an entirely new geopolitical reality. Any analysis of the EU's current public tasks must take that historic episode into account. European integration then passed through the 'gateway' of the 1992 Maastricht Treaty, a milestone on the journey of deepening the integration process that the Communities had embarked upon in 1986 with the Single European Act, but whose historical context had been dramatically altered by the fall of the Berlin Wall in 1989. By passing through this 'gateway', the European Union increasingly entered politically controversial territory, a process fuelled by the politicisation of its traditional economic policy domain.

The Europe of European integration left behind the Cold War period and the division of Europe and Germany and entered the multipolar world of the twenty-first century, fundamentally changing both the circumstances *and* the process of European integration. The EU gained more competences in more policy domains and in 1993 embarked on a major enlargement process, mainly by welcoming Central and Eastern European countries as new Member States. At the same time, the EU remained predominantly intergovernmental in nature regarding matters that lay beyond the remit of the internal market (the first pillar of 'Maastricht') and associated areas such as the environment and consumer protection. While it is true that politically sensitive policy domains, such as asylum and justice, became EU matters, they were initially decided by unanimity (the third pillar). The Common Foreign and Security Policy (CFSP) was also added, but remained intergovernmental in nature (the second pillar).

The Maastricht Treaty thus represented a major step towards diversifying the methods of integration. In addition to integration in accordance with the Community method—in which the Commission functions as a supranational institution, initiator of legislation and guardian of the Treaty organisation, the Council of Ministers takes decisions by majority, and the European Parliament (EP) serves as co-decision-maker—other forms of integration emerged: multi-speed (e.g. regarding EMU), intergovernmental alternatives, and new hybrid forms of supranational and intergovernmental governance, such as the Open Method of Coordination (OMC, the process of coordinating policies without resorting to the harmonisation decrees based on the Treaties).

In many respects—and certainly with regard to the first pillar of the EC Treaty—the process initiated in Maastricht can be viewed as a completion, refinement and constructive amendment of the traditional integration process begun by 'the Six' with the European Coal and Steel Community (ECSC) of 1951, which from 1957 onwards came to focus on the common market of the European Economic Community (EEC, later EC). In addition, the Maastricht Treaty kick-started emu (including the UK's and Denmark's opt-outs) and, from 1993 onwards, a package of harmonisation measures introduced the free movement of goods, persons, services and capital on a Community-wide basis (including opt-ins by Norway and other non-EU Member States as participants in the European Economic Area (EEA)). Thus did de facto varied cooperation commence.

The Maastricht Treaty amended the Community Treaties and established the European Union, including the new pillar structure. Although the EU's politically-tinged ambitions became institutionalised in this way—asylum, justice and other more sensitive policy domains became European matters and the aim of a CFSP was made explicit—the general attitude in Europe remained largely one of 'business as usual'. In other words, despite being confronted by new challenges and unforeseen historical events, such as German unification, European unification, and the emergence of a multipolar world with greater independence for Europe, the process of European integration continued as if there was little need to alter (Western) Europe's self-image or the political and democratic embeddedness of the integration process.

In short, in the new reality following the Cold War, the Europe of integration continued to place its trust in the Europe of the European Communities as it was shaped in the post-War period. Given the success of the European Community and what many considered the historic victory of 'Western' societies over their communist rivals, this was not surprising. Even after 1989–1991, the Europe of integration continued to define itself on the basis of the old Cold War order, the order to which the Treaty of Rome had given birth. It sought solid footing in policy programmes, institutions and practices inspired by the West European order of the second half of the twentieth century.[6] As mentioned above, there were understandable and valid reasons for this, but it did so in an altered international context in which the EU was forced to address more politically controversial issues,[7] and in an integration process characterised by a growing level of diversity. This growing diversity was fuelled, among other things, by:

1. treaty-related and institutional changes associated with the structure of the new EU (such as the UK's and Denmark's partial opt-out in the Maastricht Treaty), of which the European Community—in conjunction with the European Atomic Energy Community, still a legally distinct entity established by the Euratom Treaty, the second Treaty of Rome alongside the Treaty establishing the EEC—was now part[8];
2. the enlargement from 12 to the present 28 Member States, which led to much greater economic, cultural-historical and administrative disparities within the process of European integration;
3. the widening and deepening of European integration.[9]

At the same time, an important step was taken in the Maastricht Treaty to connect the European project with the citizens of the Member States by establishing European Union citizenship, in addition to national citizenship. The Treaty not only consolidated existing rights relating to the free movement of persons, but also highlighted civil and political rights (the citizen as voter and electoral candidate) and their relationship to other fundamental rights. It was not until 2009 that the EU

Charter of Fundamental Rights, proclaimed in 2000, became fully legally binding, albeit with many reservations with regard to fundamental social rights.

In the period following the signing of the Maastricht Treaty, confidence in the traditional approach to European integration remained high. This confidence may have also been underpinned by the assumption that time would do its job: European integration would crystallise further, the basis was solid, and whirlwind changes were unnecessary and probably unwise. Considerations of this kind fostered a 'muddling through' and 'wait and see' approach, even with respect to extremely far-reaching new projects such as EMU, and the unprecedented enlargement of the Union with Central and East European states.

In short, the changes affecting European integration were enormous, but the way they were handled remained much the same as in the past. The EU staked its future on tried-and-tested formulas. There was frequent discussion of the need to radically reconceive the institutions of the 'Rome order'—with a view to aligning them more closely to the process of deepening and widening European integration in the post-Cold War world—but only some of these discussions resulted in action.[10] Core elements of the integration process clearly remained in place, such as mutual recognition as a basis for market access, convergence (of economies) and the Community method as the driver of integration.[11]

2.3 After 'Maastricht'

The inclination to rely on familiar formulas of integration after 'Maastricht' does not mean that there were no signs that such reticence would eventually lead to problems.[12] Following the signing of the Maastricht Treaty, pressure mounted, slowly but surely, on the famed 'permissive consensus' (implicitly assumed support for the EU project),[13] long regarded as the solid democratic basis underpinning European integration. Latent support for integration burgeoned into mistrust among ever larger groups of citizens.

That emerging mistrust found expression in public debate and in the results of the elections and referendums held since 2005. *De sociale staat van Nederland*[14] reveals that support for membership of the European Union is higher in the Netherlands than in any other EU Member State.[15] However, the share of the population who believe that Dutch membership of the EU is a good thing has fallen significantly in recent decades, from 75% in 1996 to 58% in 2016/2017.[16] In 2017, 45% felt that European integration was going too far.[17] According to Dekker, Dutch attitudes towards the EU are generally multidimensional and ambiguous.[18] That is why the SCP[19] has concluded that 'Dutch public opinion appears to regard membership above all as something unavoidable'.

This shift in the public mood may well have decelerated the functioning of the Community institutions,[20] in turn possibly reinforcing apolitical reticence and institutional caution in European policymaking, which reinforced the 'muddling through' and 'wait and see' approach.

These mutually reinforcing forces produced a paradoxical result: as the 1990s marched on, the political challenges facing the EU grew more and more acute even as it was less and less able to cope with those challenges. Of course, the EU engaged in politics despite this inability, but it did so in the disguise of depoliticisation, thereby creating a widening breach between institutional structure and reality.

Alongside the traditional, rather apolitical issues of functionality in European integration (e.g. regarding economies of scale and oversight), urgent matters of justice, distribution, transparency and humanity required more and more attention (e.g. to deal with the Yugoslav Civil Wars, the structuring of the monetary union, and the enlargement). The issues that arose in this second category were, in essence, politically and morally charged, making them hard to resolve within the existing policy rationality and corresponding instruments.

In cases where a functionalist rationale is absent as a grounds for transferring competences and when solidarity is not self-evident, it is difficult to legitimise possible European-level solutions democratically. Such a situation manifests itself in political inertia, leading in turn to a loss of confidence. This dilemma has now reached the point that even attempts to solve apolitical problems are often met with great resistance. The acute nature of this dilemma shows that the focus on extending European integration in the direction of a 'regulatory state',[21] rooted in the functionalist rationale of the common market, has prevented more political and democratic mechanisms of legitimisation from developing to the point that they can function with sufficient credibility in the present day. Perhaps there was no immediate need for this, in fact.

Box 2.1. The Effect of Historiography

How can we explain the fixation on the status quo? To an important extent the explanation probably lies in what one might call the notion of 'progressive functionalism'.[22] This notion is one of the most important underpinnings of the 'Rome order'. It has also long been a driving force in academic research. For decades, the historiography of European integration was overshadowed by functionalist explanations and their theoretical challengers.[23] As a result, academic debate was confined to theories of utility maximisation and rational choice (focusing on the economic and/or geopolitical considerations of the actors in the integration process).

Once researchers began in the 1980s to gain access to more archives, they found that such theories did not adequately explain why things were going the way they were. Less rational, more historical-political or identity-inspired forces frequently played a defining role too, as did coincidence.[24] For the time being, these insights have not yet broken the surface of political and public debate. The functionalist narrative still dominates, not least because the success of EU market integration has lent retroactive cogency to 'rational actor theories', which appeared to provide evidence mainly for various functionalist or rational choice development concepts (see also Sect. 2.3).

The persuasiveness of these theories in fact may distort history, leading ultimately to incomprehension and alienation.

In the past two decades, the public debate on European integration has been marred by problems associated with an overly functional approach. In many respects, these problems have revived the existential struggles of the early stages of European integration in today's EU. In the decade following the end of the Second World War, the credibility of the whole enterprise rested on an idealistic European movement—the UK's former Prime Minister Winston Churchill advocated the creation of a 'United States of Europe'—but that movement had to win over the suspicion and reluctance of national movements in a battle for priority.

Today, the political debate about European integration is taking place in a completely different historical context, as well as in a much wider and more diverse integration process. The grave problems facing the EU increasingly raise the question of whether European integration is sustainable at all at a time when prosperity is stagnating or declining, or outside the borders of a core West European group of highly integrated, similar societies. Viewed from a historical perspective, the 'Rome order' and the 'Maastricht order' are not necessarily aligned.

The paradox between change and inertia that became manifest in the relationship between the EU's internal and external space (profound change within and around the EU, but at the same time a growing reluctance to respond to it) also emerged in the way the EU dealt with the institutional order of European integration. While diversity became increasingly central to European integration, and 'Maastricht' even forced the issue within certain policy domains (by permitting multi-speed integration, for example with regard to EMU), the Community method and the notion of reciprocity between all Member States remained the undisputed frame of reference, including a firm expectation of convergence.

All this obscured the fact that, after 'Maastricht', various forms of differentiation, i.e. lead groups and opt-outs, gradually became possible outside the traditional domain of the internal market. Such flexibility remained almost invisible in the public and political domains, however. In those instances when flexibility was openly accepted, it was usually as a last resort, after every possible attempt had been made to reach a solution 'together' through the Community method. Variation thus took the form of 'ad hoc dealmaking', often in an attempt to limit damage. As late as 2015, the Dutch Government responded with extreme reticence to the aforementioned advisory report by the Advisory Council on International Affairs (AIV), which recommended making more extensive use of the options for internal variation.[25]

The ad hoc approach has exceeded its sell-by date, a point driven home by the White Paper on the future of the EU published by the European Commission

(EC) in early 2017. In it, the EC sketches five scenarios for Europe by 2025 in an attempt to steer a debate on the future of Europe. Variation is the key concept in these scenarios, with the need for change being paramount.

Box 2.2. The Way Ahead According to the European Commission
The European Commission's input for the Rome Summit of March 2017 is contained in a White Paper in which it presents five scenarios for how the EU could evolve by 2025, against a backdrop of structural changes in Europe's international position. The main point is that Europe's place in the world is shrinking as other, emerging, economies beyond its borders grow. Europe's relative economic power is waning. In the EC's view, this accentuates the need for Europe to speak with one voice on behalf of its own interests.

These changes have fuelled doubts about the ability of the EU's social market economy to ensure that every generation will be better off than the previous one. Such doubts have been felt most strongly in the euro area. The EC believes this highlights the need to complete emu and strengthen the convergence of economic and social performances. The EC also cites a number of major challenges of our time: Europe's ageing population, the growing pressure on its social protection systems, the changing nature of work, and climate change. It is difficult to close the gap between expectations and the EU's capacity to deliver. That challenge is made all the greater by the complexity of the EU, i.e. the Member States and institutions such as the EC and the ECB combined; it is, for example, by no means easy to understand who does what.

In its White Paper, the EC states that the EU must choose: it can let its future be shaped by unexpected events, or it can try to carve out a different future for itself. The EC considers that the five scenarios presented in the White Paper can help steer the debate on the future of Europe.

The starting point for each scenario is that the Member States will move forward together as a Union. The five scenarios are not detailed blueprints or policy prescriptions; form must follow function. The EC recognises that all too often, the discussion on Europe's future comes down to a binary—and misleading—choice between more or less Europe. It is up to the EU27 to decide together which combination of features from the five scenarios will best help advance the European project.[26]

Scenario 1: Carrying on ('muddling through')

In this scenario, problems are tackled as they arise. The speed of decision-making depends on overcoming differences of views. The unity of the EU27 is preserved but may still be tested in the event of major disputes. Decision-making remains complex and the capacity to deliver does not always match expectations.

The internal market is strengthened, including in the energy and digital sectors. The EU actively pursues progressive trade agreements. The functioning of the euro area and management of external borders will improve. There is also progress towards a common asylum system and improved coordination on security matters. Progress is expected on closer defence cooperation and on speaking with one voice on foreign affairs.

Scenario 2: Nothing but the internal market

The functioning of the single market becomes the main *raison d'être* of the EU27. Rights derived from EU law may be restricted. Decision-making may be easier to understand but the capacity to act collectively is limited. This may widen the gap between expectations and delivery at all levels.

Progress is easier to achieve for the free movement of capital and goods than in other areas, such as the free movement of persons and services, which can no longer be guaranteed. Given the sharp focus on reducing regulation at EU level, differences persist in consumer, environmental and social standards, leading to a 'race to the bottom'. Cooperation in the euro area is limited. There is no common migration or asylum policy; as a result, there are more systematic internal border controls. Coordination on security is dealt with bilaterally.

Scenario 3: Those who want more do more (multi-speed Europe, 'lead groups')

The EU27 proceeds as today but certain Member States that want to do more in common work together in specific policy areas. As was the case for the Schengen area or the euro, such cooperation can build on the shared EU27 framework. The status of other Member States is preserved, and they have the option of joining those doing more in time. Citizens' rights derived from EU law vary depending on whether or not citizens live in a country that has chosen to do more. Transparency is an issue because the different layers make decision-making complex.

At the very least, the EU27 follows scenario 1 by acting in unison in all policy areas. As in scenario 1, the internal market is strengthened and the EU27 pursues progressive trade agreements. Regarding EMU, a number of Member States deepen cooperation in areas such as taxation and social standards. They also do so with regard to security, defence and justice matters.

Scenario 4: Doing less more efficiently

In this scenario, there is a consensus on the need to better tackle certain priorities together. The EU27 decides to focus its attention and limited resources on a reduced number of areas, allowing it to act much quicker in a number of policy domains while doing less in other fields. In choosing its new priorities, the EU27 seeks to better align expectations and delivery. This clearer division of responsibilities helps European citizens to better understand what is handled at which level, helping to close the gap between promise and delivery.

The EU has real difficulty in agreeing which areas it should prioritise, however. The EC in any event proposes dealing with trade exclusively at EU level but setting common standards in the internal market to a minimum. Several steps are also taken to consolidate the euro area to guarantee its stability, but the EU27 does less in employment and social policy. Cooperation on border management, asylum policies, counter-terrorism matters, foreign policy issues and defence (the creation of a European Defence Union) are further examples of deepening integration, according to the EC.

Scenario 5: Doing much more together

In this scenario, all the Member States decide to do much more together across the board. As a result, decisions are agreed faster at European level. Citizens have more rights derived directly from EU law, but there is the risk of alienating parts of society that feel that the EU lacks legitimacy or has taken too much power away from national authorities.

The internal market is strengthened through harmonisation of standards and stronger enforcement. Trade is dealt with exclusively at EU level. Economic, financial and fiscal Union is achieved as envisaged in the *Five Presidents' Report*. Cooperation on border management, asylum policies, counter-terrorism, foreign policy and defence is deepened.

2.4 An Historical Perspective on the Present

It is not only the present uncertainty and astonishing succession of recent crises that explain the situation as it stands today. The problems of inertia and credibility that have come so sharply to the fore also have long historical roots.

We have only a limited understanding of what perhaps lies at the very heart of the integration process: the political processes that led governments to set up multilateral and supranational institutions, thereby placing unprecedented restrictions on their own freedom of action.[27] Those restrictions are most visible when Member States must face the fact that they have transferred authority to institutions, such as the EC and the ECB, whose competences eclipse those of their own national governments in certain areas. When the ECB takes interest rate decisions that are contrary to the position of the President of the De Nederlandsche Bank (Netherlands Central Bank) (DNB) but nevertheless binding on the DNB, then it becomes clear that certain matters are no longer national affairs.

On top of this, since 'Maastricht' these self-imposed restrictions have become much more visible, not least for the Member States in the euro area. When that is combined with a limited understanding of the political 'how' and 'why' of the transfer of powers, a loss of confidence in European integration becomes almost inevitable. This is particularly true at a time when circumstances are driving the EU to pursue crisis intervention policy, as in recent years. Its responses to the euro crisis and the tensions surrounding the arrival of refugees are striking examples. Almost by definition, European crisis intervention policy involves interfering radically in national policy autonomy, and it forces the Member States to take ad hoc decisions on grounds that many consider obscure. This is at odds with democratic legitimacy and public support in the national political arena.

In the current uncertainty, the question of the 'how' and 'why' of the political processes that drive integration will only grow louder and echo far beyond the boundaries of policymaking and academia, for decades the only arenas to have addressed this question. In the meantime, the 'how' and 'why' of European integration has become a central issue in elections in the EU Member States. 'Why have things gone the way they have?' 'How did "we"—a sovereign state—get ourselves into this situation?' 'Can the tide still be turned?' Questions such as these are now setting the tone in public debate in almost all EU Member States, but politicians and policymakers have yet to follow up on them in any concrete way.

As more research is conducted into the history of European integration, it is becoming increasingly clear that the outcomes of European politics and rulings of the Court of Justice have frequently defined the integration process in ways unanticipated by the participating Member States and institutions.[28] In other words, no one conceived of the integration process in its present form. In fact, the form that European integration took was, in most cases, entirely unforeseeable. It was something unexpected that belonged to everyone and no one, depending on the circumstances and the *zeitgeist*—which does not mean that the result is necessarily wrong, of course.

The unpredictable nature of European integration becomes obvious in the Maastricht Treaty. The Treaty was an attempt by the 'Europe of the Twelve', as it was known, to respond to the unexpected challenges posed by the fall of the Berlin Wall and the end of the Cold War. Its response, however, revealed the two faces of European integration. On the one hand, the Treaty appeared to confirm the relevance of European integration and its capacity for change in the post-Cold War era. In that respect, 'Maastricht' provided a promising practical basis for a constructive approach to German and European unification in a radically new context. The EU was forward-looking. On the other hand, the same Treaty responded to the new challenges of the post-Cold War world with tried-and-tested, somewhat old-fashioned forms of European integration. The most obvious example is how it presented the monetary union as the completion of the common market, with the 'Maastricht order' hailed as the crowning glory of the 'Rome order'. The EU sought justification for such a radical change mainly in the past.

In the twenty-five years since its signing, the Maastricht Treaty's inherent tension has, slowly but inevitably, fuelled a growing strain between the EU's self-image (based on the wildly successful apolitical 'Rome order', whose aim was social and economic convergence between the Member States) and a fundamentally different European and international reality, which left scope for greater diversity within the EU and assigned an increasingly important role to (geo)politics within and around Europe.

It has become clear in recent years just how stubborn this paradox between self-image and reality has become in today's Europe, but also how aptly the same paradox describes what has often been characterised as 'European impotence', from 'muddling through' and a belief in convergence on the one hand to the disruptive events of international politics on the other.

2.5 The Concept of Functionalist Development

The tension between the EU's self-image and its reality becomes even more evident when we juxtapose the unforeseen outcomes described above with the 'traditional form' of socio-economic and legal convergence, as described in detail in social sciences research. Such research is based on a functionalist concept made up of three closely interwoven, highly principled components: (1) the *sui generis* momentum of market integration, (2) spill-overs between sectors, and (3) their consolidation by supranational institutions.[29] These three components are interlinked and therefore mutually reinforcing.

It was this functionalist concept that was also used to justify the construction of a supranational legal order.[30] In that sense, it served as a political spur for the transfer of competences from the Member States to the supranational level.

(1) **Market integration**

The mechanism of market integration works in the following way. The first phase in creating and optimising a 'level playing field' is negative integration. This is meant to remove national barriers to trade and the free movement of goods, persons, services and capital. For example, import and export duties are prohibited between Member States, and Member States are not allowed to impose quotas or other obstacles to free movement. In practice, however, merely removing such barriers is often not enough. After all, each Member State sets its own requirements and upholds its own standards for products, services, diplomas and the like. Only when the Member States agree on the 'mutual recognition' of one another's requirements, or when the EU introduces its own standards, is there truly a level playing field within a single European market. Even when standards are harmonised, however, differences—for example between the general economic or monetary policies of the Member States—can have an impact on the ability to operate successfully in an internal market. A recent example of this phased process is the attempt to create a capital markets union and a banking union in the euro area following the elimination in the 1980s of restrictions on capital movements, meant to promote a European capital market.

(2) **Spill-overs between sectors**

Spill-overs between sectors happen when market integration in a small number of economic sectors (such as Coal and Steel or Atomic Energy) induce new integration processes in adjacent sectors. This process has gained additional momentum through the internal market. The four freedoms that are the essence of the European market and stimulate harmonisation processes (see above) also create incentives for far-reaching spill-overs between sectors. Examples include European integration processes in the areas of traffic and transport, climate, consumer protection, the fight against crime and—in association with the free movement of persons—migration and asylum.

(3) **Consolidation by supranational institutions**

The third functionalist development is the establishment of supranational institutions as guardians of the order created in the internal market and by spill-overs. In this phase, harmonisation and spill-overs are consolidated by supranational bodies. Examples include the High Authority of the ECSC, its successor the European Commission (EC), and the European Court of Justice (ECJ). In turn, however, these supranational institutions serve not only as 'guardians' but also as 'drivers' of spill-over processes, thus giving rise to an independent functional development that often has a basis in the law. This process is visible in the discourse concerning the approximation of laws in policy domains not directly covered by the Treaties. The harmonisation process is undertaken at supranational level and takes the form of what is primarily a technical operation in pursuit of the economic objective of market integration.

One significant form of consolidation is the legal materialisation of the above: the confirmation of the functionalist concept in European case-law. Here, it is the supranational court, the Court of Justice (ECJ), that is the supreme authority in matters concerning the interpretation of the Treaties and their enforcement. This judicial practice has gradually developed its own powerful momentum, in tandem with the momentum of market integration and spill-overs, which are more economically driven. The Court has contributed in two decisive ways to this whole. First of all, it supports an often fragile political will to regulate matters at European level with the doctrine of *supremacy* of European law over national law and the doctrine of *direct effect*. Second, it is extremely flexible about the nature and scope of Europe's legislative powers (thereby facilitating Europeanisation). The supremacy of European law over national law, confirmed by the Court in its established case-law, has bestowed a quasi-constitutional higher rank on the numerous operational provisions currently set out in the TFEU.[31] That has greatly narrowed the scope for variation in applying EU law and in amending it in the light of experience.

2.6 Conclusion: Integration Through Variation and the Politics of Circumstance

The political processes that underpin European integration have not traversed a straightforward, preordained path; instead, they were forged by the pressure of circumstance, the result of what Van Middelaar[32] calls 'event-driven politics'—a form of policymaking that was decisive for European cooperation from the outset. The functionalist concept sets the tone for the integration process, but the image it leaves us with is distorted; in the real world of political cooperation, there was much more variation and flexibility. Functional theories can also be mutually reinforcing, which is why they remain a dominant force in the process of European integration.

The dominant nature of this image means that the 'credible reflection' of real needs and requirements emphasised at the beginning of this chapter falls short. There is very little interest in the possibility of flexibility and variation and their actual implications, leaving them unknown and unloved. It also means that flexibility and variation are only used in emergencies, when all the functionalist routes have been exhausted. Using them merely as damage limitation mechanisms, however, is unhelpful in the ongoing 'politics of circumstance' so typical of European cooperation.

The legitimacy of ever-closer integration based on the interplay of the functionalist concept is now under growing pressure in the societies of the EU Member States. In other words, it is becoming increasingly difficult to apply the functional rationale that was transferred wholesale from the 'Rome order' to the 'Maastricht order'. As the next chapter will reveal, that has implications for the civil and political embeddedness of the European project and the confidence that citizens and peoples have in it.

Notes

1. The United Nations Vienna Declaration on Human Rights (1993) asserts that states should focus on this, both individually and in cooperation with one another.
2. Piris (2012), AIV (2015), Martinico (2012).
3. European Commission (2017d).
4. E.g. Bauman (2004), Joas (2001, 2008, 2013).
5. It is important to note that although the Treaty of Lisbon (2007) further consolidated new institutional forms, this process had already been initiated during and by the historical circumstances of 'Maastricht'.
6. See Jabko (1999).
7. International events, such as the wars in the Balkans, soon led to the EU having to face issues of a more (geo)political nature.
8. The ECSC ceased to exist in 2002, when the ECSC Treaty expired after 50 years.
9. Dyson and Sepos (2010: 3–23).

10. Striking examples of this are the attempts to streamline the institutions and simplify the frameworks of the Treaties during the negotiations leading to the Treaties of Amsterdam (1997; when this task was also described as the 'Maastricht leftovers') and Nice (2000), and the failure of the Constitutional Treaty in 2005.
11. For an explanation of the 'normative core'—broken down into 'Transnational Non-domination' and 'Transnational Mutual Recognition'—on which these core elements are based, see: Nicolaïdis (2013), here: p. 358–360. Partly on this basis, Nicolaïdis argues for an EU as a 'Union-as-demoicracy', a democracy with demos in plural, which 'should remain an open-ended process of transformation which seeks to accommodate the tensions inherent in the pursuit of radical mutual opening between separate peoples'. Building on this, Lindseth suggested that this 'demoicracy' could be developed into a model of European 'administrative governance', in which the relationship between national and supranational actors leads to 'mediated legitimacy' based on 'polycentric constitutional principles on the national level' Lindseth (2014).
12. See Tietmeyer (1994), Metten and Van Riel (2000), Schäuble and Lamers (1994), Delors (1985).
13. Cini (2016: 414), Rood (2016).
14. SCP (2017).
15. SCP (2017: 77).
16. SCP (2017: 76).
17. SCP (2017: 77).
18. Dekker (2017: 8).
19. SCP (2017: 78).
20. See Sternberg (2013).
21. Majone (1993).
22. See Lindseth (2014: 551–552).
23. Anderson (2009), Milward et al. (1994), Cini and Perez-Solorzano Borragan (2016).
24. See Pierson (1996: 123–163), Segers (2012).
25. AIV (2015); Kamerstukken II 2015–2016, 34350 V, nr. 50.
26. The White Paper seeks to launch an open and wide-ranging debate on how Europe should evolve in the coming years. The EC will organise a number of 'Future of Europe Debates' in national parliaments and cities in the EU in the near future. The EC will contribute to the debate in the coming months by publishing a series of reflection papers on the European social dimension, deepening EMU, globalisation, the future of European defence, and the future of EU finances.
27. See Fioretos (2011), Lindseth (2014: 550).
28. See Fioretos (2011: 9), Bronk and Jacoby (2013).
29. See Moravcsik (1998), Anderson (2009).

30. The functionalist theory of European integration has a long and venerable history; core texts and recent applications and variants of the theory include: Haas (1958), Sandholtz and Stone Sweet (1998), Niemann (2006), Catherine Barnard (2016), *The Substantive Law of the EU—The four Freedoms*, Oxford University Press, 5th Edition, p. 14–17.
31. Grimm (2016).
32. van Middelaar (2017).

Chapter 3
Growing Frictions

3.1 Introduction

Since the early years of the common market, the Community legal order has focused on removing obstacles to the free movement of goods, persons, services and capital; in other words, on creating a single market.[1] Social protection remained in place in national legislation; harmonisation was sought where politically feasible, but 'Europeanisation' has remained limited in this domain. Free competition was promoted through a European-level anti-trust policy and by counteracting preferential treatment by national governments. As a Member State of the European Union, the Netherlands is part of an internal and external economy of unprecedented power, with more than half a billion consumers and a combined Gross Domestic Product (GDP) of 14,714 billion euros (2015), the largest GDP in the world. Two thirds of the EU's trade in goods takes place between EU countries, with a volume of 3070 billion euros (2015). Approximately 72% of Dutch goods exports (measured in terms of their value) go to EU countries, and more than half of its imports come from EU countries (2015).[2]

With the removal of barriers as the starting point, the Netherlands, like its neighbouring countries, is closely intertwined with its European biotope. Dutch legislation is embedded in European legislation in almost every area, and in fact it must be, because differences would be susceptible to exploitation in the single market. Even technical requirements for appliances must not differ too much from country to country, as they would otherwise create an obstacle to European trade or give one or other country an undesirable competitive advantage. Since the reforms of recent decades, virtually all relevant legislation is the result of joint decision-making by the European Parliament and the Council of the European Union, at the initiative of the European Commission. The Member States are represented in the Council by a minister; decisions are taken by qualified majority, which means that for a decision to pass, at least 55% of the Member States, representing at least 65% of the population, must be in favour of it. The weekly

E. Hirsch Ballin et al., *European Variations as a Key to Cooperation*,
Research for Policy, https://doi.org/10.1007/978-3-030-32893-1_3

publication of important new rulings in the Dutch case-law reports *Nederlandse Jurisprudentie* (NJ) almost always begins with the case law of the Court of Justice of the European Union, for example on fraud prevention or the abuse of transactions carried out in another Member State.

In a striking contrast to this everyday reality, the people's trust in politics has plummeted, causing some—a minority—to argue in favour of leaving the European Union. It is difficult to fully explain why, in part because public opinion fluctuates, and preferences remain unclear, but we can certainly identify a number of frictions associated with changes in the international context and the way in which the European Union is socially embedded. That is what this chapter addresses.

3.2 The Western Context of 'Embedded Liberalism'

The international context in which European integration has advanced in recent decades differs considerably from the decades of recovery in which it began immediately after the Second World War. In those initial stages of European integration, there was a broad consensus among the main political movements that the social dimension should be an integral part of the European market economy. This ambition was no illusion, as it turned out. The more international coordination (e.g. in the Bretton Woods Institutions) and European integration took shape in the post-War period, the clearer it became that economic integration need not obstruct the growth of national welfare states.

Gradually, a system developed internationally that the American political scientist John Ruggie described in 1982 as 'embedded liberalism'. The promotion of free trade and multilateral coordination was 'embedded' in a large measure of autonomy for the participating states. Within their own borders, they were free to create a welfare state as they saw fit and shape the social policy most appropriate to it, in line with the views of their national, domestic democracy. Regarding the first decades of the post-war West, we can describe this system as 'Keynes at home, Smith abroad': welfare state within one's own borders, free trade outside. Western Europe explored and developed this system extensively within the institutional frameworks of European integration. In this model of embedded liberalism, the philosophy of *ordoliberalism* (as developed by the Freiburg School, initially in the 1950s) was influential on certain critical points.[3]

Ordoliberalism maintains that the market should operate with as few restrictions as possible within statutory frameworks that are enforced by independent institutions. The core principles of those frameworks are the protection of property rights, free and fair competition, and monetary prudence. Social policy is essential as a complementary and corrective measure, with due respect for the principle of subsidiarity. In Europe, this means that social policy is largely a national affair. The free movement of workers within Europe is facilitated by arrangements indicating which state is responsible for social security.

There are sound reasons for the importance that Ordoliberalism attaches to subsidiarity. It is preferable for different institutional models of socioeconomic organisation to co-exist within the space created by framework agreements; not only is it then possible to accommodate regional circumstances, but it also reveals which models set a 'good example', which the other members can then follow. Reinforcing the weakest links in this way benefits the entire community or union. The influence of Ordoliberalism is still visible today in Article 3 of the TEU, which describes the EU as a 'social market economy'.

3.3 Social Protection Gives Way to Market Liberalisation

As the decades wore on, the social dimension of European integration, despite frequent references to it in EU documents (for example in the preambles to the Treaties), remained a national affair and the responsibility of the Member States. At the same time, the market became increasingly integrated. From the 1980s onwards, this led to a trend that cast the European Community, and later the EU, into the role of European guardian of market liberalisation. Viewed from the perspective of the Member States, then, the institutions of European integration increasingly emerged as yet another external force favouring the reform or retrenchment of their welfare states. In brief, this also meant that the 'Keynes at home' element of the system that had prevailed in the initial decades of European integration was slowly undermined, with the EU's institutions regularly featuring as one of the driving forces behind this development.

European responsibility for social cohesion and for assuaging socioeconomic demands was thus relegated to the background. The image of European integration as a mere project of market integration, and the EU as the 'liberalisation engine' driving it forward, became much more powerful and realistic. That image has only gained force since the financial and economic crisis, in part because the crisis put the 'promise of convergence'—which was meant to replace the promises of the national welfare state to some extent—under so much pressure that suspicions of misrepresentation were roused.

The European promise of convergence embraced the notion that deeper economic integration would shrink differences *between* the Member States, while care would be taken *within the national welfare states* to distribute the benefits of economic cooperation fairly. In the first decades of the integration process, this promise yielded genuine benefits, in the form of unprecedented stability and economic prosperity. Indeed, the European model acted in many respects as a 'convergence engine' during that period: the poorer, less-developed Member States were pulled along by the economic growth of the richer Member States, resulting in prosperity growth in *all* Member States and making the aim of progressive social cohesion, both within and between Member States, appear feasible in this manner. That period has come and gone, however.

The emphasis shifted between 1986 and 1993. The completion of the common market was given greater priority at that time, for example by privatising public utilities. The climax of this trend was the heated, protracted European debate on the Services Directive at the start of the twenty-first century. Europe shifted emphasis in many respects; it was less interested in harmonising legislation and more interested in abolishing it, in the expectation that free competition would undoubtedly produce the best possible results. This is precisely why the EU has not produced restrictive legislation but has instead weakened a number of protective rules and structures (such as those protecting companies providing services of general economic interest, in disregard of Article 36 of the Charter of Fundamental Rights of the European Union[4]). 'Free movement' has become the main touchstone of the institutions of European integration. In many decisive moments, the EU in fact seemed to be focused on the liberalisation of the international market.

Customs tariffs, and later customs and border checks on persons, have been abolished at the internal borders, with some exceptions in the latter case. External trade relations are also necessarily a Community matter. However, there are many cases where it is precisely the desire to prioritise market forces that has led to detailed new rules and oversight procedures. After all, market imperfections can originate anywhere. All the Member States have established market authorities, often giving them far-reaching powers of investigation and sanctioning. There are thus two faces to liberalisation.

Convergence between Member States is waning in the EU and the euro area of the twenty-first century,[5] whereas social inequality appears to be increasing. Large numbers of Europeans see this as the 'downside' of the policy as actually implemented, undermining confidence in European integration. The tensions induced by the threat of terrorism, the persistent problems with the banks in the wake of the financial and economic crisis, and the inability to collectively manage the arrival of larger numbers of asylum seekers are, for many, proof that the EU is incapable of taking effective action. Moreover, large numbers of Europeans no longer feel that they are in control of their own lives—a feeling that they did appear to have in the era of embedded liberalism.

3.4 Globalisation and the Problem of Alienation

The imbalance between economic growth and social protection is contributing to the crisis of confidence. The malfunctioning of the 'convergence engine' and the laborious efforts required to combat the financial crises have undermined the credibility of the euro area and the EU. The response to the crisis, the bank bailouts and nationalisations, confirms that the financial sector behaved irresponsibly and has aggravated people's sense of vulnerability.

For large groups of Europeans, then, 'euro' and 'EU' have become synonymous with austerity, the decline of the welfare state, and more uncertainty about the future. Market integration and the removal of economic barriers have a growing negative association with globalisation.[6] One typical example is the polarised debate about the trade agreements with Canada and the United States, CETA and TTIP, the latter having now proved unfeasible.

In addition, terrorist violence and foreign political crises, such as the tense relationship with Russia, the war in Syria and the related destabilisation of the region, raise doubts about peace and security. The EU's inability to formulate a collective response to these issues is, for many, proof that it is failing—even if the same facts also furnish arguments in favour of strengthening it.

The loss of confidence has consequences. Support for European integration goes hand in hand with a willingness to show solidarity at European level. The responses to the major crises that the EU has faced in recent years show, however, that mutual solidarity has waned considerably. On top of the financial and economic crisis, the climate crisis and the migration crisis, there is now also a European solidarity crisis, and this latest crisis has furthermore arisen in a context in which problems of legitimacy and 'democratic alienation' are setting the tone.[7] Even though the outcome of the Brexit referendum was partly because Britain's feelings of remoteness from the 'Continent' had never been overcome and because the electorate was misled about the consequences, it seemed indicative of a more widely felt, and growing, sentiment. As the negative impact of Brexit became clearer in the UK, support for the EU began to grow again on the Continent.[8]

3.5 Solidarity and 'Demoicracy'

The international context has continued to change in recent years: after the UK's decision to trigger the exit process under Article 50 of the Treaty on European Union (TEU), a political tidal wave in the United States threw the European Union back on its own resources to a greater extent, with the expectation that France and Germany together would bring new élan to the integration process. In this new context, there is, seemingly, a tendency to make greater allowance for real socio-economic, socio-cultural and administrative differences between Member States and for the need for a familiar and protective national context.

This points to more varied cooperation within the EU. More specifically, this would mean that the EU would no longer do everything with all its Member States in the same way (see the paper by the European Political Strategy Centre of September 2017, *Two Visions, One Direction. Plans for the Future of Europe*).[9] Such an approach would also allow Member States to maintain or regain more policy autonomy, and give them more clear-cut choices as to whether they should join in efforts to deepen their cooperation.

The big question, however, is what this will mean for EU solidarity. More varied cooperation would probably put that solidarity to the test even more than is presently the case. After all, will it not become more difficult to find common ground if the notion of communality were to be further abandoned as a guiding principle? Some argue that a 'European polyphony' could actually work *in favour* of integration. The idea is that polyphony promotes harmony because it leaves somewhat more room for diversity.[10]

Such notions of polyphony are also compatible with calls to cease regarding the European 'demoicracy' (a democratic system encompassing various *demoi*, i.e. peoples) as incomplete or as a 'half-way house' (something that an overarching *demos* at European level would transcend), but instead accept it as established practice or even as a guiding principle.[11],[12] This would entail seeking grounds for European legitimacy in the diversity that is, rather than in a unity that has yet to be. Difference comes first in this approach, not as an end in itself but as a feature of European reality. It may refer to a difference in social and cultural-historical circumstances and backgrounds, a difference in the public sphere and the media landscape, a difference in the problems that arise, but also to a difference in the way groups of citizens are affected by such matters, both favourably and unfavourably. In this way, diversity becomes a guiding principle in the fulfilment of public tasks, rather than an obstacle to be overcome.

A *demoicracy* should address those issues that affect not only Member States but also Europeans in differing formations; in a certain sense, the demoicracy that is the EU already does this. This reality, which is trans-European in nature, gives rise to the need for European public tasks. The plural of *demos*, *demoi*, therefore refers not so much to the co-existence of Member States' electorates as to the cross-border issues affecting citizens in differing Member States. Such cross-border issues are at the root of the public tasks that Europe must take up, as are global risks, which are equally cross-border in nature and concern such matters as financial stability, security and mobility. One of defining traits of such issues is that they can both unite and divide Europe.[13]

The diversity and variability of these issues imply that variation (both in the form that cooperation takes and in differences in each policy domain) can be regarded as a permanent feature rather than as a temporary gateway to closer cooperation or integration. What remains decisive is to show mutual solidarity, even—and perhaps even more so—when undertaking more varied methods of cooperation. The question is which notions of cooperation, integration and solidarity would apply in scenarios that allow for more variation. Whatever the answer to this question may be, it is clear that this is primarily what Habermas[14] refers to as a *political* form of solidarity. This 'political solidarity' distinguishes itself from other forms—such as moral (obligatory) and legal (enforceable) solidarity—through the 'joint involvement in a network of social relations', a situation that can perhaps best be described as a form of institutionalised solidarity.

That involvement fosters greater confidence that the other members of the network will continue to respect the principle of reciprocity in the future. Such 'benefits' of joint, institutionally embedded involvement are crucial to its survival. Political cooperative relationships operate in a context that must be actively reproduced, over and over again, if they are to endure. In other words, to be sustainable, political solidarity must help preserve the precarious social alliance that supports joint involvement. This implies that political solidarity can only be sustained if it is rooted in a subtle feeling for relationships and mutual dependencies.[15]

Throughout the history of European integration, political solidarity came about because political parties broadly supported the principles that (1) people are bound together by mutual dependencies, (2) social cohesion is the aim of European cooperation, and (3) the state is there to offer protection to individuals (and not the other way around)[16]. Christian democrats, social democrats and social liberals were united in the conviction that market integration and multilateral coordination of trade, financial, economic and monetary policy should go hand in hand with maintaining social cohesion at national and regional level. This conviction dovetails with the concept of the 'social market economy' discussed above.

In parallel with the 'social embeddedness' of post-war multilateralism in the construction of national welfare states, however (see Sects. 3.1 and 3.2), this same multilateralism was also 'embedded' in the construction of an international and European legal order. European integration was a constantly evolving part of this post-war multilateralism and its 'double embeddedness' (in national welfare states and in a special type of international legal order).

3.6 Conclusion: Social Embeddedness Under Pressure

The European social market economy developed in a context in which an international and European legal order was being constructed, based on human rights, including fundamental social and economic rights; it was 'embedded' from the outset in the construction of that legal order. This second 'embedding' took its cue from the 'Four Freedoms' presented by President Roosevelt in 1941 (freedom of speech, freedom of worship, freedom from want, and freedom from fear). Among other things, these ideas offered firm foundations for creating the Council of Europe and the European Communities and a basis for establishing structures that would protect fundamental rights in the Member States of these European organisations. Social and economic rights were also included, as they are in some national constitutions, and were reinforced by the protective structures of fundamental rights.

It should be noted that, in the early years, the safeguarding of human rights was the task of the Council of Europe alone. Since then, this task has been defined in greater detail in the European Convention on Human Rights and Fundamental Freedoms (ECHR) and in the intensive scrutiny of the European Court of Human Rights; it was also gradually taken up by the European Communities and later by the EU with the adoption of the Charter of Fundamental Rights of the European Union.

Besides the tensions that have now arisen within this 'second embedding' of European integration in human rights (for example concerning the refugee issue), the 'social embeddedness' of market integration has also been under pressure for some time. In the 1990s, the 'Washington Consensus' (the name given to the IMF's neoliberal economic reform programmes) became increasingly popular within the EU, and in particular within the emu. It manifested itself in the European Treaties, in the governance of the EMU, and in a selective and market-driven penchant for negative integration (by removing barriers to trade and privatisation). Article 36 of the Charter of Fundamental Rights of the European Union 'recognises and respects access to services of general economic interest as provided for in national laws and practices…in order to promote the social and territorial cohesion of the Union'. Nevertheless, in the policies as actually implemented, market forces often outweighed social cohesion.

In this context, the dividing line between public and private interests grew fainter within the EU itself, for example, and issues such as the level of social protection or the 'social dimension' of European integration faded increasingly from view.[17] The pursuit of peace, security and social and economic stability was superseded by a narrow focus on market forces and globalisation. For a growing number of Europeans, then, European integration became a risk rather than a source of protection.

This development is now putting political solidarity in the EU under severe pressure. In the euro area, for example, it is now doubtful whether political solidarity can be attained at all, for instance between northern and southern countries.[18]

It is an observation that raises important questions about the state of European integration. Integration and disintegration sometimes go hand in hand. Both are typical of the integration process. The crucial question, however, is to what extent they fall under the heading of common purpose and joint protection of shared public tasks. Where do the fracture lines appear? To answer these questions, we will outline an analysis framework for describing and explaining these developments in the following chapter. We do so based on the premise that harmonisation and growing uniformity do not exclude variation. This framework will be applied in Appendix 1 to analyse some of the EU's most urgent issues.

Notes

1. The creation of a common market was at the heart of the original concept of the European Communities. To a large extent, European integration has taken shape through this common market. In this newly formed single market, integration (joining different components under a single common denominator) incited (and still incites) conflicts between market freedoms and public interests. After all, the Member States' national policies may prohibit the free movement of goods, persons, services or capital within that single market. In addition to obvious barriers at the border, such as customs tariffs and import bans, provisions meant to protect citizens (e.g. against harmful or polluting substances, but also against the downside of market liberalisation) can lead to differences in competitiveness. There are several ways in which European integration can balance these different interests. For example, it can limit itself to prohibitions, i.e. 'negative' integration, meaning that barriers to the internal market must be removed, or it can issue European standards or jointly formulated principles. The latter, known as 'positive' integration, is achieved by means of European laws. The provisions banning discrimination on the grounds of nationality and thus protectionism or barriers to intra-Community trade —'negative' integration—can be found in the European treaties themselves.

2. Kamer van Koophandel (n.d.) *Interne Markt*, available at https://www.kvk.nl/over-de-kvk/kvk-en-europa/interne-markt/.
3. Segers (2019).
4. 'The Union recognises and respects access to services of general economic interest as provided for in national laws and practices, in accordance with the Treaty establishing the European Community, in order to promote the social and territorial cohesion of the Union.'
5. See M. Dauderstädt, Friederich Ebert Stiftung (2014) *Konvergenz in der Krise - Europas gefährdete Integration*. http://library.fes.de/pdf-files/id/ipa/10941.pdf.
6. van den Hoeven (2016).
7. 'This is a phenomenon that is occurring at present in many democracies where a growing number of citizens feel increasingly unable to identify with the decisions taken by the legislature or government, no matter how much the democratic procedures are observed.' Council of State of the Netherlands, Advisory Division, W01.12.0457/I, 'Report on the embedding of democratic control in the reform of economic governance in Europe to combat the economic and financial crisis', 18 January 2013, p. 6.
8. B. Stokes, R. Wike and D. Manevich (2017) *Post-Brexit, Europeans More Favorable Toward EU*, Pew Research Center 15 June. http://www.pewglobal.org/2017/06/15/post-brexit-europeans-more-favorable-toward-eu/.
9. In effect that was already the case; not all the Member States, for example, participate in the euro or in Schengen and there are various opt-outs, but the actual intention is otherwise.
10. Zielonka (2014: XII).
11. Bohman (2007), Nicolaïdis (2012), Lindseth (2014)
12. In line with Weiler's statement that 'the European Union is a community of others, not brothers', Nicolaïdis (2012) describes the EU as a demoicracy, but now in the positive (appreciative) and idealistic sense of the word: 'A Union-as-demoicracy should remain an open-ended process of transformation which seeks to accommodate the tensions inherent in the pursuit of radical mutual opening between separate peoples.'
13. Beck and Grande (2007).
14. Habermas (2015).
15. Habermas (2015).
16. Segers (2013), Stjerno (2011).
17. See Mazower (2013: 408–412).
18. See Streeck (2015a, b).

Chapter 4
Beyond the Institutional Form: Motivations for Collective Action

4.1 Introduction

The previous chapter described how globalisation, the erosion of embedded liberalism and social protection, and pressure on mutual solidarity between Member States have led to growing frictions in the European Union. These frictions have usually had a combination of causes: external events, internal choices, or the unforeseen consequences of compromises that turned out better for one country or one segment of the population than for another.

While such frictions have become almost a fixed pattern, they have undermined Europeans' support for the project of integration in its current form. For a more complete picture of the sources of these frictions and how they affect European integration, this chapter surveys the various different motivations for cooperation and the variety of institutional forms within the EU. The factors that cause the frictions are multifaceted and ambivalent, after all. To understand the differing and sometimes opposing trends, this chapter examines what goes on behind the institutional forms of European integration. Anyone who looks beyond these forms will discover that motivations for collective action play a crucial role. Examining them will give us a better understanding of what is happening in the EU today and the sources of its current problems. In this chapter, we visualise this approach in the form of a matrix that, besides the dimension of the institutional order, also considers what lies behind it: the dimension of collective action and the motivations for such action. Our visualisation is not meant to offer explanations or solutions. It should be regarded as a tool that acknowledges the underlying motivations of Member States when charting the possibilities and impossibilities of public tasks. Our approach also allows for a more precise assessment of where changes in European integration might be appropriate, where scope for further variation exists, and how it should be effectuated.

The appendix includes an exposition showing how the matrix presented in this chapter can be applied 'dynamically'. It places several urgent European issues, such

E. Hirsch Ballin et al., *European Variations as a Key to Cooperation*, Research for Policy, https://doi.org/10.1007/978-3-030-32893-1_4

as the free movement of services, the resettlement of asylum seekers and European border surveillance, within the matrix, using concrete examples of policy instruments to identify the push-pull forces at work. For example, it examines the content-based positions of these issues in the European field of influence by emphasising the 'why' behind them and by relating them to obstacles to and opportunities for other institutional approaches. This will help us to better understand the current discussions on the EU and to explore, more consciously and proactively, other approaches to cooperation.

4.2 Introduction to the Matrix: Two Axes

We often have high expectations of the EU. For example, we expect it to protect the Community against external threats, protect individuals against the negative aspects of globalisation, and take action in response to migration and climate issues.

Our projection of what the EU should or can do assumes that it can deliver public goods that the Member States are unable to produce on their own, for example a stable and fair socio-economic order, a sustainable living environment, or international security and freedom. It is not necessarily a given that the EU should take over its Member States' tasks, however. The point is to produce the desired public goods reliably, not to confirm European institutional structures. However, producing those goods often requires a level of organisation and teamwork beyond that of intergovernmental cooperation. This means that the EU's institutional structures should be derived from European public tasks (linked to desired public goods), and not the other way around.

Despite this, we often see the institutional order at the heart of European policy. Policy discussions focus on the *form* of cooperation—which Member States are participating and which are not and what is the corresponding transfer of competences? The European public tasks that are to be fulfilled—i.e. the *content*—are thus relegated to the background. It is only when the process of European integration shifts focus from form to content, in other words from institutional order to European public tasks, that the 'why' of collective action becomes apparent. That then provides the basis for considering which institutional forms are or are not possible.

This book uses the matrix below to illustrate the possibilities and impossibilities of a number of European public tasks. The purpose of the matrix is to cross the possible institutional order within European cooperation (horizontal axis) with the motivations for collective action (vertical axis) and to investigate how they relate in the production of public goods. We begin by providing theoretical underpinnings for the concept of European integration as a collective action. The following paragraphs explain the axes and cells in greater detail.

4.3 European Integration as a Collective Action

According to Olson (1965),[1] the more members there are in a group, the less likely that they will be able to spontaneously advance their common interests through collective action. This is true even where the group is unanimous about the public good and the method to be used to produce it. In the world of European integration, this conclusion—that spontaneous collective action is virtually impossible—implies the following.

As the number of Member States increases, it becomes less and less likely that individual Member States will be prepared to help achieve the EU's official, established goals. In other words, Member States will aid in achieving those goals only if the EU offers them enough selective incentives. Specifically, this means that European integration must hold out the prospect of penalties and rewards to each Member State from which non-members can be excluded.

One important qualification here, however, is that an organisation—like any other form of collective behaviour—can also achieve official goals without any of its members aiming to achieve those goals through its actions. The same can be said of the EU. It is quite conceivable (and there is empirical evidence in specific cases) that the EU can attain the official goals of European integration without its Member States themselves pursuing such goals. For example, the history of European integration offers us frequent examples of Member States that, despite unequivocally putting their national economic interests first, promoted prosperity by opening up their national economies to one another and accepting supranational enforcement of such reciprocity. Individual considerations and official organisational goals are not, by definition, at odds with one another.

Since the 1990s, a distinction has been made in the literature on collective action between the 'logic of appropriateness' and the 'logic of consequences' in interpreting individual modes of action.[2] In this book, an actor or group of actors—here, EU Member States—that adhere to the 'logic of appropriateness' will take decisions that follow rules of appropriate or exemplary behaviour. In such behaviour, normative considerations outweigh cost-benefit considerations.

Institutions that refer to the 'logic of appropriateness' add an ethical or moral dimension to their practices and the expectations that they raise. In the reality of the EU, they see an idealistic level of solidarity as the desired mode of action for fulfilling European public tasks. But this mode of action has its downside as well. When put forward as a decisive argument for cooperation, the 'logic of appropriateness' has certain moral and ethical overtones that risk its being perceived, at some stage and within a certain institutional order, as a straitjacket without adequate democratic underpinnings.

The alternative is 'the logic of consequences', i.e. cost-benefit analyses based on individual self-interest or the collective interest. When this highly rationalistic mode of action prevails, the institutional order that emerges is regarded as an aggregate of individual interests achieved through processes of negotiation and coalition formation—and not much more than that. Cooperation is based on rules governing these processes, rather than on norms and values.

The two 'logics' need not be mutually exclusive. They can be regarded as the extremes on a continuum of modes of action. This continuum runs from a laser-sharp focus on national interest or autonomy at one end to idealistic interstate solidarity at the other, with hybrid forms such as 'situational or ad hoc solidarity' in the form of 'reciprocity' in between. The two logics can also reappear in very different types of agreement, ranging from mandatory rules to calls for more solidarity, which together create a framework of checks and balances for cooperation (see for example the work of Ostrom[3] and the WRR report *Publieke zaken in de marktsamenleving*[4]). Issues of European integration, which are by definition complex and multi-faceted, require the Member States to constantly consider this entire spectrum of options, although it is scarcely visible as such, if at all. Its breadth and significance almost always fades from view when officials attempt to explain the course of events and the decisions taken. That is often counterproductive, because it narrows the debate on European integration to one of 'more or less Europe', rather than focusing on the question of 'why?' and 'what kind of Europe do we want to live in?' It also obscures our view of the public tasks that are ultimately at stake (see the first section of this chapter). The problems that this creates have become more and more obvious in recent years.

The creation of the European Communities, and subsequently of the EU, was based on the understanding that vital public tasks can be better, or in fact only, fulfilled by a permanent alliance that has its own political legitimacy. Although the supranational nature of European legislation, governance and court rulings was accepted in the 1950s and 1960s, direct political legitimacy took longer to achieve. Important steps have been taken towards democratisation: a European Parliament whose members are elected directly by the people was founded in 1979; European citizenship was established in 1993; and the European Parliament was given almost full co-legislative competences in 2009. Nevertheless, the results of various referendums—most recently on the Ukraine-EU Association Agreement in the Netherlands and on Brexit in the UK—show that alienation and centrifugal forces are impairing the European project more than ever before.

This experience is yet another reason why the EU should avoid once more embarking on an institutional reconstruction, as it did when it founded the European Convention that produced the failed Treaty establishing a Constitution for Europe. Nor is institutional destruction recommended; the United Kingdom is already experiencing major difficulties as it cancels its membership of the EU. Far too little thought has so far been given to the possibility that the dissonance between the EU and its citizens is caused precisely by its failure to fulfil its public tasks. After all, when citizens feel abandoned, the authorities with which they are least familiar—in this case, those of the European Union—are the first to bear the brunt of their mistrust and rejection.[5]

4.4 Motivations for European Collective Action

It is important to acknowledge how diverse the expectations, interests and preferences involved in European integration are. After all, the motivation, public interest or normative framework that colours how Europeans view integration determines which policies will and will not have their support.

The motivations for European collective action differentiated in this book form a type of continuum. In the matrix below (Fig. 4.1), they are shown on the vertical axis.

(1) **National autonomy: Self-governance is critical.**

Motivation: *Cooperate with other countries only when unavoidable.*
In this approach, the aim is to be as independent as possible from other states or other actors, and to retain as much power as possible to make one's own laws and rules. A state that takes this approach to European cooperation does not, in principle, think cooperation offers enough advantages to relinquish some of its power of self-governance. It will therefore minimise European cooperation and only cooperate if there is no other option. It is difficult to reconcile this approach with structural cooperation, interstate solidarity and supranational institutions.

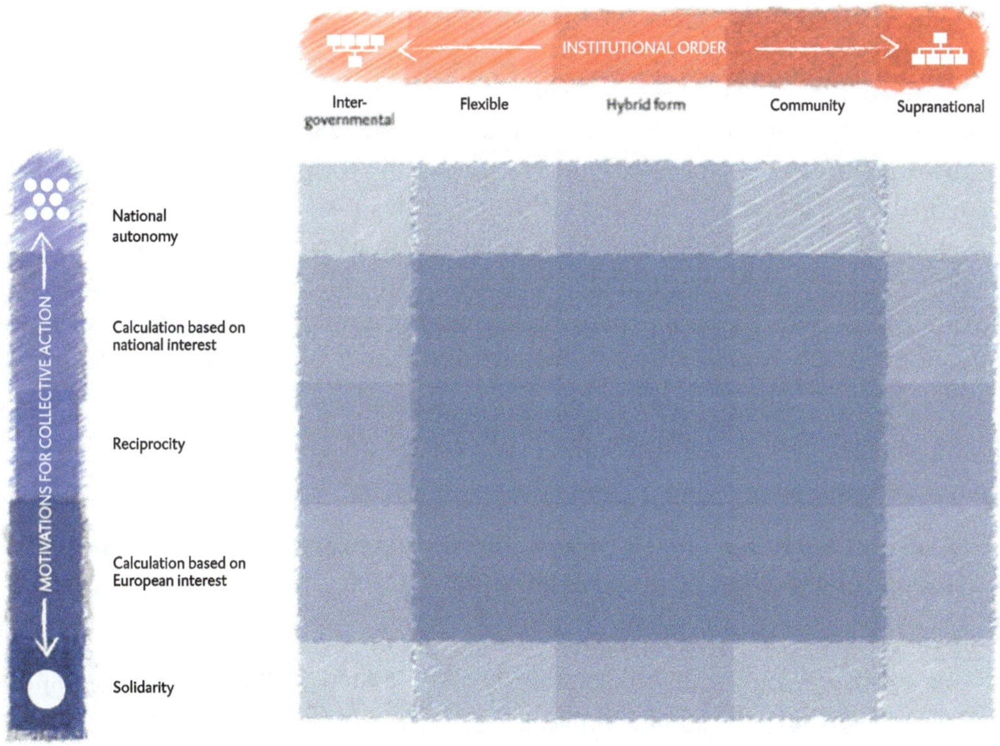

Fig. 4.1 Introduction to the matrix

Example: Agreements on cross-border issues, such as inland shipping on rivers that transcend national borders.

(2) **Calculation based on national interest: Recognising that cooperation can be advantageous.**

Motivation: *The advantage is immediately evident.*
In this approach, European cooperation is accepted if it is advantageous to the individual state. That means that the state has estimated or agreed in advance what cooperation will yield. The advantage may be short-term or long-term in nature, but the state is more likely to go after short-term goals and associated advantages, as they are generally more predictable. The behaviour of the cooperating partners must also be stable. Predictability and quantifiability are crucial in this form of cooperation, but solidarity is not required.

Example: Pooling of defence equipment.

(3) **Reciprocity: One good turn deserves another, playing by the rules to create a level playing field.**

Motivation: *Surrender policy autonomy in favour of market access and expected convergence.*
In this approach, states decide to cooperate in Europe based on the notion of reciprocity. They are prepared to delegate their autonomy in a policy domain to supranational institutions because it will ultimately benefit them to do so. This means that certain 'losses' (material or in terms of autonomy) are accepted in the expectation that they will be compensated in the long term. In anticipation of this positive result, they invest in long-term cooperation. Sahlin (1972)[6] refers to this form of reciprocity as 'balanced' or 'symmetrical' reciprocity. It requires all the participating partners to comply with the rules as they have been agreed. Compliance and enforcement are crucial and are (in part) entrusted to supranational institutions, to avoid 'free riding' problems. After all, collective standards lose credibility as soon as certain participants cease complying with the agreements. Situations are conceivable in which a certain degree of solidarity is required to correct distortions in reciprocity.

Example: Opening the market to goods and services from other Member States and mutual recognition.

(4) **Calculation based on European interest: Absorbing possible individual losses for the good of the greater whole.**

Motivation: *The collective advantage is immediately evident.*
In this approach, European cooperation is taken a step further on the assumption that it is advantageous to all the partners as a group. The expectation is that the collective benefits of cooperation will ultimately accrue to the individual states as well, even though it may be detrimental to national interests in the short term.

Example: The European Commission negotiates in the WTO on behalf of its Member States. A single, strong economic bloc is better than several small European states on the world stage. Another example is the asylum quota proposed by the European Commission in response to the refugee crisis.

(5) **Solidarity: Interstate solidarity as a principle. Making sacrifices for a higher purpose.**

Motivation: *Idealistic solidarity and values.*
In this approach, the larger whole serves a higher purpose than merely meeting national or material goals. Individual losses are accepted, and the losses of one or more partners are also borne by the others. The transfer of autonomy is inherent and may be necessary to enforce idealistic solidarity. The general, overarching aim is to maintain cooperation in anticipation of the tangible and intangible benefits that it will bring, including peace, human rights and social cohesion.

Example: Structural and cohesion funds to reduce disparities in prosperity between Member States and regions.

4.5 Institutional Order

Multiple institutional orders co-exist in the process of European integration. We go through them in this section to clarify our matrix. It is important to note that these are institutional *forms* whose basis lies in the decision-making method and the participating Member States. In other words, a categorisation of institutional orders offers a simplified version of reality. It serves to illustrate existing tensions concerning European public tasks and to show that such simplification does not lead to solutions. We have *omitted* various types of legislation (regulations and directives) as parameters from the categorisation.

This approach makes it clear that other issues play a role in the background, for example different (interpretations of) motivations for collective action, but also that variations are possible which are not immediately obvious. In the matrix above (Fig. 4.1), the various institutional orders can be found on the horizontal axis. We begin our description of this axis with the two idealised extremes on the left and right. We then look at the intermediate forms.

The two extremes:

(1) **Intergovernmental: Agreements are reached by consensus or unanimity.**

In this framework, agreements are made between governments to advance cooperation on a particular issue. There is no interference from institutions to which the cooperating states are subordinate; competences are not transferred and are retained at the national level at all times. Decisions can thus only be taken after full agreement has been reached, and they require the consent of all participating countries. States therefore have a right of veto on each issue, guaranteeing their full policy autonomy.

Example: Past cooperation within the EU's second and third pillars (and prior to that, within the framework of TREVI)

(2) **Supranational: Only supra-state agreements and supra-state enforcement.**

This institutional form involves the *complete* transfer of national policy autonomy to the supranational institutions of the European Union. In a hypothetical variant where this framework would apply to all policy domains, there would be a federation into which the Member States, as federal states, have been absorbed. Enforcement, initiation, democratic legitimacy and oversight of European policy implementation would be entrusted to supranational institutions, regulatory bodies and a supra-state parliament. Variations whereby Member States would or would not participate are not possible in this form of cooperation.

Example: The competences of the Commission in certain matters, such as competition policy or international trade, and the ECB come closest to this institutional framework

The intermediate forms:

(3) **Community: Member States play a greater role in concluding supra-state agreements.**

All EU Member States participate.

The cooperation established within the Community framework applies equally to all participating Member States and is based on (1) supranational institutions as initiators and guardians of the Treaty order, (2) qualified majority voting in the Council as the representation of the Member States and (3) co-decision-making by the European Parliament. As such, it is the same as the ordinary legislative procedure. Community cooperation differs from the supranational institutional framework in that it is possible for Member States to form blocking minorities, for example in the Council. It differs from the flexible arrangements (described below) in that all EU Member States participate in the Community. Variations whereby Member States do or do not participate are impossible in this form of cooperation.

Example: Internal market

(4) **Flexible: Differentiated arrangements based on participating Member States and decision-making.**

The flexible institutional framework allows states to decide, by policy domain, whether or not they wish to participate. Decision-making can take place both through intergovernmental arrangements and under the ordinary legislative procedure. This framework accommodates differentiated cooperation, such as opt-outs in certain areas, differing degrees or speeds of integration (variable-geometry and multi-speed Europe), lead group or sub-group formation, or closer cooperation.

Example: Common European Asylum System (CEAS)

(5) **Hybrid form: Encompasses all of the foregoing institutional elements.**

The institutional framework described here as a 'hybrid form' has intergovernmental, supranational and Community elements, and is also flexible, with opt-outs permitted in certain areas. This institutional framework comes closest to the description of the current EU as a whole.

4.6 Conclusion: Community Cooperation and Its Limitations

The institutional order that has traditionally been appropriate for European integration differs from other forms of international cooperation. This difference is particularly noticeable in how the EU institutions cooperate with one another in the ordinary legislative procedure (the European Commission, the European Parliament and the Council). Adhering to the Community method of cooperation reinforces a tendency to seek solutions through deeper integration and uniformity, by having *all* Member States participate. It is a tried-and-tested formula in the history of European integration. Based on this 'policy rationality', motivations for collective action are then identified, often by appealing to an overarching European interest and interstate solidarity (see the vertical axis).

There is growing public and political resistance to closer European integration based on this policy rationality. Increasingly, political circles at national level advocate moving away from the EU (seeking solutions in the institutional orders located more to the left on the horizontal axis of the matrix). These new arguments correspond with a shift in the motivations for collective action towards more national autonomy, evident in the politics of almost all Member States (see the vertical axis).

Applying the matrix to the current reality reveals a critical fault line in European integration. If we take Community cooperation and the associated policy rationality as our basis, then we soon arrive at the following motivations for collective action: 'calculation based on European interest', 'solidarity' and 'reciprocity'. These motivations are often based in part on 'the logic of appropriateness' and correspond with the Community and supranational institutional orders, or possibly a hybrid form. In Fig. 4.2, the blue arrows pointing to the bottom right-hand side of the matrix visualise the trend induced by Community cooperation and the associated policy rationality.

The phenomenon of 'democratic alienation' in response to European integration is the opposite of this, in a certain sense (see Chap. 3). It manifests itself as a desire for maximum autonomy on the part of the national state. The Brexit campaign's 'take back control' slogan was a poignant example. 'Calculation based on national interests' can also serve as a motivation for collective action when political

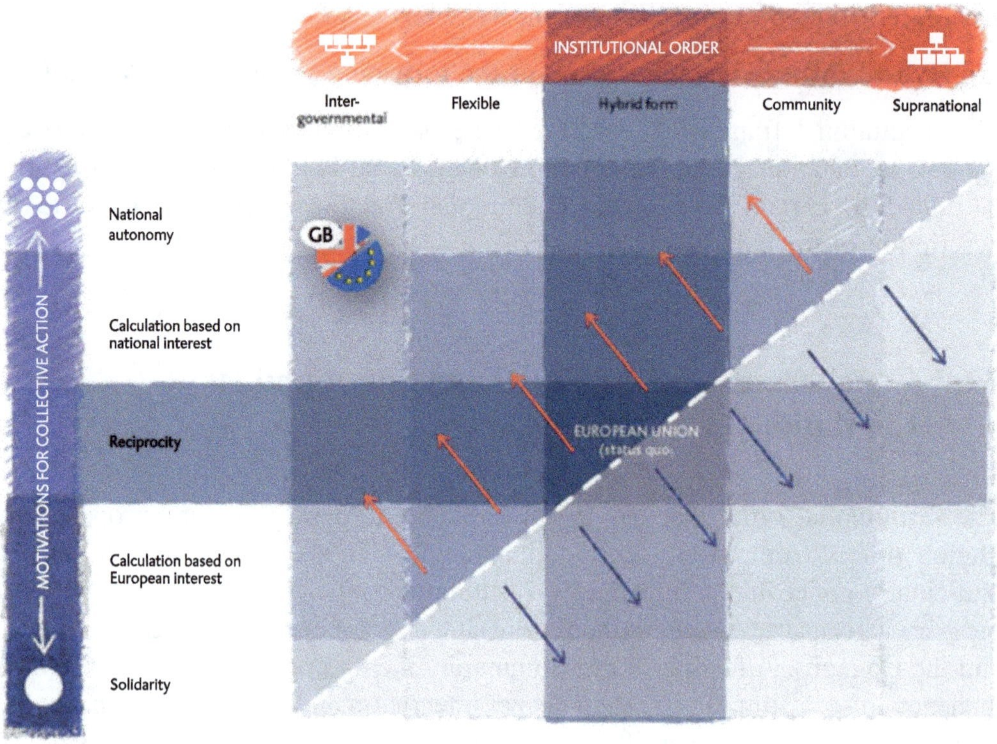

Fig. 4.2 Matrix of opposing trends

legitimacy is perceived to be lacking because it involves cooperation solely in the pursuit of individual short-term interests, something that is usually easier to justify in the domestic politics of the Member States. These two motivations are based on the 'logic of consequences'. They can usually only be advanced through an institutional order that takes the form of intergovernmental or flexible cooperation with a number of like-minded Member States. In Fig. 4.2, the red arrows pointing to the upper left-hand side of the matrix visualise the trend towards greater autonomy.

The original concept behind the European Communities involved the pursuit of free competition and a level playing field in a European single market. This European legal order would make it possible to remove obstacles to the common market without completely dismantling social protection in national legislation associated with the movement of goods, persons, services and capital. Social protection would also be guaranteed by *harmonisation.* Within this legal order as established by the Treaty of Rome, the notion of reciprocity (and hence the expectation of convergence), combined with Community cooperation, guided the evolution of European cooperation. See Fig. 4.3 for the visualisation.

The transition to the Maastricht order in 1993 cast European integration into the shape of the European Union. In the EU, the main institutional order increasingly evolved into a hybrid form that now includes supranational, Community, intergovernmental, but also flexible elements. The overall approach of reciprocity

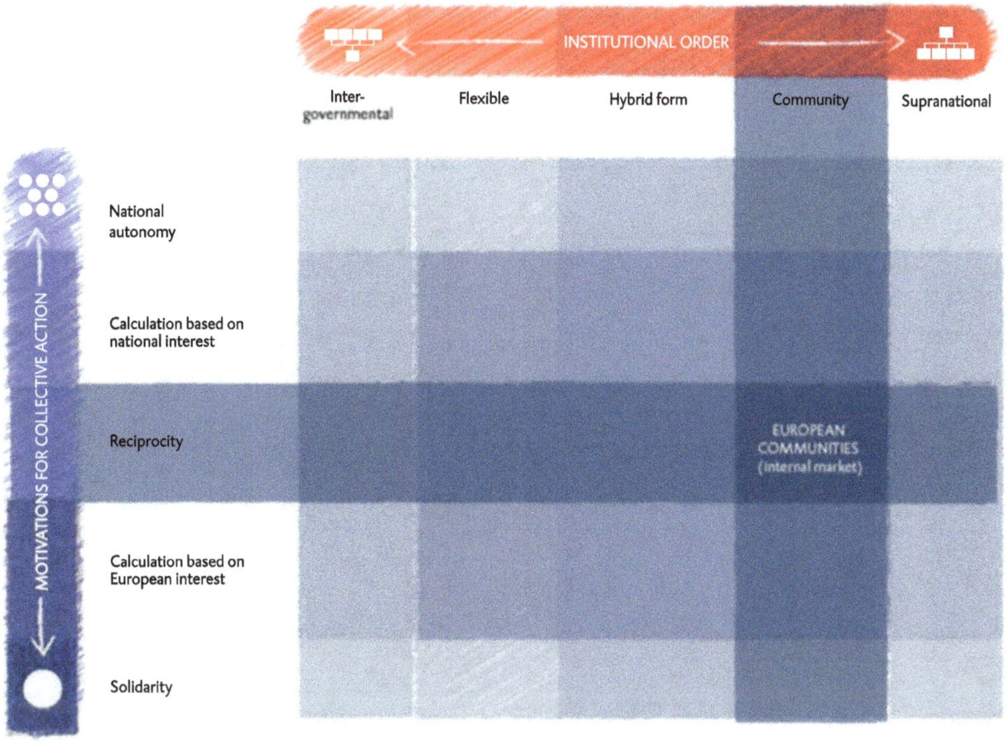

Fig. 4.3 Matrix showing the position of the European Communities

remained unchanged, however, and is still at the heart of Europe's self-image and how it handles policy measures.

Figure 4.4 shows that, in its present form, the EU is positioned precisely in the middle of the diverging trends described above. The opposing forces are at their strongest there, largely because EU Member States have a range of different motivations for collective action, often due to differences in how they prioritise public interests. Oftentimes, the motivations are neither recognised nor acknowledged, however. Instead, they are forced into the straitjacket of mutual recognition (in the expectation that this will encourage ever greater harmonisation and convergence) and 'playing by the rules'. All the while, the EU's institutions remain focused on Community cooperation with all the Member States. The frustrating inertia to which this leads may, in the long run, be detrimental to EU unity, as Brexit has recently demonstrated (Fig. 4.5).[7]

There are alternatives, however, that become possible by consciously allowing for more variation.

The matrix introduced in this chapter explains (1) the motivations for collective action and (2) the existing forms of institutional organisation within the process of European integration, and shows how the two relate. As we cautioned, this is a simplified version of reality. Significantly, what the matrix does not show is that even if different Member States choose the same motivation for collective action, they may have based that choice on completely different interpretations of the

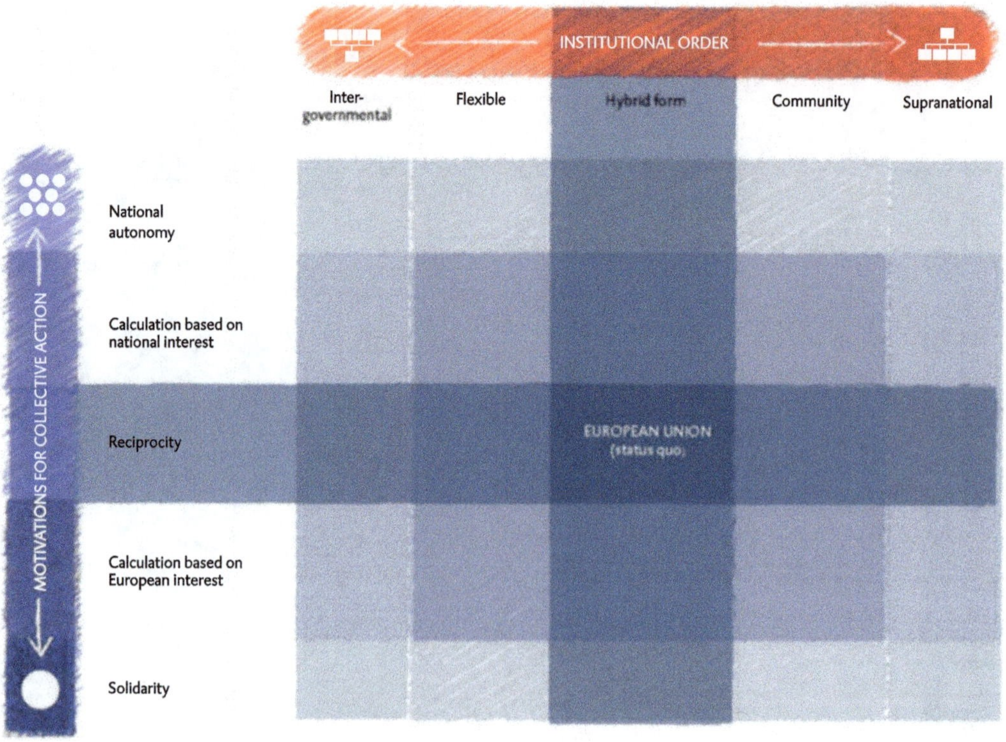

Fig. 4.4 Matrix showing the position of the European Union

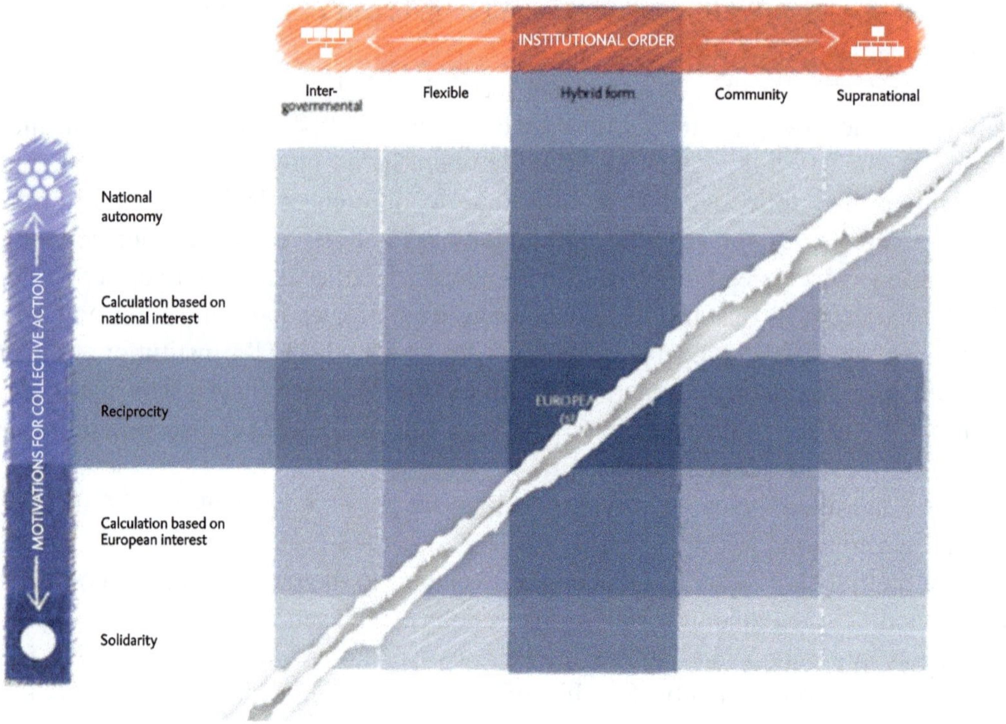

Fig. 4.5 Matrix of fault lines

situation in question. This is particularly important with regard to motivations suggesting a constructive attitude towards European solutions. For example, two Member States that have the same motivation may be pursuing two different public interests or have different priorities within those interests.

In such a case, even when Member States share the same motivation for collective action, it may be impossible to arrive at a constructive European policy because the underlying interpretations differ too much. If we include such differences in interpretation in our analysis, then we get the following new option on the vertical axis of the matrix: Member States have the same motivation, but based on different interpretations of the situation. This is the third possibility alongside the more obvious ones in the matrix, namely 'Member States have the same motivation for collective action (and therefore interpret the situation in the same way)' and 'Member States have different motivations'.

When the motivations for collective action differ, scope for cooperation can be created by allowing variation in membership and/or the decision-making procedure. This is already apparent in the various 'flexible' and 'hybrid' institutional orders on the horizontal axis of the matrix and fits in with its set-up (which is based on membership and decision-making procedures as defined for the various institutional orders). However, variation in membership and/or decision-making is not enough in the third option, in which the motivation is the same but the underlying interpretations (which Member States use to defend their chosen motivation) differ. In that case, variation must be sought along a third dimension, in addition to membership and decision-making, namely the content of the relevant policy. One way to do this is to work with minimum standards and allow variation beyond that minimum (instead of seeking harmonisation). Even in the current quest for methods to strengthen the euro area and emu, variation in policy content offers scope for arriving at innovative solutions within the existing Treaty frameworks. The appendix provides a number of examples illustrating the above.

The EU's current problems thus demand that we not only break away from the notion of reciprocity and Community cooperation, but also that we examine the option of 'flexible' arrangements more closely by exploring the possibility of variation in policy content. The following chapter will reveal that 'policy variation' has existed since the founding of the European Communities, but has not always been recognised as such. We see this at the very heart of the Union, the internal market. There are no opt-outs there, no lead groups being formed, but rather—thanks in part to national discretion in policymaking—a continuous balancing of European public interests, for example between the four freedoms and other fundamental values arising from the embeddedness of European integration in social and human rights. The following chapter explores the theme of variation in more detail and analyses what forms of diversity in cooperation already exist in Europe. It examines existing variation practices in the internal market from a legal perspective, in particular with regard to the political legitimacy of variation in policy content and its significance for the four freedoms.

Notes

1. Olson (1965).
2. March and Olsen (1995).
3. Ostrom (2009, 2010).
4. WRR (2012).
5. In three areas crucial to European societies, integration stalled halfway and came to a juddering halt. The introduction of the euro led to deeper economic and political entanglement than the institutional structure of the time could bear. Complementary to the free movement of persons was a Common European Asylum System, the details of which were put into place procedurally between 1999 and 2013, but which lacked genuine cohesion: the Reception Conditions Directive allowed for extreme differences in national policies and a common refugee return policy was never agreed. The Common Foreign and Security Policy was established in 1993 but has never got off the ground. As a result, following earlier disagreements about the wars in former Yugoslavia and the Iraq War, the European Union has been unable to play an effective role either in the civil war in Syria or in the Ukrainian crisis.
6. Sahlins (1972).
7. In March 2017, during a discussion with Emmanuel Macron and Sigmar Gabriel, Habermas described this state of affairs as 'a furious standstill' (see: https://www.blaetter.de/archiv/jahrgaenge/2017/april/europa-neu-denken).

Chapter 5
Variation and the Internal Market

5.1 Introduction

The internal market, which encompasses the free movement of goods, persons, services and capital, is at the heart of European cooperation. The Treaty on the Functioning of the European Union (TFEU) prohibits Member States, and in some cases private organisations, from introducing measures that impede free movement. In addition, there are provisions in the Treaty that prohibit companies from obstructing competition in the internal market. Legislation, including directives and regulations, completes its legal architecture[1] and is meant to eliminate differences between national rules that might disrupt the internal market process and to set common standards for the 28 Member States.

Ever since the Treaty of Lisbon came into force, the EU has had a 'social market economy' as its aim. The crucial question is what that means and to what extent variation is compatible with that aim and with attempts to meet the needs of different groups of citizens. More specifically, how divisible (or indivisible) is the internal market? Is it politically and legally conceivable and beneficial to society to separate the four freedoms from one another and thus for each Member State to no longer guarantee all freedoms? But also, how conceivable and beneficial is variation *within* each of the four freedoms? For example, concerning the precise definition of the free movement of persons: to what extent can national exceptions be permitted?

The question of the divisibility or indivisibility of the internal market is crucial because it is important for the overall direction of European integration, and because it must be settled at Treaty level with the agreement of all the Member States. Variation within the individual freedoms has more to do with everyday political practice, where the emphasis is much more on how European legislation should be fleshed out in specific terms, depending on the policy objective. The questions this involves include what sort of European standard or level of protection is required, how much discretionary scope can be left to the Member States, and what kind of legal or policy instruments are appropriate.

E. Hirsch Ballin et al., *European Variations as a Key to Cooperation*, Research for Policy, https://doi.org/10.1007/978-3-030-32893-1_5

Three phenomena come to light repeatedly when analysing such questions. We will come across them time and again in this chapter.

1. First of all, the process of European market integration is constantly disrupted by various factors. Those factors include national legislation and rules that are meant to protect national public interests but that may simultaneously create obstacles to free movement within the EU. In other words, there is tension between Europe's interest in market integration and national public interests. For example, safeguarding market integration may have negative consequences for the national social domain.
2. Second, while harmonisation of national rules is important for eliminating market distortions while protecting national interests at European level, it does not always require homogeneity and convergence across the full breadth of internal market rules. On the contrary, allowing for national differences can also strengthen support for the EU, for example because it is more in keeping with the temporary—and constantly evolving—nature of many EU arrangements or with special circumstances in a particular Member State. The internal market is not based on a simple 'one-size-fits-all' approach but instead leaves scope for divergence. In fact, the way in which the single market deals with distortions and allows for variation in national public interests can also provide interesting insights into other policy domains.
3. Third, market integration and the enactment of European legislation in the internal market can also be distorted from the outside, for example by non-EU countries. The internal and external worlds of European market integration are inextricably linked. The completion of the internal market therefore also depends on the arrangements and rules agreed with the outside world.

5.2 A Social Market Economy: Work in Progress

It is clear that not everyone benefits to the same extent from the free market and sees their standard of living improve as a result, even if the *economic added value* of the European internal market is widely acknowledged.[2] By estimates, almost a quarter of the EU's population is currently at risk of poverty or social exclusion. Employment levels and living standards vary widely not only between Member States but also between regions within Member States. There are also major differences between Member States in terms of working patterns, education, health and social security.[3] Many people are therefore worried about how the EU is tackling the social problems associated with an open (labour) market. According to the 2017 *Eurobarometer*, more than eight out of ten Europeans see unemployment, social inequality and migration as the three most important challenges facing the Union and expect a free market economy to go hand in hand with high levels of social protection. Seven out of ten feel that social and unemployment policies are poorly managed and support decision-making at both national and EU level.[4]

Since the entry into force of the Treaty of Lisbon in 2009, Article 3(3) TEU provides that the EU shall work for the sustainable development of Europe, based, among other things, on a 'highly competitive social market economy, aiming at full employment and social progress'. Other objectives mentioned in Article 3(3) support these aims, namely combating social exclusion and discrimination and promoting social justice and protection and solidarity between generations. These passages flesh out the more general aim of Article 3(1), namely that the Union's objective is 'to promote peace, its values and the well-being of its peoples'. But well-being goes beyond safeguarding the social dimension in the above sense; it also implies protecting other public interests, for example the environment, sustainable development and consumers. Ancillary policy of this kind is therefore also important in shaping the internal market.[5] The Union is founded[6] on the values of 'respect for human dignity, freedom, democracy, equality, the rule of law and respect for human rights, including the rights of persons belonging to minorities. These values are common to the Member States in a society in which pluralism, non-discrimination, tolerance, justice, solidarity and equality between women and men prevail'.

However, opinions differ considerably as to the form that the social market economy and related aims and values should take.

Article 26 TFEU defines the internal market as 'an area without internal frontiers in which the free movement of goods, persons, services and capital is ensured in accordance with the provisions of the Treaties'. This definition says nothing about how the internal market should be shaped, the intensity of EU regulation, the relationship between national and European public interests, or the idea of a social market economy. It is also unclear exactly what the relationship is between the four freedoms and whether there may be a hierarchy between them.[7] Article 151 TFEU, on the objectives of Europe's social policy, also refers to the internal market. Objectives such as the promotion of employment, improved living and working conditions, proper social protection, lasting high employment and the combating of exclusion are linked explicitly to the internal market.

The task of developing the social dimension of the internal market and safeguarding other public interests going forward is literally a work in progress. The two defining factors in this context are the existing principles of market organisation (e.g. the fundamental rights set out in the Charter of Fundamental Rights of the European Union), but also the possibilities and impossibilities arising from 'political will'.

Two factors: Principles of market organisation and political will

The first factor is that the Member States are not entirely free to define the Union's socio-economic objectives and core values. Specifically, we can identify a number of market organisation principles in EU law that constitute important legal and political benchmarks for their further elaboration. In the first place, there are the fundamental rights of citizens and other residents of the Union as now enshrined in the Charter of Fundamental Rights of the European Union. The Charter includes provisions on human dignity and freedoms, solidarity, citizenship and justice.

These not only guide the Union legislator and—in the policy domains covered by Union law—the Member States, but also the Court of Justice in its judicial reviews of the relationship between the internal market and national public interests. We will discuss this in the sections below.

What is important here, however, is to take a closer look at solidarity as a key principle for the Member States and its possible significance for citizens. It is not yet clear what this principle encompasses or precisely what it requires of them,[8] but what *is* clear is that it is acquiring growing political and legal relevance. In terms of the Treaties, it is not only identified as one of the core values of the Union but is also referred to in Article 3 of the TEU, i.e. in terms of ensuring solidarity between generations and between Member States and promoting economic, social and territorial cohesion. In practical terms, the EU pursues the latter aim by redistributing funds through the Structural and Investment Funds, including the European Regional Development Fund and the European Social Fund.[9] However, the importance of solidarity between Member States is also reflected in the Union's external policies,[10] the common foreign and security policy,[11] migration and asylum policy,[12] and in the internal market, even if the Treaties do not refer to it specifically in this context.[13] There, solidarity is referenced indirectly in the Court's judgments on the free movement of services and persons, but also in the political assessment that takes place in the legislative process. Solidarity can also be regarded as an important factor in loyal cooperation, not only between the Member States and the Union's institutions, but also between the Member States themselves.[14]

The TFEU also contains a number of 'mainstreaming principles' (Articles 8–13) that oblige Union institutions to afford public interests other than purely economic ones a high level of protection when adopting any European legislation, rules or policy. Article 9 TFEU specifically provides that:

> In defining and implementing its policies and actions, the Union shall take into account requirements linked to the promotion of a high level of employment, the guarantee of adequate social protection, the fight against social exclusion, and a high level of education, training and protection of human health.

The other provisions concern combatting discrimination and promoting equality on various grounds, integrating requirements to promote sustainable development, and taking consumer protection requirements into account.[15] Regarding the single market, the main legal basis for internal market legislation (Article 114 TFEU), which we will discuss further below, states that 'any proposals must take as a base a high level of protection concerning health, safety, environmental protection and consumer protection'.

These socio-economic aims, core values and market organisation principles together constitute the framework for the second factor: determining precisely what level of social protection and progress is being pursued in the context of European decision-making, how much guidance that requires of the EU, and how much discretion is left to the Member States is above all a question of political assessment. The initial expectation, i.e. that establishing the common market would improve standards of living, implied that there was no need to transfer significant national competences in the social policy domain to Europe. When reality proved otherwise, however, the political will to make social protection an essential element of the internal market expressed itself through other channels in legislation, including directives derived from the legal basis for the internal market set out in Article 95 of the EC Treaty (now Article 114 TFEU). Examples are the Directive on the safeguarding of employees' rights in the event of transfers of under-takings,[16] the Directive on the protection of employees in the event of the insolvency of their employer,[17] and various directives on equal treatment of men and women.[18] Although the EU's legislative power to implement social policy was and still is limited, for example in relation to employment policy and social security, the Union legislator has interpreted its competences in internal market matters broadly so as to guarantee the social rights of workers as well. In that sense, we can say that the EU has a certain social *acquis*.[19]

The political guidelines for the social *acquis* are set by the European heads of state or government, together with the President of the Commission and under the leadership of the President of the European Council, while the legislative and regulatory details are negotiated by the Council of Ministers together with the European Parliament upon proposals from the Commission. As our discussion of various cases below will make clear, amendments or adjustments to European legislation may also be deemed necessary as insights into the downsides of market forces change. In other words, the EU's legal framework leaves plenty of scope to weigh up the interests of the economic market and other public interests politically, and so the matter of how to flesh out the social market economy is, above all else, a question of political choice.

The European Commission's recent proposal to establish a European Pillar of Social Rights reaffirms the importance of both factors in achieving a more 'social' internal market.[20] On the one hand, the twenty principles and rights covered by this pillar deploy the principles of market organisation in a legal and policy-related sense. On the other hand, the joint adoption by the Commission, the Council and the European Parliament of the European Pillar of Social Rights at the Social Summit for Fair Jobs and Growth in Gothenburg on 17 November 2017 expresses the political will to implement the principles and rights under the pillar. The pillar is about delivering on equal opportunities and access to the labour market, fair working conditions, and social protection and inclusion.

The courts play a reactive role in the internal market in that they review national laws and rules in the light of the EU Treaties' free movement provisions whenever the public or companies are disadvantaged by them. The Union legislator has a proactive role in that it creates rules and policies to protect various public interests. Coordinating policy measures are also needed, however, and are now provided for in the European Pillar of Social Rights, for example concerning employment policy in relation to the European Semester for economic policy coordination and the convergence process within the EMU.[21]

Assessing public interests in the internal market

The EU Treaties have various provisions prohibiting rules and conduct that impede free movement. The Court of Justice, which plays a major role in interpreting more general Treaty provisions, stipulated early on in the history of the European Communities that these provisions must be applied and enforced by Member States through their own courts. The Court described European law as an autonomous source of law, binding Member States and citizens alike to the rules governing the common market. As a result of this 'normative-functional' integration method, which emphasised market liberalisation and the removal of barriers to movement, the law governing the internal market, in which the four freedoms play a crucial role, has proliferated and extended into virtually every domain of economic and social life.[22] These market rules thus provide normative frameworks for national measures and actions, even when they pursue public objectives and guarantee social rights.[23]

Although they are applied broadly, the four freedoms are not absolute in nature. The Member States may restrict freedom of movement to a certain extent to safeguard non-economic interests, for example the fundamental rights of citizens, including social rights, which may be guaranteed under certain conditions and within the boundaries of the four freedoms. Case law has recognised that Member States may restrict freedom of movement to safeguard non-economic interests, provided that the relevant national measure is proportionate. It therefore makes allowance for certain public interests, typically national values or ethical or politically sensitive issues such as the protection of vulnerable groups of consumers, a regional language, or the regulation of gambling.

The scope that is created in this way makes a balanced assessment possible that can be used to protect social rights and interests. There are, however, certain situations in which the Court's judgments subordinate social rights to the rules of free movement. In the Viking and Laval cases,[24] the Court restricted the trade unions' right to strike, something for which it was criticised.[25] Its approach here conflicts with the underlying principle of the Charter of Fundamental Rights of the European Union, which requires a balanced assessment between economic freedoms and the fundamental rights of citizens. After all, the Charter implies that the freedoms of the internal market are no more important than fundamental rights or public interests.[26] The economic freedoms and the guarantee of social rights are by no means mutually exclusive, however, but complementary, something that became apparent in the 1968 Regulation on freedom of movement for workers within the Community, which stipulated that workers employed in the territory of another Member State must enjoy the same social and tax advantages as national workers.[27] In its judgments, the Court has interpreted the term 'social advantages' broadly to include non-financial advantages, such as the right to require the use of a certain language in court proceedings[28] and the right of residence for the unmarried companion of a worker who is a national of another Member State, which the Court asserts must be regarded as social advantages within the meaning of Article 7(2) of the Regulation.[29]

The Court of Justice has also issued key rulings on the importance of the free movement of persons versus that of maintaining national social security systems, i.e. between transnational and national social solidarity. It has, in fact, promoted transnational solidarity between citizens by increasingly granting them access to national social security rights, based on the notion that Member States must treat their own nationals and the nationals of other EU Member States as equals. It has used the principle of proportionality to interpret social solidarity in a way that affords citizens the right to social assistance, but within the limits of the available resources.[30], [31] The Court requires Member States to show solidarity towards the nationals of other Member States, depending on the length of time an individual has resided in the host Member State—an indicator of his/her level of integration—and on the condition that the individual does not become an unreasonable financial burden on the host Member State.[32] A similar dilemma between transnational and national solidarity can be seen in case law concerning the free movement of services in relation to access to medical care in other Member States, where the Court has guaranteed individual citizens access to such care under certain conditions.[33] On the one hand, we can say that the Court's approach to citizens' rights has added a dimension of social solidarity to the economic internal market paradigm that extends beyond the customary beneficiaries of the free movement provisions.[34] On the other hand, its championing of individual rights has been criticised for weakening the social solidarity that underpins the national social security systems. Newdick refers meaningfully in this connection to 'citizenship, free movement and health care: cementing individual rights by corroding social solidarity'.[35] It is, in any case, clear that the free movement of persons and services has impacted the guarantee of public interests through social security systems grounded in national social solidarity.

Negative integration is thus based directly on the norms of the Treaties and involves assessing national public interests within the framework of EU law, with the Member States being obliged to take the interests of free movement into account in that assessment and not to interfere disproportionately with the four freedoms. By interpreting internal market law, the Court of Justice plays a guiding role, and that role is decisive for the discretion that remains to protect national public interests. The fact that the Member States are largely in charge of creating social policy and that the Union legislator has little or no input gives the Court of Justice the final say in assessing how national social interests weigh up against the EU rules on free movement. After all, whenever the exercise of national competences affects freedom of movement within the internal market, a private individual can invoke the free movement provisions of the Treaty and challenge the social law provisions in court. It is then up to the Member State to show that its policy is meant to safeguard social interests.

The situation is different when the Union legislator takes the initiative. It is empowered to assess public interests within the context of the internal market (positive integration). The fact that it possesses such legislative competence already implies that the internal market is about more than simply removing barriers to trade. That is why legal specialists and other researchers have now come to regard the internal market as a 'battlefield of values and interests'.[36] As noted above, the Treaties require the Union legislator to take other interests into account, for example a high level of protection for health, safety, the environment and consumers (Article 114(3) TFEU). The question then is how the various interests are weighed up and accommodated in the practical sense. Our analysis of two key pieces of legislation that concern interests other than the elimination of internal market barriers, i.e. the Posting of Workers Directive and the General Data Protection Regulation (GDPR), has given rise to a number of findings. The following questions are central to the analysis:

1. How does the EU weigh up public interests against the removal of barriers to free movement?
2. How is this assessment made manifest in legislation?
3. How much discretion do individual Member States have to vary policy content?

Sometimes the importance of removing barriers to the four freedoms of the internal market is diametrically opposed to other public interests. In the original proposal for the Posting of Workers Directive, the Commission stated that it was a question of 'finding a balance between two principles which find themselves in contradiction'.[37] On the one hand, there is the free competition between companies. That requires a 'level playing field' eliminating unfair competitive advantages under national rules. On the other hand, Member States wish to protect workers—for example by setting minimum pay levels—in a way that takes the relevant country's circumstances into account. In the directive as ultimately enacted, the free movement of services is mentioned explicitly as one of the objectives of the Community (in recital 1).

We also see another tension in the assessment of public interests in the Posting of Workers Directive. Not only is the protection of free competition and the free movement of services at odds with the protection of workers, but there is also the related issue of the level at which that public interest should be protected: the first two interests require the Union legislator to take action, whereas the protection of workers—as interpreted by the Commission—requires action on the part of the Member States.

The interests involved in data protection are not diametrically opposed. At stake here are the protection of privacy on the one hand and the free movement of personal data on the other, the latter being viewed as an aspect of the internal market (indeed, some argue that the free movement of knowledge and data should be considered the fifth freedom of the internal market).[38] Whether enshrined in the GDPR or the old Data Protection Directive, these interests remain the same (although the wording is slightly different). The reason for the new Regulation lay mainly in the rapidly changing social and technological context, referred to as the 'datafication' of the economy,[39] which has made the exchange of data within the EU crucial for prosperity growth.

The legal system also assumes that protecting privacy does not necessarily undermine the free movement of data. On the contrary, the Commission's argument was that a uniform system of privacy rules would boost confidence in personal data protection and thus ease the free movement of data. While this belief is not based on any empirical evidence, the new Regulation is designed in such a way that if organisations comply with a range of privacy safeguards, the free flow of data will be guaranteed by the absence of diverging national regimes.

Similar trade-offs between free movement and other public interests can also be found in other legislation. The Audiovisual Media Services Directive[40] strikes a balance between free movement and cultural interests, for example. The Directive's preamble states that the growing importance of audiovisual media services for societies, democracies, education and culture justifies the application of specific rules that restrict the operation of the internal market. It follows from the Directive's articles that other interests are also at stake, such as the protection of minors, the right of those with visual or auditory disabilities to access media, and the diversity of television programming.[41] The revised Payment Services Directive (PSD2) weighs the free movement of payment services against the protection of individuals (data protection).[42] The Directive opens up the market for payment services but at the same time improves consumer protection—although there are doubts about how effective that protection really is.[43] Finally, in its public procurement law, the EU now (since a review round) gives contracting authorities more leeway to include environmental and social aspects in contract award criteria.[44]

The political assessment of public interests is fleshed out in European legislation. The content of EU legislation answers the question of how the Union legislator weighed up public interests, what weight it assigned to each of those interests, and what balance it ultimately struck between them. Our analysis of the two legislative case studies shows, however, that other factors also play a role in this assessment. Two of these are of critical importance for the above questions: the chosen legal basis, and the role of the Court of Justice.

The legal basis and the role of the Court

The Union legislator does not have a general mandate but must rely on the legal basis laid down in each sector in the Treaties. With regard to the internal market, the Treaties provide a broad legal basis for action, in particular in Article 114 TFEU. The question is: to what extent does the chosen legal basis influence the assessment of public interests at stake?

Our analysis of the two legislative cases reveals that the Court considers free movement very important whenever the Union legislator refers to one of the legal bases of the internal market as justification for a directive or regulation (see also the Court of Justice's Laval judgment below). This is understandable: as a legal basis, free movement is intended precisely to create an internal market. The fact that the Treaties define these legal bases in terms of broad, general objectives has led to major problems and allowed economic interests to prevail over non-economic ones. Nevertheless, the importance attached to free movement is not indisputable. The Court of Justice has ruled that a measure grounded in such a legal basis may certainly serve other public interests, as long there are guarantees that it will also have a positive effect on free movement. In fact, pursuant to the principles of market organisation identified above, other interests and principles must also be taken into account. The Court has even accepted that the primary objective of internal market legislation may concern a public interest other than the improvement of conditions for the free movement of goods, persons, services and capital. In a judgment concerning the Tobacco Advertising Directive, which was clearly meant to protect public health, the Court ruled that this was acceptable as long as the measure also contributed to improving the conditions for the functioning of the internal market.[45] If legislation grounded in the legal bases of the internal market does indeed contribute in such a way, then it is valid. Such legislation may also be applied in domestic situations. For example, individuals may invoke the rights stemming from the Data Protection Directive (now the GDPR) even if they reside in the same Member State as the person against whom they are invoking those rights.

Legislative practice reveals, however, that the legal basis does influence the assessment of public interests. The GDPR makes that clear. The legal basis of the old Data Protection Directive was the internal market (Article 114 TFEU), whereas the new Regulation has a special, new legal basis (Article 16 TFEU)[46] leading to a different assessment of the interests of free movement versus those of privacy. The Regulation imposes new obligations on data processors (e.g. on data portability, how to respond if citizens wish to exercise their 'right to be forgotten', how to act in the event of data breaches, etc.), extends the conditions under which organisations appoint data protection officers, increases organisations' responsibility for demonstrating compliance with the law, and inflicts severe penalties in the event of non-compliance. These and other elements show that the balance has shifted in favour of privacy protection.

The current Posting of Workers Directive also shows that the chosen legal basis can advance the interest of free movement—because it is given greater weight than social interests—especially when combined with the role of the Court of Justice (see below). However, a new Posting of Workers Directive has now been agreed that will tip the scales towards the protection of workers, in response to criticism that the current Directive focuses too much on free movement. The Sociaal-Economische Raad (Social and Economic Council of the Netherlands) (SER) argued that the current Directive failed to strike the right balance in this respect.[47] It saw opportunities to broaden the basis of support for the internal market with a 'trust offensive' consisting of measures intended to eliminate the unequal treatment of labour migrants. The revision envisaged by the SER was meant to create a level playing field for companies and workers, in particular by addressing ambiguities in the period of posting and the concept of remuneration. Its proposals have now been incorporated into the agreement concerning the revised Posting of Workers Directive. The revised text emphasises the temporary nature of posting by imposing a 12-month cap on posting (with the possibility of a six-month extension). Regarding the concept of remuneration, the principle of equal pay for equal work will prevail; before, it was the minimum wage. The Directive will also be extended to all sectors of the economy, with special conditions applying in the transport sector, thus creating a level playing field there too. These changes are meant to restore the balance between the freedom of companies to provide services and the protection of posted workers.

Both legislative case studies show that, in the context of the internal market, public interests are assigned different weights over time and that the relevant legal bases also provide leeway for this. While free movement is clearly subordinate to other public interests in these case studies, that is not always so, as the Services Directive demonstrates.[48] Even there, however, the interests of the internal market were undoubtedly set off against social interests at the time, with the Commission's original proposal undergoing a major revision as a result. For example, the country of origin principle was eliminated during the negotiations for that reason, and certain sectors and services excluded from that principle.[49] It is therefore difficult to draw general conclusions about the direction of this trend. Legislative and other decision-making processes and their outcomes are often impenetrable. Not even the objectives targeted by EU legislation are always made explicit, for example.[50] The data protection case also shows that other actors can significantly influence these processes in ways that are not equally clear to all. In this instance, the Article 29 Data Protection Working Party (WP29)—a group composed of representatives of the national supervisory authorities and two EU representatives—played a role. The Working Party's official task was advisory in nature, but in fact it exercised considerable influence on the interpretation of data protection law.[51] The Working Party has now been superseded by the European Data Protection Board. In addition, data and privacy considerations within the context of European law are also influenced by other parties, notably the United States.

From a legal point of view, then, there is leeway in the internal market for the pursuit of other public interests. There are no restrictions on the type of public interest that can be protected under internal market legislation. At the same time, it should be noted that this leeway is not yet being exploited to its full potential. In many cases, it is unclear how much weight has been assigned to the various interests, an ambiguity that could very well undermine the political and democratic underpinnings of the assessment.[52]

The Posting of Workers Directive is a particularly good example of the way in which the Court of Justice protects the interests of free movement. First of all, the Member States must interpret the Directive in the light of the free movement of services. This means, for example, that legitimate limitations provided for in the Directive must be interpreted restrictively. As regards the application of EU law, on the other hand, the Court is inclined towards a broader interpretation, for example of the key concepts of the Directive. The Court has also ruled that only the country of origin (and therefore not the host country) may offer more extensive social protection than the minimum provided for in the Directive.[53]

The role of the Court of Justice is exceptional for another reason. The Court does not always adhere to the intentions of the Union legislator (in so far as they can be ascertained). A gap may therefore arise between the Court and the Union legislator in the *interpretation* of EU law and its underlying aims. After all, the Union legislator's intentions are only one factor among many considered by the Court. At least as important is the position of the directive in the larger body of EU law, in particular the Treaties, 'the objectives pursued by the legislation of which they form part'. The Court, moreover, sometimes describes those objectives in its own unique way. The *Easycar* and *Brüstle* cases, for example, offer striking examples[54] in that the Court's interpretations of provisions and key concepts do not necessarily correspond to what the Commission, the Council and the European Parliament had in mind. But the Court's role may go even further. It may even invalidate legislation that it regards as contrary to fundamental rights, for example. The *Schrems* case is notable in the area of personal data protection. The Court ruled that the Commission was wrong to assume that the United States provides sufficient safeguards for the protection of personal data in the event of data transfer from Europe. The ruling had enormous consequences: data transfer to the US was prohibited and the EU's political institutions were forced to negotiate entirely new agreements with the US.[55]

The Court regularly comes under fire for its judgments, such as in the aforementioned *Laval* case in which it ruled that an employer who employed posted workers could not be forced to agree on a minimum wage with the trade unions, the customary procedure in Sweden. Although most legal specialists understood the ruling, others were fiercely critical. Many commentators felt that the Court had allowed the free movement of services to take precedence over the social protection of workers.[56] The proposal for a new Posting of Workers Directive shows, however, that the Union legislator need not take note of the way in which the Court weighs up the interests at stake. After all, the Court's role is limited to interpretation; it cannot disregard explicit provisions in Union legislation concerning the scope of concepts, or the inclusion of specific rights to protect employees.

More recently, the Court has been much more vigorous about protecting fundamental rights, particularly in the context of the internal market.[57] Fundamental rights became more firmly embedded in the constitutional structure of the Union when the Charter of Fundamental Rights became binding on the Union legislator on 1 December 2009. As a result, the Court has taken to assigning more weight to fundamental rights when they are at odds with the four freedoms.[58] In doing so, it applies the rule-of-reason analysis, also used in assessing conflicts between free movement provisions and public interests. In addition, it interprets internal market legislation in a manner conducive to fundamental rights. For example, it interpreted the old Data Protection Directive in a 'privacy-friendly' manner.[59] It is less inclined to do this when other public interests are at stake, however; in such cases, the Court's protection depends more heavily on the way in which the Union legislator has made those interests explicit in the relevant legislation.[60] The Union legislator bears more responsibility in such instances.

5.3 Variation Within the Internal Market

The foregoing implies that Member States have the discretion to protect public interests in the context of both 'negative' and 'positive' integration. National variation is therefore possible, but the question is how much variation the system can take, because national differences that result in the restriction of free movement will be disruptive to the market. In other words, how homogenous must the internal market be and how much heterogeneity is allowed to create a European social market economy while protecting national public interests at the same time? How can we reconcile the conflict between economic freedoms, public interests and fundamental rights? In the following, we first consider the possibility of variation after EU legislation has been enacted, and then explore variation within the wider context of the internal market and the EU's external trade policy.

By applying a combination of deregulation and re-regulation, the law has always played a crucial role in the completion of the internal market.[61] The single market must be guaranteed by removing national barriers and by establishing common rules that are interpreted and applied uniformly. After all, 'unilateral action by the Member States leads to fragmentation of the market and affects the Community legal order'.[62] We must, however, rethink the idea that Member States' hands are tied by the rules once EU legislation has been adopted. In reality, this is by no means always the case. Although the Member States now have less room for manoeuvre in certain areas, such as consumer and data protection, most EU legislation does give them some discretion to make their own choices. The best-known example is minimum harmonisation; in fact in some domains, the Union legislator is prohibited from going beyond the minimum. That is not the case in the internal market, but even there, the Union legislator frequently limits itself to establishing a certain minimum set of rules. This is one way to resolve the tension between free movement and other public interests.[63] It means that public interests are assessed partly by the EU and partly by the Member States themselves. It should be noted, however, that the Member States must explicitly take the interests of free movement into account in their assessment.

Policy discretion can also be the outcome of open standards and concepts in EU legislation, which identifies general objectives but not the means to achieve them, and of legislation that allows Member States to decide on the precise scope of certain standards.[64] The legislative case studies that we have analysed also feature different forms of policy discretion. The proposal for the new Posting of Workers Directive, for example, creates greater leeway for collective agreements and thus offers the Member States more tools for regulating their own labour markets. Replacing the concept of 'minimum wage' by the broader concept of 'remuneration' also gives Member States more latitude to protect employees.

In the data protection domain, on the other hand, policy discretion is being restricted. Article 5 of the old Directive allows Member States to determine the conditions under which the processing of personal data is lawful, within the limits of the Directive. The new GDPR is much more restrictive because it raises the bar with respect to protecting privacy. It also contains detailed rules that establish the legal relationships between parties directly (i.e. without the intervention of the Dutch legislator). Nevertheless, it still offers the Member States some discretionary powers, not only to supplement the rules but even to derogate from them in specific situations or to restrict the rights of data subjects (for a comprehensive analysis of the various forms of policy discretion provided by the Regulation, see the Dutch Data Protection Authority's Opinion on the Personal Data Implementation Act (*Uitvoeringswet Algemene Verordening persoonsgegevens*).[65] Examples include the possibility of providing for more specific rules to protect personal data in the employment context (Article 88), and of permitting further conditions to be introduced for specific types of personal data, including data concerning health (Article 9). As is often the case in EU legislation, the Member States have discretion with regard to regulating oversight, enforcement and legal protection (although the Regulation also contains rules regarding key aspects in this respect, such as the power of supervisory authorities to impose fines). The GDPR is thus a good example of the way in which the Union legislator combines mandatory rules with the discretion to interpret certain elements of the law.

Differences in the way countries deal with the policy discretion provided for in EU legislation can lead to national variation. In the case of the GDPR, for example, the Dutch legislator has opted for the principle of 'policy neutrality', i.e. maintaining existing national law as far as possible, unless the Regulation disallows this (see the Dutch Data Protection Authority's Opinion referred to above). As a result, the previous regulatory framework (in this context, the 2001 Dutch Personal Data Protection Act) continues to set the tone in discretionary policymaking as provided by the Regulation. Member States regularly choose a relatively 'bare-bones' implementation of EU legislation, thereby avoiding the delays in implementation that could arise if they were to extensively rethink the policy discretion available to them. In doing so, however, they may be overlooking an opportunity to allow for changes in circumstances (in the case of the GDPR, technological advances) or to express their policy preferences in the way that they deal with their national policy discretion. With reference to the GDPR, the Dutch Data Protection Authority cites the possibility of regulating the processing of the personal data of deceased persons. In cases where the Union legislator allows the Member States discretion, it accepts that the applicable law may vary from one Member State to another. This may impede the creation of a 'level playing field' between Member States, but it is a risk that the Union legislator is prepared to accept in the light of Member States' interests. It is therefore important that Member States do not simply choose, automatically, to interpret their policy discretion in a way that alters as little as possible in their own legislation.

As the number of objectives and competences has grown and fundamental rights have been included, variation is becoming more of a possibility—or is the internal market already so heterogeneous that bilateral arrangements between Member States are also conceivable? We consider this below in connection with the four freedoms and how they relate to other policy domains, i.e. competition law, social policy, and external trade policy.

The four freedoms: coherence and divergence

One important goal of the four freedoms and European competition law is to 'unite the national markets into a single market reproducing as closely as possible the conditions of a domestic market'.[66] The unity of the market is critical here; it must be safeguarded by common rules that are applied uniformly.

If we consider the relationship between the four freedoms, we see that the case law of the Court of Justice is largely consistent.[67] The freedoms granted under the Treaties apply only in cross-border situations and in reference to an economic activity, a concept that the Court interprets broadly.[68] The Court also embraces the 'market access test' in the enforcement of all fundamental freedoms. According to this test, both discriminatory and non-discriminatory measures are basically prohibited if they result in restrictions on free movement. And, as noted above, Member States may justify the imposition of restrictive measures by invoking a wide range of exceptions, either in the Treaty or in case law. The rule of reason doctrine introduced by the Court with regard to all fundamental freedoms has been applied consistently. This doctrine asserts that restrictions on the freedom of movement may, by way of exception, be justified if they are designed to satisfy urgent requirements in a public interest that have not already been provided for explicitly in the Treaty. In its case law, however, the Court of Justice recognises that, although a Member State may safeguard such public interests, the validity of a national measure depends on whether European harmonisation legislation already exists that takes such interests into account and whether the measure meets the requirement of proportionality. The implication is that a Member State must be able to demonstrate that a national measure is both appropriate and necessary to safeguard the interest that it invokes, and therefore does not go beyond what is necessary.

Nevertheless, there are differences between the four freedoms and the prohibitions with regard to their scope of application. For example, unlike the other freedoms, the free movement of goods basically does not apply to legislation concerning such market conditions as shop closing times or advertising. It is also not possible to simply invoke the free movement of goods when challenging the trade-impeding measures of trade unions, banks, online companies and other organisations, whereas the other freedoms have been recognised as valid grounds. The Court's case law is erratic when it comes to accepting horizontal direct effect in the free movement of goods. The free movement of capital also extends to liberalisation of free trade with third countries. In terms of the free movement of persons and, more specifically, provisions concerning EU citizenship, the Court has come up with its own method of assessing whether the rights of EU citizens are not being undermined, even in internal situations under specific circumstances.[69] Moreover, the fundamental legal dimension that underpins the free movement of persons is obvious, and that affects the scope of these provisions.[70]

We also see that, when applying the principle of proportionality, the Court of Justice examines some cases more scrupulously than others, depending on the interest that has been invoked and the procedure followed.[71] There is very extensive case law in which the Court has applied only a limited test of proportionality to allow for characteristic national values or ethical or politically sensitive issues, such as the protection of vulnerable groups of consumers, a regional language, or the regulation of gambling.[72] In other judgements, however, the Court has applied the proportionality principle more scrupulously, thereby limiting the discretion of Member States or private parties to safeguard consumer or social interests.[73]

Regarding the activities of the Union legislator, we see that variation is possible within the context of the internal market either because the legal basis itself permits Member States to adopt more far-reaching measures, for example concerning the environment (Article 193 TFEU), or because the Union legislator has a range of harmonisation methods at its disposal, such as minimum harmonisation or total harmonisation. Variation is also possible under Article 20 TEU and Articles 326–334 TFEU, for example, which allow for closer cooperation between some Member States. Such cooperation must not undermine the internal market, however, emphasising the importance of market unity. The question is how seriously this prerequisite is applied.[74]

Although the foregoing instruments thus permit variation and national policy discretion, and although the case law is erratic, consistency between the freedoms remains crucial. The political wish not to separate the four freedoms is also consistent with the Treaty's aim of establishing a social market economy that not only liberalises trade but also creates an area founded on the principles of equality, freedom and solidarity.[75] This area is changing constantly owing to social trends and technological advances that blur the dividing lines between production factors and make it even more difficult to separate the four freedoms.[76] Some even favour the introduction of a fifth freedom, the free movement of data. However, data—also known as 'digital gold'—has certain characteristics that make it unlike goods or services. As we explained above, the legal framework for *personal data* has largely been set by the GDPR. The Regulation does not cover 'non-personal data', i.e. data in general, nor is there a clear-cut legal framework in this regard. A Commission proposal for a new European regulation appears to remedy this[77]; it aims is to ensure the free movement of data—i.e. data mobility—for non-personal data. Article 3 of the proposal defines such data as data other than personal data as referred to in the GDPR. This would include facts and statistics collected for purposes of reference or analysis. Non-personal data cannot be used to identify individuals. Since the Commission proposal does not provide a definition of non-personal data, the Court of Justice may be asked to provide clarification.

Introducing the free movement of non-personal data is regarded as an important step in the completion of the *digital* single market and is particularly important for businesses. In a press release, the Commission says that it will achieve this by removing 'unjustified or disproportionate national rules that hamper or restrict companies in choosing a location for storage or processing of their data'.[78] Examples include professional secrecy rules that imply local data storage and supervisory authorities advising financial service providers to store their data locally. The prohibition on such data localisation requirements curtails national differences with regard to non-personal data, with variation between Member States only being permitted if public security is at stake—a concept that the Court normally interprets narrowly in its case law.

The four freedoms and competition rules: coherence and divergence

The four freedoms, EU competition rules, and harmonisation of laws are among the building blocks of the internal market. There is considerable coherence between competition law and all other areas of substantive European law. That coherence is expressed in various ways, for example in the territorial scope of the freedoms, in the 'effect on trade' as a necessary condition for the application of competition rules, in the concept of economic activity, and in such principles as non-discrimination and market access. The broad applicability of the four freedoms and competition law means that virtually no socio-economic policy domain escapes the effects of internal market law.[79]

Of further note are the efforts made within the context of competition law to allow for public and social interests that are safeguarded by companies. For example, collective agreements between the social partners do not, in principle, fall within the scope of the prohibition on restrictive agreements (Article 101 TFEU) if they concern wages and working conditions.[80] The Court of Justice has also ruled in a number of cases that specific interests defended by companies, for example in sports, may constitute a justified exception to the prohibition on restrictive agreements.[81] In the Wouters case, the Court even ruled that public interests defended by the Bar of the Netherlands [*Nederlandse Orde van Advocaten*] constitute a justified exception to the competition rules.[82] These rulings are not so broad in their interpretation that they carve a path to a blanket exception for public interests in competition law, however. In addition, the Treaty includes an exception for 'undertakings entrusted with the operation of services of general economic interest' (Article 106(2) TFEU).

There are, nevertheless, significant divergences from the free movement provisions. For example, the Court of Justice's case law suggests that the requirements of environmental protection may outweigh the economic importance of a free movement provision.[83] This is much less the case in competition law. In the CECED case, the European Commission granted an exemption to washing machine manufacturers that had made a restrictive agreement for environmental protection purposes.[84] Its decision, however, depended on the environmental benefits arising from the agreement resulting in a quantifiable economic benefits, which, moreover, had to accrue to consumers. That is because consumer welfare is at the heart of EU competition law, alongside the interests of the internal market. The aim of consumer welfare is often interpreted narrowly, leaving the European Commission and the Netherlands Authority for Consumers & Markets (ACM) little leeway to pursue general interest aims in their practices. This limited view of competition law has come under increasing fire[85] and is not compatible with mainstreaming principles. Although the European Commission has put environmental and social policy objectives at the heart of its long-term strategy, *Europe 2020*,[86] it apparently does not yet see a broader interpretation of the concept of consumer welfare as an effective means of achieving this.

The question, then, is to what extent European competition law can encompass both national public interests and a social market economy. There have been proposals to introduce the 'capability approach' in competition law, with more emphasis on the role that companies play in achieving environmental objectives or reinforcing social cohesion in cities.[87] Fundamental rights and social welfare would then play a more significant role in how competition rules are applied. That is the strategy put forward in the Dutch government's coalition agreement, but because Dutch competition law is based on European competition law, the legal latitude is very limited.[88]

The four freedoms and social policy: coherence and divergence

The Treaties, and in particular Article 151 TFEU, assume that the functioning of the internal market will contribute to convergence between national social welfare systems and thus help improve living and working conditions, provide adequate social protection, achieve lasting high levels of employment, and combat exclusion. In reality, however, such 'spontaneous' convergence or harmonisation has proven much more problematic; in addition, the EU lacks legislative competence to impose harmonisation. This is, in part, the reason behind the 'open method of coordination' (OMC), which emerged in the 1990s as a 'third option' midway between independent national policy and harmonisation within the Union, initially in the field of employment policy. The open method, now laid down in Article 153(2)(a) TFEU, implies that policy objectives are set jointly at EU level, but that it is left to the Member States to achieve them. It is also used for other aspects of social policy, such as combating social exclusion. The point is not to harmonise national legislation but to only use 'soft law' mechanisms to coordinate national policies and steer them towards convergence. The first aim of coordination is to identify common policy objectives and then to achieve real policy convergence by sharing expertise and success stories and by using peer reviews and applying peer pressure to detect, criticise and change bad practices. One of the basic assumptions of the OMC, then, is that convergence between the Member States' social policies can be achieved through many different national measures, as long as such measures contribute to attaining the policy objective set at EU level.

The four freedoms and the common commercial policy: coherence and divergence

Based on the assumption that the EU's internal and external areas are connected—as we emphasised in the introduction to this book—we must also consider how the internal market relates to the EU's common commercial policy vis-à-vis third countries and other international organisations. The common commercial policy is one of the Union's areas of exclusive competence (Article 3(1) TFEU), and the most critical element of its economic relations with the world outside and its external actions in general.[89] The EU's exclusive competence in this policy area implies that the European Commission plays a key role, for example in trade negotiations with third countries and in international organisations such as the World Trade Organisation (WTO). External trade policy is therefore often regarded as an external dimension,[90] the external face,[91] or a complement to the internal market and as a logical consequence of the interaction between internal and external trends and events in world trade.[92] The Court of Justice ruled as long ago as 1975 that: '[s]uch a policy is conceived … in the context of the operation of the common market, for the defence of the common interests of the Community, within which the particular interests of the Member States must endeavour to adapt to each other. Quite clearly, however, this conception is incompatible with the freedom to which the Member States could lay claim by invoking a concurrent power, so as to ensure that their own interests were separately satisfied in external relations, at the risk of compromising the effective defence of the common interests of the Community.'[93]

The foregoing also explains the EU's exclusive competence in external trade relations. Unilateral action by Member States in this area would undermine the economic foundations of the internal market.[94] It should be noted here, however, that European trade policy is based on a different institutional structure, uses different instruments and, to a certain extent, pursues different objectives than those of the internal market. Moreover, the Union's external trade policy has always been closely linked to the multilateral system of the General Agreement on Tariffs and Trade (later WTO), concluded some ten years before the Treaty of Rome was signed. The EEC framework was therefore inspired, in part, by the gatt model.[95] That is why the Union's external trade policy should not be seen as a simple expansion of the internal market to outside the EU, but rather as a necessary or even indispensable consequence of the internal market in the external sphere.[96] Larik[97] argues that European trade policy is 'a necessary corollary for the maintenance of its internal market'.

We can get a better idea of the evolving relationship between the internal market and the common commercial policy by considering how the scope, objectives and instruments of trade policy have developed over time, from a common customs tariff to the dispersal of fundamental rights. The original reason behind the external trade policy—which was related directly to the development of the internal market—was the need to establish uniform rules for the customs union, in particular the introduction of a common customs tariff for Member States' relations with third countries (now Article 28 TFEU).

The Treaty of Nice and, in particular, the Treaty of Lisbon have given the external trade policy an extra push, mainly by increasing the EU's powers and by placing the entire policy within the framework of non-economic principles and objectives. In particular, the Treaties have broadened considerably the principles on which the external trade policy is based, as well as the associated instruments. Those instruments now include trade agreements on services, the trade-related aspects of intellectual property, and foreign direct investment.[98] This means that the EU is now also competent to conclude international trade agreements on certain aspects of capital and establishment. In this respect, the EU's competences in the area of trade policy increasingly reflect the scope of the internal market. The precise scope of those competences is currently the subject of fierce discussion, but that subject is beyond the remit of this book.

The most notable addition to the EU's competences in the area of external trade policy can be found in the final sentence of Article 207(1) TFEU: 'The common commercial policy shall be conducted in the context of the principles and objectives of the Union's external action.' Article 205 TFEU clarifies the mandatory nature of the general objectives and principles with which the common commercial policy must comply.[99] Since the Treaty of Lisbon, then, the Union has pursued its external actions and, in particular, its commercial policy explicitly within the framework of Article 21 TEU, basing them on the principles of democracy, the rule of law, human rights and fundamental freedoms 'which have inspired its own creation, development and enlargement'.[100] In addition, in its common commercial policy, the Union pursues the various political and non-economic objectives enumerated in the second paragraph of Article 21 TEU, for example to safeguard its values, fundamental interests, security, independence and integrity and the principles of international law, to preserve peace and strengthen international security, to foster the sustainable development of developing countries in order to eradicate poverty, to encourage the integration of all countries into the world economy, and to improve the quality of the environment and to ensure sustainable development.

Article 21 TEU thus reflects the content of Articles 2 and 3 of the Treaty to a certain extent, but adds its own unique elements. Formally speaking, however, there is no hierarchical relationship between all the principles and objectives of trade policy; they are all equally valuable and significant.[101] That means that there is also no hierarchical relationship between the economic and non-economic objectives of the common commercial policy. Finally, the Treaty of Lisbon stresses the need to guarantee coherence between the Union's external and internal actions.[102] This raises the question of how to address potential conflicts between trade liberalisation and the non-economic objectives set out in Article 21 TEU. We should emphasise here that the Union has already used external actions, and trade policy in particular, to promote broader and non-economic objectives.[103]

With multilateral trade negotiations within the context of the WTO at a long-standing impasse, the Union has sought alternative ways of fostering economic cooperation with the world beyond. Increasingly, it has focused on concluding bilateral and regional trade agreements with third countries. Free trade agreements are certainly nothing new for the European Union.[104] Within the context of its European Neighbourhood Policy, for example, it has concluded partnership, cooperation and, more recently, association agreements. The strategy published by the Commission in 2010[105] does not represent a break with the past, but does imply a number of shifts in emphasis. The Commission proposes to focus more on concluding bilateral free trade agreements, in particular with the EU's neighbouring countries, with the aim of gradually integrating these countries into the internal market. A new generation of Deep and Comprehensive Free Trade Agreements has been introduced in this context, the Association Agreement with Ukraine being one example. This new generation of free trade agreements goes far beyond tariff reductions and trade in goods and services and shows that this form of bilateral economic cooperation has become the main instrument of the Union's external trade policy.[106] The Treaty of Lisbon and the Union's expanded competences have therefore given bilateral economic cooperation an additional boost.

The EU now has the widest range of free trade agreements in the world, with considerable variation between them. Practically every agreement provides for a different model of market integration. Often, they are part of a broader political agreement, such as an association agreement. The EU also concludes economic partnership or cooperation agreements that are more geared to its trade partner's development. For example, if we compare the EEA Agreement, CETA, the EU-Ukraine Association Agreement and the EU-South Korea Free Trade Agreement, we see that liberalisation can take different forms across the four freedoms. The EU's values and principles, as well as its objectives and its social market economy, are reflected in all these bilateral agreements, but to varying degrees and with differing emphases. They are also underpinned by different processes that vary in intensity and impact, with the third countries adapting their own legislation to the EU *acquis* or confining themselves to dialogue and cooperation. Ultimately, it seems, there is no hierarchical relationship between the different principles and objectives.

5.4 Conclusion: Principles Leave Room for Manoeuvre

The European internal market is as politically and economically significant today as it ever was. In terms of social welfare, however, the current structure falls short because it does not offer a sufficiently solid safety net to the losers in an open, free market. This chapter has considered whether EU law offers a framework for promoting not only economic but also other public interests within the context of the internal market, and how variation might contribute to this. In the light of the aforementioned core elements of market integration, as well as the 'logic of appropriateness' and the 'logic of consequences', we can draw the following conclusions from our analysis.

First of all, we must question an approach that claims that national public interests and fundamental rights can distort economic market integration. The internal market is not an end in itself but supports a social market economy. Public interests and fundamental rights should in fact serve as important indicators for the completion of the internal market. That is something that the Union legislator but also the Court of Justice must take into account when determining whether a specific national measure is compatible with the internal market provisions. The internal market's legal framework is so flexible that both the legislator and the Court can weigh economic market interests against other public interests, the former from a political and the latter from a legal perspective. It is even so that the 'logic of appropriateness' has, over time, become increasingly important as a basis for the structure of the internal market. That is because the current organisation of the internal market reflects the explicit pursuit of a social market economy and the view that fundamental rights and the principles of solidarity, proportionality and 'mainstreaming' (which mirror public interests) are important principles of market organisation under the Treaty. Moreover, the Treaties assume that the functioning of the internal market will contribute positively to the public's well-being and standard of living.

Given the close connection between the internal market and competition law, limiting the assessment of interests under competition law to economic interests versus consumer welfare is not consistent with the rationality of the internal market. It would be more logical for competition law to place greater emphasis on other public interests too, and to weigh them against the interests of the market. Competition law still appears to be firmly rooted in the logic of consequences than in the overarching pursuit of a social market economy and the safeguarding of other public interests. These require a coherent approach in which the policy domains closely associated with the four freedoms evolve in accordance with the same guiding principles. On the other hand, one could argue that competition law is geared towards companies and that such companies do not necessarily promote public interests in the way that government institutions are obliged to do.

This brings us to the risks of greater variation. As the above shows, variation between the guiding principles of the internal market and closely associated policy domains raises problems when it comes to establishing a social market economy. Variation in the way the Member States interpret the four freedoms would also pose a major risk not only to the economic completion of the internal market but also to the safeguards afforded to the associated social and public interests. The general principles of Union loyalty and effectiveness of Union law limit such variation, in any event.

At the same time, however, we also see that the broad spectrum of principles underpinning the internal market does, in fact, offer more scope for national variation, especially where no EU legislation applies. These principles allow for variation by permitting Member States to apply certain rules and practices that protect certain public interests in preference to the interests of the internal market. It should be noted, however, that it is precisely when the Member States have more discretion in policy-making that their responsibility for considering the interests of free movement and the internal market increases. The assessment framework for the four freedoms developed by the Court for such national rules has remained uniform and therefore offers legal certainty. The absence of a 'level playing field' for commercial parties and individuals in the Member States is a given in internal market law, however. Coherence and divergence thus go hand in hand and a sustained commitment to the internal market cannot be guaranteed without allowing the Member States a certain degree of policy discretion. The problem now is that the Court sometimes leaves little leeway for national variation with respect to social rights and social policy, something that the Union legislator cannot always compensate, given its limited competence in this domain.

Parallel coherence and divergence is an established feature of internal market law in other respects as well. On the one hand, there is a large measure of convergence in the interpretation and scope of the four freedoms, which contributes to the uniform application of internal market law and to legal certainty; on the other hand, the Treaty has already recognised some variations in their scope of application, for example, by providing for the free movement of capital not only within the EU but also vis-à-vis third countries. In addition, variation is inherent to the mechanism of harmonisation by means of directives for the purpose of completing the internal market. These give the Member States room to exercise discretion in various ways, for example by establishing minimum harmonisation measures, allowing possible exceptions, and introducing concepts that are open to interpretation. Finally, there is variation in the way Court interprets the scope of application of the four freedoms, but also, for example, in the degree to which it recognises their horizontal effect.

The rationality of the internal market also has implications for the institutional dimension, i.e. the role of the various actors at both European and national level in contributing to a social market economy and safeguarding public interests. Thinking in terms of shared principles and responsibility rather than a division of competences might help to mitigate the technocratic nature of European cooperation.[107] It is also the responsibility of the Member States themselves to ensure that the European social market economy becomes reality; this depends on how they formulate general policies within the context of the European Council and how they fulfil their role on the Council as Union co-legislators with respect to the internal market, competition law and trade policy. The same applies to the way they exercise their powers in the context of European social policy. The Union is competent primarily to coordinate policy, and so much depends on the Member States themselves taking steps to achieve the policy objectives they have jointly set at EU level. An open process of political and democratic decision-making and a broad public debate about how public interests are assessed would also help to mitigate the technocratic complexion of the EU. At the moment, it is not always clear exactly how that assessment has taken place within the Council, the European Parliament and the Commission, and what influence powerful lobbies have had, for example on the protection of privacy. When it comes to sensitive issues such as the protection of privacy and the posting of workers, or whether to ban agricultural pesticides that may pose a threat to the environment and public health, a public debate can help to assess the interests at stake, an assessment that will ultimately find its way into European rules.

Notes

1. Union law on the internal market is largely based on Article 114 TFEU, which provides for decisions to be taken in accordance with the ordinary legislative procedure, as laid down in Article 294 TFEU. In this context, the Union legislator is the Commission as the initiator and the Council and the European Parliament as the bodies that jointly adopt a legislative act.
2. Single Market, Four Freedoms, Sixteen Facts—Economic Effects in the EU, National Board of Trade, 2015, see: https://www.kommers.se/Documents/dokumentarkiv/publikationer/2015/Publ-single-market-4-freedoms-16-facts.pdf.

3. European Commission (2017b).
4. European Commission (2017b: 20).
5. de Vries (2006).
6. Pursuant to Article 2 of the TEU.
7. The Spaak report referenced above appears to contradict this.
8. Domurath (2013).
9. 5 Article 174 TFEU.
10. Article 21 TEU.
11. Articles 24 and 31 TEU.
12. Articles 67 and 80 TFEU.
13. However, solidarity is also mentioned in connection with economic policy (Article 122 TFEU), energy policy (Article 194 TFEU) and in the 'solidarity clause' in the event of a terrorist attack or natural or man-made disaster (Article 222 TFEU).
14. Article 4(3) TEU and, more explicitly, for example in Article 24(2) TEU.
15. Articles 35, 37 and 38 of the Charter of Fundamental Rights of the Union impose a similar obligation as regards public health, environmental protection and consumer protection.
16. Directive 77/187/EEC, OJ 1977, L 061/26.
17. Directive 80/987/EEC, OJ 1980, L 283/23.
18. Directive 75/117/EEC on the approximation of the laws of Member States relating to the application of the principle of equal pay for men and women, OJ 1975, L 45/19, adopted on the basis of Article 100 of the EEC Treaty; Directive 86/378 on the implementation of the principle of equal treatment for men and women in occupational social security schemes, OJ 1986, L 225/40, adopted on the basis of Articles 100 and 235 of the EEC Treaty.
19. For a concise overview, see the Commission Staff Working Document, 'The EU social acquis', SWD (2016) 50 draft, of 8 March 2016.
20. Communication from the Commission Establishing a European Pillar of Social Rights, COM (2017) 250 final, 26 April 2017.
21. As long ago as 1990, the Social and Economic Council of the Netherlands explicitly stressed the importance of the social dimension of the European internal market, which was to be completed in 1992, in the light of its far-reaching liberalisation as provided for in the Single European Act of 1986; Advies Sociale dimensie Europa 1992, SER Advisory Report 90/11.
22. Weatherill (2013: 14), de Vries (2016: 9).
23. Mortelmans (1985: 10).
24. ECJ 11 December 2007, C-438/05 (Viking Line) ECLI:EU:C:2007:772; ECJ 18 December 2007, C-341/05 (Laval) ECLI:EU:C:2007:809.
25. Weatherill (2015).
26. See Conclusion ag Trstenjak in C-271/08, (European Commission V Germany), ECLI:EU:C:2007:809, recitals 186–188.
27. Regulation 1612/68, now replaced by Regulation 492/2011 on freedom of movement for workers within the Union, OJ 2011, L141/1. See also

Regulation 883/2004 on the coordination of social security systems, OJ 2011, L166/1.
28. ECJ 11 July 1985, C-137/84 (Mutsch) ECLI:EU:C:1985:335.
29. ECJ 17 April 1986, C-59/85 (Reed) ECLI:EU:C:1986:157.
30. Domurath (2013).
31. ECJ 17 June 1997, C-70/95 (Sodemare), ECLI:EU:C:1997:301, par. 29.
32. E.g. ECJ 12 May 1998, C-85/96 (Martinez Sala) ECLI:EU:C:1998:217; ECJ 15 March 2005, C-209/03 (Bidar), ECLI:EU:C:2005:169, par. 60.
33. E.g. ECJ 23 April 1998, C-120/95 (Decker) ECLI:EU:C:1998:167; ECJ 28 April 1998, C-158/96 (Kohll) ECLI:EU:C:1998:171.
34. Domurath (2013).
35. Newdick (2006: 1645).
36. Davies (2015: 4).
37. Commission (1991: 9).
38. The argument was initially put forward by Janez Potočnik, former European Commissioner for Science and Research (2007).
39. Moerel (2014).
40. Directive 2010/13/EU on Audiovisual Media Services, OJ 2010, L95/1.
41. de Witte (2012: 40).
42. The Commission has now adopted a proposal amending this directive. According to the Explanatory Memorandum, the Commission's new proposal reflects market, consumption and technology changes; it extends the scope of application of the Directive, improves the protection of minors and lays down rules on advertising (European Commission 2016, Proposal for amendment of Directive 2010/13/EU, com 2016 287 FINAL).
43. Directive 2015/2366 on payment services and the internal market (PSD II), OJ 2015L 337/35.
44. See Article 41 of Directive 2014/23/EU, OJ 2014, L 94/1 and Article 67 and recital 92 of Directive 2014/24/EU, OJ 2014, L 94/65 (Procurement Directives).
45. ECJ 5 October 2000, C-376/98 (Tobacco Advertising), ECLI:EU:C:2000:544.
46. In addition to the privacy aspect, Article 16 TFEU also grants authority to regulate the free movement of personal data.
47. SER Report—*Arbeidsmigratie* (2014).
48. de Witte (2012).
49. 'Editorial Comments', *Common Market Law Review* (2006), Barnard (2008).
50. de Witte (2012).
51. For examples, see Prins and Moerel (2017).
52. Davies (2012).
53. See Brink et al. (2019b).
54. ECJ 10 March 2005, C-336/03 (Easycar) ECLI:EU:C:2005:150; ECJ 18 October, C-34/10 (Brüstle) ECLI:EU:C:2011:669.
55. ECJ 6 October 2015, C-362/14, ECLI:EU:C:2015:650.

56. Joerges and Rodl (2009), Lindstrom (2010), Garben (2017).
57. de Vries (2016).
58. A critical judgment in this respect is ECJ 12 June 2003, C-112/00 (Schmidberger) ECLI:EU:C:2003:333.
59. See, for example, ECJ 27 February 2012, C-131/12 (Google v Spain) ECLI:EU:C:2014:317. For a comprehensive overview of privacy-friendly rulings of the Court of Justice, see: Van den Brink et al. (2019a). *Differentiatie en uniformiteit in EU-wetgeving: detachering en gegevensbescherming*, section 3.3, WRR Working Paper.
60. See, for example, ECJ 6 September 2012, C-544/210 (Deutsches Weintor) ECLI:EU:C:2012:526; and ECJ 22 January 2013, C-283/11 (Sky Osterreich) ECLI:EU:C:2013:28.
61. Mortelmans (1998: 105).
62. Prechal (2006: 14).
63. Dougan (2000).
64. van den Brink (2015).
65. Available at: https://autoriteitpersoonsgegevens.nl/sites/default/files/atoms/files/advies_uitvoeringswet_avg.pdf.
66. ECJ 21 May 1985, C-47/84 (Gaston Schul) ECLI:EU:C:1982:135.
67. de Vries (2006), Nic Shuibhne (2013).
68. This is not the case for internal market legislation, which may apply to purely national situations.
69. ECJ 8 March 2011, C-34/09 (Ruiz Zambrano) ECLI:EU:C:2011:124.
70. Prechal and de Vries (2009).
71. de Vries (2006, 2016).
72. See, for example, ECJ 20 May 1976, C-104/75 (De Peijper) ECLI:EU:C:1976:67; ECJ 24 March 1994, C-275/92 (Schindler) ECLI:EU:C:1994:119; ECJ 28 November 1989, C-379/87 (Groener) ECLI:EU:C:1989:599; ECJ 16 December 2010, C-137/09 (Josemans) ECLI:EU:C:2010:774; ECJ 14 October 2004, C-36/02 (Omega Spielhallen) ECLI:EU:C:2004:614.
73. See, for example, ECJ 2 February 1994, C-315/92 (Clinique); ECLI:EU:C:1994:34; ECJ 14 July 1988, C-407/85 (Drei Glocken) ECLI:EU:C:1988:401; ECJ 11 December 2007, C-438/05 (Viking Line) ECLI:EU:C:2007:772.
74. Weatherill (2017: 31).
75. VerLoren van Themaat (1982).
76. See also White Paper on the Future of Europe, Reflections and Scenarios for the EU 27 by 2025, COM (2017) 2025, 1 March 2017.
77. Proposal for a Regulation of the European Parliament and the Council on a framework for the free flow of non-personal data in the European Union, COM (2017) 495 final.
78. European Commission (2017e).
79. de Vries (2006).

80. ECJ 21 September 1999, C-115/97 to C-117/97 (Brentjens) ECLI:EU:C:1999:434; ECJ 12 September 2000, C-180/98 to C-184/98 (Pavlov) ECLI:EU:C:2000:428.
81. ECJ 18 July 2006, C-519/04 P (Meca-Medina) ECLI:EU:C:2006:492.
82. ECJ 19 February 2002, C-309/99 (Wouters) ECLI:EU:C:2002:98.
83. van de Gronden and Mortelmans (2001).
84. EC 24 January 1999, comp.F.1/37.894 (CECED).
85. de Vries (2016).
86. See Communication from the Commission. *Europe 2020: A strategy for smart, sustainable and inclusive growth*, COM (2010) 2020 final.
87. Claassen and Gerbrandy (2016).
88. Gerbrandy (2017).
89. Dimopoulos (2010).
90. van Vooren and Wessel (2014).
91. Cremona (2017: 498).
92. van Vooren and Wessel (2014).
93. Opinion No 1/75 of the Court of Justice of 11 November [1975] ECR 01355, Part B (2).
94. van Vooren and Wessel (2014).
95. Larik (2011).
96. Cremona (2017).
97. Larik (2011: 16).
98. Article 207(1) TFEU.
99. Krajewski (2012).
100. See Article 21 TEU.
101. Krajewski (2012).
102. Article 21(3) TEU.
103. See, for example, the Generalised Scheme of Preferences (GSP). The GSP+, introduced in 2006, is a European trade policy instrument aimed at supporting sustainable development in developing countries. It is a preferential tariff system that incentivises developing countries to comply with basic international agreements on human rights, labour rights, the environment and good governance.
104. A complete list of all agreements concluded and under negotiation can be found at http://ec.europa.eu/trade/policy/countries-and-regions/negotiations-and-agreements/#_in-place. At present, 33 treaties are in full force and effect.
105. European Commission (2010).
106. Bungenberg (2010).
107. Habermas (2011).

Chapter 6
Variations in the European Union

6.1 Introduction

The previous chapter discussed the existing forms of variation within the internal market. The remainder of this book discusses forms of variation that fall both within and outside the current framework of European Union Treaty law. This chapter connects the various dots to reveal a broad range of variation options.

6.2 Three Dimensions of Variation

Variation has three dimensions, associated with: (1) policy content, (2) decision methodology, and (3) the Member States. Based on these dimensions, the options for variation can best be presented as a three-dimensional continuum whereby the degree of uniformity in each dimension runs from minimum to maximum.

Variation in policy content

The first dimension concerns the scope for variation within the content of policy, i.e. the leeway that each Member State has to interpret how certain public interests, objectives and values are to be achieved. This means that Member States can have different priorities and interpretations but continue to participate in a political form of solidarity. More specifically, they are given more policy discretion in directives involving minimum harmonisation or open standards. Such directives employ concepts that allow the Member States to shape national policy as they see fit. This form of variation also includes European 'guidelines' established within the OMC, which afford the Member States maximum autonomy in their interpretation of policy. At the other extreme are regulations that limit national policy discretion. The chapter on the internal market offers examples of existing forms of variation in that specific policy domain.

E. Hirsch Ballin et al., *European Variations as a Key to Cooperation*, Research for Policy, https://doi.org/10.1007/978-3-030-32893-1_6

The room for manoeuvre created in this manner prevents the tensions caused by diverging aims from resulting in opt-outs, for example. *Variation in policy content* makes it possible to incorporate the Member States' diverse motivations into the process of European integration without compromising unity. The process of policymaking must then reveal, time and again, how much room for manoeuvre there actually is.

Trade-offs are also possible within a policy area. One example of this is 'flexible solidarity' within the context of migration, asylum and borders. Variation in this domain is not meant to ignore the basic principle of solidarity, but it does mean paying greater attention to differences between countries. This means that those regions where public support and opportunities for personal development are greatest (Northwest Europe, the 'destination countries') can expand their asylum policies. The impossibility of full harmonisation does not mean that solidarity cannot be achieved in other ways. Allowing countries to buy their way out of quota obligations with larger financial contributions is not the only alternative. In the future, transit countries in the East and South could, perhaps, play a larger role in circular migration, once their economic structures and employment rates so permit.

Variation in the decision-making method

This dimension concerns the way in which policy and legislative decisions must be taken: in an intergovernmental context, via the Community method, or perhaps even at supranational level.

Within an intergovernmental framework, there is no interference from institutions to which the cooperating states are subordinate; competences are not transferred and are retained at the national level at all times. Decision-making thus requires unanimity. In effect, states have the right to veto policy and legislation, guaranteeing that their policy autonomy is preserved. The open method of coordination (OMC), which does not involve legislative competences and in which decisions are taken on the basis of unanimity, is one example of this form of variation.

Policies and legislation developed according to the Community method apply equally to all participating Member States and are based on (1) supranational institutions as initiators and guardians of the Treaty order, (2) qualified majority voting in the Council and (3) co-decision-making by the European Parliament (ordinary legislative procedure). The difference between this and a fully supranational decision-making framework is that, in the Community method, qualified majority voting makes it possible to form blocking minorities, for example in the Council. Unlike in the supranational method, a simple majority is not enough to reach a decision.

Variation in membership/members

The third dimension concerns membership. If the Member States' 'motivations for collective action' differ too much to fulfil public tasks by means of the Community method or *variation in policy content*, the Member States can switch to the most extreme form of variation, i.e. *variation in membership*. In this form of variation, the Member States do not see sufficient reason to undertake collective action and must pursue a different type of relationship with one another. Examples include opt-outs, establishing lead groups beyond the EU structures, transition periods, and close cooperation.

Figure 6.1 shows the three dimensions of variation in the shape of a cube. The X-axis represents variations in decision-making, with the degree of uniformity in decision-making rising from intergovernmental to supranational. The Y-axis represents variations in EU membership. The minimum form of integration here is the 'lead group' and the maximum form is 'all EU Member States', with opt-outs positioned midway between the two. Finally, the Z-axis represents variation in policy content. Examples include 'policy guidelines' within the OMC or 'trade-offs' within the same policy domain as a minimum form of integration. The maximum form is far-reaching harmonisation (e.g. by means of regulations). In between these two extremes, the Member States have more or less latitude to develop their own policy within EU directives and other frameworks that are more or less specific. We illustrate the variation options by positioning a number of specific legislative and policy instruments within the figure.

For the Union to utilise the variation options in actual practice, it must keep an open mind to the opportunities afforded by the existing Treaties by (1) considering the relationship between motivations for collective action and the possible institutional orders, and thus (2) relinquishing its fixation on the Community method and the resulting compulsion to rely on certain motivations for collective action.

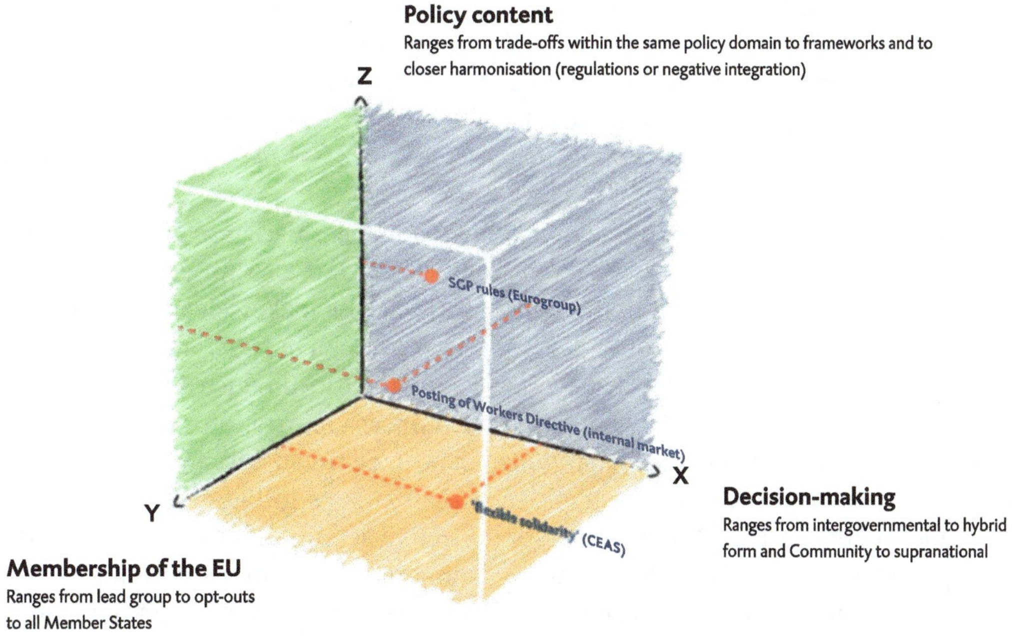

Fig. 6.1 A three-dimensional representation of variation options in the EU

6.3 A Guideline to Variation

The uniform model of integration—in which all Member States have the same rights and obligations—has dominated the integration process, and in particular the *thinking* about that process, since the end of the Second World War. The predominance of this model is largely due to the expectation that a single European market would produce mutual benefits in terms of efficiency, growth and jobs. The fact that these expectations were largely fulfilled in the decades following the Second World War, but also the fear of being deprived of the benefits, boosted the dominance of the uniformity model even more. Nevertheless, from the outset European integration has also involved all sorts of variation in policy implementation, often based on and firmly anchored in the principle of subsidiarity, and variation in membership. Gradually, the different forms of variation have developed into instruments that can be used to find a solution to the central problem of collective action, which we can describe as follows: although the outcome of cooperation is clearly beneficial for all the participating states, one or more parties still impede such cooperation because they consider their individual advantage more important than the collective advantage. This is a constant struggle within the context of European integration.

Relinquishing the fixation on greater uniformity also offers new opportunities for a discussion on the future of European integration that does more justice to reality. This new approach makes it possible to get beyond the simplified debate of national state versus federation. This stylised juxtaposition, while simplifying the debate, does not do enough justice to the multifaceted reality of cooperation, integration and interdependence. Nevertheless, it is a juxtaposition that has dominated the debate on the future of European integration, as if that debate ultimately involved a stark choice between one ideal or another, and as if it were the institutional order of cooperation alone that defined the reality of Europe. Both assumptions hamper the pursuit of real solutions, something that is perfectly possible within the existing frameworks.

Variation is not equally possible in all policy domains. Variation can create room for manoeuvre, but it also has its limitations. There are also different forms and degrees of variation, as the introduction to this chapter makes clear. We can now use the analysis framework constructed in the previous chapters and the variation options in the internal market that we have identified to produce a guideline that prioritises variation in policy content in European integration, simultaneously linking it to variation in membership/members, which can serve as a remedy in extreme cases. The guideline for applying variation is as follows:

If the Member States' 'motivations for collective action' differ too much to fulfil European public tasks according to the existing variation options permitted under the Treaties and the Union's institutional order, i.e. variation in policy content or trade-offs in a policy domain, the Member States can switch to the most extreme form of variation, i.e. variation in membership/members.

Applying this guideline may produce new insights, and in particular lead to a reappraisal of the existing diversity in the EU. That is already a step forward, if only because, in many respects, diversity has been at the heart of the process of European integration in recent decades. Nevertheless, such diversity has not always been sufficiently acknowledged. For us, this is the most important reason for recommending that the matrix presented in the previous chapters be used to analyse the tasks of the European Union. Doing so makes it possible to identify which institutional order and which grounds for collective action should be applied. In some instances, this is likely to lead to a fundamental review of the choices that have emerged from the negotiation process; in others, it will lead to improvements and firmer arguments. These analyses heighten the value of variation and make its implementation more precise.

In addition to variation within the European internal market as described in the previous chapter, there are various other forms of variation in today's EU. For example, better-known and more striking forms of variation in membership/members include the Schengen area, the euro area and the opt-outs of EU Member States in various policy domains. There are, however, also many lesser-known alliances within the EU that illustrate variation in membership/members, such as EU Battlegroups,[1] the G6 meetings on law enforcement and security matters,[2] the 'EU big three'[3] or the target interbank payment system.[4]

The approach proposed here not only offers improvements in governance. It is vital for politicians to abandon the old habit of presenting European decision-making as an obstacle that must be removed purely in the national interest. A proper analysis of the interests at stake will also allow politicians and others involved in decision-making processes to explain variation in a different and more convincing way, by arguing that, in the light of the EU's internal socio-economic and socio-cultural differences, variation in policy content and in membership/members is and can be useful and in the interests of both the Member State and the EU as a whole.

In the following two sections, we delve deeper into where variation in membership/members stands (as the most extreme form of variation) and make suggestions for dealing more constructively with it than has hitherto been the case.

6.4 Variation in Membership/Members

Variation in membership/members is by no means a new phenomenon in European integration. Even before the Treaty of Amsterdam laid the foundations for 'enhanced cooperation', there were ways of downplaying uniformity in European policymaking. When the European Communities were established, it was stipulated that the Treaty provisions would not preclude the existence or completion of the regional unions between Belgium and Luxembourg or the Benelux (now Article 350 TFEU). Territorial clauses allow variation in the conditions under which the Treaties are applied in the 'outermost regions' of the Member States and some other territories. This variation in membership/members has also existed since the founding of the Communities, now provided for under Article 349 TFEU.

The main variation in membership/members can be found in the Title on Economic and Monetary Policy (Title VIII of Part Three of the TFEU), which distinguishes between Member States that do and do not have the euro as their currency. The financial and economic crisis and the impending financial collapse of some euro-area Member States led to a system of separate treaties and decision-making structures being developed on that basis.[5] The inclusion of transitional provisions upon the accession of new Member States has always been established practice, although such derogations from the *acquis* have become much more pronounced in the more recent accessions.

There are other examples of variation in membership/members, including the limited participation of some states in the cooperation between police and judicial authorities in the area of freedom, security and justice (Title V). Two Member States (Poland and the United Kingdom) have even been granted a special status with regard to the judicial enforcement of the Charter of Fundamental Rights of the European Union,[6] an exception that is at odds with the fundamental values of the Union. Article 31 TEU allows a Member State to abstain from applying a decision within the context of the Common Foreign and Security Policy. Article 42(2), second paragraph, accepts variations within the context of the Common Security and Defence Policy depending on whether or not EU Member States belong to NATO. The execution of military missions may be entrusted to a group of Member States (Article 42(5) and Article 44). Article 42(6) and Article 46 permit a group of Member States to establish permanent structured military cooperation with one another.

The picture that emerges is further defined by the fact that some non-Member States participate in elements of EU policy and the associated legal rules. We illustrate this in Fig. 6.2.

The question, then, is not so much *whether* variation should be permitted to ensure that the European project can continue successfully, but rather *how* variation can best be used to revitalise the European Union in a meaningful and more persuasive manner. That may be in existing policy domains, whenever uniformity appears to breed too much tension, or in new areas of cooperation.

There are two routes to more variation within the existing structures of the EU.[7] One is the enhanced cooperation procedure, put in place by the Treaty of Amsterdam (1997) and revised several times since then. It is now set out in Title IV of the TEU. Member States may establish enhanced cooperation within the framework of the Union's non-exclusive competences, making use of its institutions. The other route involves concluding separate agreements which, although they operate outside European Union framework, are nevertheless linked to it, such as the additional treaties on monetary cooperation. The Prüm Convention on combating terrorism, cross-border crime and illegal migration, which was concluded by a number of Member States in 2005, was also adopted and remained entirely outside the Union framework until 2008, when it was partially subsumed into EU law.

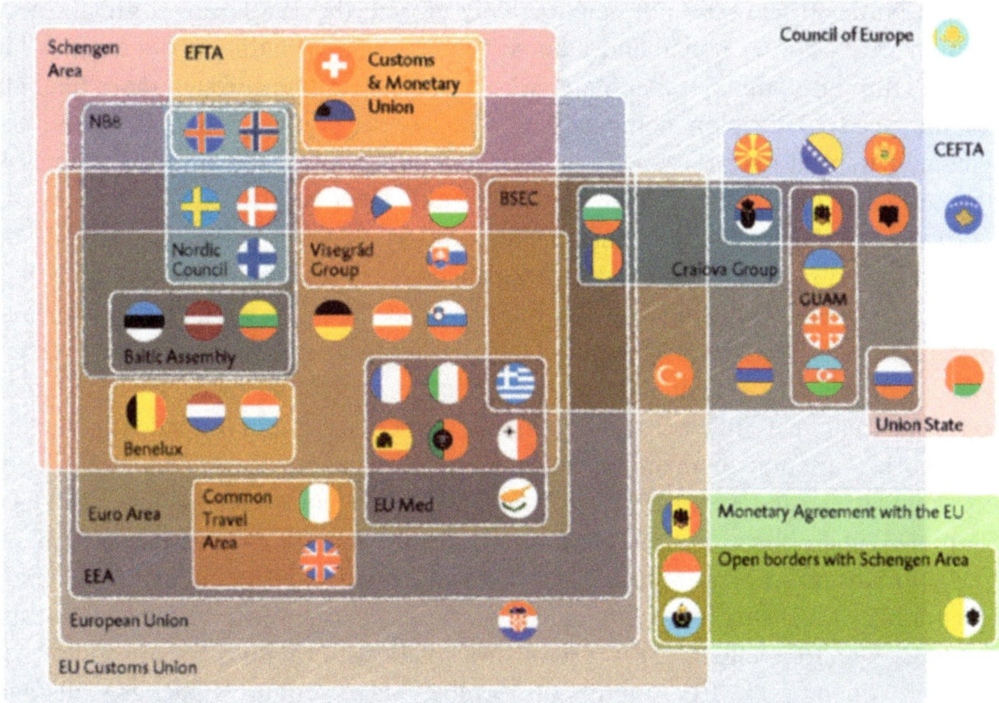

Fig. 6.2 European variation options in membership

What is notable about the existing variation in membership/members is that it usually arises from differences of opinion or differences in the speed of acceptance. What then follows can be described as a form of 'learning by doing' whereby the initial cooperation, which was not binding on all Member States, frequently leads to closer and broader cooperation at a later stage, often within the normal framework of the Union (with possible opt-outs). Examples include the Schengen treaties, which were subsequently integrated into the main body of EU law under the Treaty of Amsterdam.

6.5 Assessing the Desirability of Variation in Membership/Members

As described above, variation in membership/members is an outcome of the decision-making process. That is not the same as variation as a conscious choice. Our analyses in Chaps. 4–6 and the guidelines provided in this chapter can be used to develop variation 'as a conscious choice'. Such analyses can also provide building blocks for the necessary political arguments. The scope that these analyses allow for changes over time is crucial, since circumstances and opinions are subject to constant change. Approaching variation in this way makes it more proactive and, above all, more conscious in nature. Although the free movement of persons implied borders that could not be effectively closed, the 1980s saw a greater need for more cross-border police and judicial cooperation, including cross-border 'hot pursuit'. Similarly, the Member States whose currency is the euro are more likely to feel the need to develop common socio-economic policies. In both cases, the dynamic nature of the policy itself made it possible to avoid the pitfall of untenable institutional uniformity and come up with complicated solutions.

Variation in membership/members should imply that the participants embark on cooperation—in terms of the speed or the objectives of a certain European policy—not to circumvent stagnating decision-making procedures but rather to do justice to real differences between Member States. Variation in membership/members therefore needs to be addressed in the policy preparation stage. This will then lead to formal and informal arrangements, either within or outside the Union framework (variation in membership and accession as well as different types of economic, trade and security relationships), giving the actors on the EU stage different rights, obligations and perspectives on the integration process.

Member States may introduce some form of variation in membership/members for a variety of reasons, for example: (1) to represent certain (geopolitical) interests, (2) for its symbolic effect, (3) to establish a relationship with a certain region, or (4) when widening the EU in terms of Member States, cultures, backgrounds and wishes, to ensure that deepening also takes place. Such political motivations are not necessarily consistent with the rationale—as derived from the motivations for collective action (logic of appropriateness and logic of consequences)—for limiting the remit of a particular policy domain or a particular piece of legislation. Further variation in membership/members will therefore also need to be supported by substantive arguments that are consistent with those put forward for other policy domains. The most explicit and well-thought-out argument favouring variation in membership/members dates from 1994 and comes from the German politicians Wolfgang Schäuble and Karl Lamers, who at the time were the leader and the European Affairs spokesperson of the CDU parliamentary group in the Bundestag. Their proposal soon vanished from view, including in the Netherlands, but it has remained extremely relevant to this day,[8] so much so, in fact, that it is worth briefly reviewing the main points (see Box 6.1).

Box 6.1. The Schäuble-Lamers Paper

Wolfgang Schäuble and Karl Lamers, at that time the leader and European Affairs spokesperson of the CDU parliamentary group in the German Bundestag, penned their paper because they believed that the process of European integration had arrived at a 'critical point' in 1994. In their diagnosis, '[i]f the causes of the current dangerous trend cannot be addressed in the next two to four years, the EU will end up as little more than … a sophisticated free trade area, incapable of tackling the fundamental problems of European societies'. What causes and problems were Schäuble and Lamers referring to?

To summarise, they identified three main problems. First, there was the problem of enlargement. The EU had grown from six Member States, the founders of the integration process, to twelve when they wrote their paper, and would welcome many more if former EFTA countries Sweden, Austria and Finland were to join (which they did in 1995) and if former Warsaw Pact countries came to be viewed as potential members—something that had become increasingly plausible in 1994. Schäuble and Lamers believed that the existing EU institutions were not equipped to handle this.

Schäuble and Lamers were not opposed to EU enlargement, quite the opposite in fact. But they had noted that this process aggravated a second problem. The growing number of members had led to more divergence between the Member States' interests, a logical result of the increasing gap between the various economies in the EU. Moreover, the diverse interests and strategic visions entering the EU in this way threatened to outweigh the opportunities for compromise—the very essence of post-war European integration. This would be a major risk in the long run. Third, Schäuble and Lamers saw a dangerous trend towards what they referred to as 'regressive nationalism'. This longing for the old nation-state was growing, slowly but surely, fed by mounting fears of prosperity loss and declining well-being. These fears were kindled by the erosion of old certainties. Unemployment, a shrinking welfare state and immigration had fuelled a defensive reflex to withdraw to within the borders of the national state. This also worried Schäuble and Lamers. After all, that reflex was driven by denial of the problems of the post-Cold War era and globalisation, potentially making these problems impossible to solve.

In this context of fresh problems, the EU could only survive if the heart of the new, extended integration process remained stable. The centrifugal forces that had been unleashed could only be contained if they were counterbalanced by a far-reaching deepening of European integration. According to Schäuble and Lamers, that should have been top priority for Germany and Europe because it was the only way to exorcise the ghosts of Europe's dark past after the Cold War as well. But the big question was: how to go about it? How should a widening EU be stabilised?

Schäuble and Lamers' plan was called '*die weitere Festigung des Kerns*', a 'core Europe'. That core was to be built around a Franco-German axis, the centre of successful reconstruction during the Cold War, i.e. Western Europe.

It should be noted that this proposal was far from self-evident in 1994. After all, Western Europe's exceptional position was rapidly dismantled in the 1990s in favour of European integration. Schäuble and Lamers argued in favour of preserving the essentials of that successful Western Europe, however. The core Europe they had in mind consisted of five countries: France, Germany, the Netherlands, Belgium and Luxembourg.

A crucial point for Schäuble and Lamers was that their core Europe was merely a means to saving the EU, not an end in itself. They believed that a core Europe was the best way to reduce the dangerous tension that had arisen between EU enlargement on the one hand and deeper integration through the currency union on the other. Only a strong core Europe could show that widening and deepening could occur simultaneously.

The members of the core Europe that they envisaged were therefore the Member States that had not only demonstrated the political will to integrate but could also do so within the framework of the monetary union agreed in the Maastricht Treaty—the latter being the decisive factor.

After all, in the post-'Maastricht' EU, deepening integration meant economic and monetary integration. Italy was therefore not part of Schäuble and Lamers' core, let alone Greece. Only the five countries mentioned could actually attain the far-reaching level of European cooperation in the relevant socio-economic, budgetary and fiscal policy domains deemed necessary for a robust currency union. And only this lead group of countries was economically fit enough and had the political will to 'Europeanise' the necessary democratic control and ensure that the future currency union would remain healthy through these channels (competitiveness, political will and democratic control).[9]

Schäuble and Lamers timed their paper so that their lead group scenario could be incorporated into the Treaty texts as part of the negotiations leading to the Amsterdam Treaty (1997). The key point was that a lead group willing and able to embark on deeper integration based on hard criteria for a healthy economy should not have its ambitions vetoed by other EU members.

The Schäuble-Lamers plan was quickly shot down in the run-up to 'Amsterdam'. The Italians were angered and insulted and the French were suspicious. One of the cardinal problems was that the plan made too blatant a distinction between 'us' and 'them'. Critics openly questioned the motives of the German 'European' authors. Did their proposals not, after all, promote the very fragmentation that they claimed to want to avoid? No one therefore heard their most important message, which Lamers summed up years later as 'a little more Europe isn't possible'.

6.6 Conclusion: Dealing Proactively with Variation

The EU's current situation forces us to rethink existing variation options and to deal more consciously and proactively with them. In the forms of variation proposed above, the focus is mainly on variation in policy content, but variation in membership/members is also certainly possible. What is important here is that making more conscious use of variation can contribute to a greater sense of control and offer an alternative to relying on the 'binding effect' of the Community method on *all* the Member States and the associated convergence. This has been underscored by the European Commission's White Paper and the follow-up Franco-German initiatives (see Chap. 2), which put the option of a 'multi-speed Europe' back on the European political agenda.

There are also objections to variation, undeniably so. Variation can be a complication. Embracing it too quickly and without the necessary critical examination will not restore the credibility of the European project, and in fact could even damage it. If it does not seem to matter who does or does not commit to European policy, why is European policy important at all? Conditions must therefore be set for closer cooperation, as well as for opt-outs and forms of cooperation created outside the Union framework, to prevent the EU from becoming an à la carte menu. The following chapters will examine which conditions may apply in which situations.

Variation must be less 'opportunistic' than it has been so far. Instead, it should be reassessed in line with the EU policy domains that can be deduced from the Treaties. Not all Member States should be required to accept the EU's intervention in all these domains. Where they do, their legal order can be integrated using the Community method, as before, ensuring that no hybrid situations arise for every directive, regulation or policy measure.

Focusing too narrowly on the details of variation and the technique used—on the 'how'—may distract from the question of 'why'. That is why we proposed a different approach in the previous chapters, one that responds to the need for variation but explicitly interprets it in terms of content. That interpretation has everything to do with the need to reassess, to consider the EU's public tasks and how it fulfils them within the context of public interests, objectives and values.

The following chapters examine the options for variation by considering a number of topical issues: Economic and Monetary Union (EMU) (Chap. 7) and migration, asylum and border control (Chap. 8). Chapters 7 and 8 look in-depth at variation and the different forms that it can take by examining its existing pluriform nature and its potential. Our focus is therefore on both the *form* of cooperation (who cooperates on what, and in what way) and the *content* of the variation: how does it seek to balance the various public interests, what is the relationship between fundamental values and public goods such as stability and security. These chapters are meant to illustrate the main arguments of this book.

Notes

1. EU Battlegroups are rapid response units within the armed forces of the EU. They are made up of battalion-sized forces of about 1500 military personnel. Many of the Battlegroups are multinational, with military personnel being drawn from different EU Member States. Larger Member States sometimes form their own Battlegroups, while smaller Member States form groups together. Four non-EU Member States participate: Norway and Turkey (NATO members) and Macedonia and Ukraine (non-NATO countries). EU Member States Denmark and Malta do not currently participate in a Battlegroup.

2. The Group of Six (G6) is an unofficial group formed by the six largest EU Member States that deals with counter-terrorism, immigration policy and law enforcement The G6 was established in May 2003 as the G5, initially made up of France, Spain, the United Kingdom, Germany and Italy. Poland joined the group, whose members are the Ministers of Foreign Affairs, in 2006.
3. The 'EU big three' refers to the informal partnerships within the European defence and security policy between the three most powerful EU Member States, the UK, France and Germany, which have jumped into fill a leadership void. See C. Hill, in *The EU presence in International Organizations*, Blavoukos, S., & Bourantonis, D. (2011). Routledge.
4. TARGET (Trans-European Automated Real-time Gross Settlement Express Transfer) was a European interbank payment system, replaced in November 2007 by TARGET2, a uniform payment system run by the European System of Central Banks. Target was established to facilitate interbank payments between the various participants in the Economic and Monetary Union (EMU). International payments between commercial banks are facilitated by the national central banks, with the European Central Bank (ECB) being given the role of clearing house.
5. Fabbrini et al. (2015).
6. The provisions of this Protocol read as follows:

   Article 1

   1. The Charter does not extend the ability of the Court of Justice of the European Union, or any court or tribunal of Poland or of the United Kingdom, to find that the laws, regulations or administrative provisions, practices or action of Poland or of the United Kingdom are inconsistent with the fundamental rights, freedoms and principles that it reaffirms.
   2. In particular, and for the avoidance of doubt, nothing in Title IV of the Charter creates justiciable rights applicable to Poland or the United Kingdom except in so far as Poland or the United Kingdom has provided for such rights in its national law.

   Article 2

   To the extent that a provision of the Charter refers to national laws and practices, it shall only apply to Poland or the United Kingdom to the extent that the rights or principles that it contains are recognised in the law or practices of Poland or of the United Kingdom.

7. For a complete overview of the most important forms of variation in membership within the current Treaty frameworks, see De Witte (2018).
8. On the eve of founding the European Convention to draft a Constitution, the debate on lead groups and differentiation resurfaced. At the time, prominent voices (Fischer, Chirac, Delors) advocated setting up a permanent lead group. Nevertheless, the Laeken Declaration and the European Convention

focused on a new common framework for all in an attempt to avoid the 'second-class Member State' label.

9. It is no coincidence that the idea of a core Europe came from the German Christian Democrats. The idea, as elaborated by Schäuble and Lamers, harkens back to the 'ordoliberal' approach to economic integration. The proper functioning of the market is central to that approach. This means, first and foremost, that integration must be supported by the economies involved (which should grow more similar) and that it must happen spontaneously, without the need for a centrist bureaucracy of redistribution. In other words, economic integration is like a chain. It can only be sustainable if the links are strong enough, social security is adequate, and the individual economies are healthy enough. Each link is responsible for its own prosperity and well-being, something it must earn by means of price stability, economic prudence and a hard currency (monitored by an independent central bank). Integration can be a tremendous help but it can also frustrate these efforts, for example if it turns out to be a stepping stone to common debt or debt union because the differences between the integrating economies are too large and competition in the market is too fierce for some of the members. While this ordoliberal-inspired logic has influenced European integration, it has never been absorbed entirely, not even in the euro area.

Chapter 7
Variation and the Euro

7.1 Introduction

The European Economic and Monetary Union (EMU) and the euro and euro area to which it gave birth have often been presented as the definitive and irreversible outcome of European integration, or even as a historical necessity at a crucial time of major changes in world politics. Today, however, the story of deeper integration and unification through the single currency is being called into question. New facts have intensified doubts; for example, convergence has not lived up to its promise for several years now.[1] During the economic and financial crisis of recent years, the euro severely tested political support for European integration. On the other hand, it could be argued that, in weathering these many storms, the European integration process demonstrated its resilience.

Stabilisation of the euro area is needed, financially, economically and to bolster confidence. That will require more change. It is neither realistic nor desirable to effectuate this change by taking a quantum leap in federalisation. It is equally unrealistic and undesirable to dismantle the existing currency union, however. Drastic overhauls are also difficult[2] in the current political and social context, despite arguments favouring Treaty revision.[3] Allowing for this context, however, there are a number of feasible and desirable options in which the notion of 'variation' can be helpful. It should be noted that the euro area itself is already a form of variation within the European Union, as not all Member States participate (while some non-Member States do). This chapter explores and elaborates on such possibilities, bearing in mind the history of the monetary union to date.

Starting in 2010, parties active in the financial markets have engaged in lengthy and spirited speculation about the collapse or break-up of the monetary union, and subsequently about 'exits' from the euro area. While fragmentation and departures have so far not occurred, doom scenarios cannot be ruled out as yet, the most recent risk factor being the formation of the Lega-M5S government in Italy. The instability of the euro area has had severe consequences. Examples include disruptive

E. Hirsch Ballin et al., *European Variations as a Key to Cooperation*,
Research for Policy, https://doi.org/10.1007/978-3-030-32893-1_7

divergence in interest rates, capital outflows and the bailout of transnational banks using national tax revenues (highlighting the unhealthy interdependence between governments and banks). The debate on how to safeguard the future of the euro is also leading to polarisation in both domestic and European politics. There is constant concern about the currency union's vulnerability.[4]

Contradictions set the tone in the debate about safeguarding the future of the euro. The objectives of financial stability and competitive advantage based on economies of scale and deepening interdependence are at odds with concerns about the loss of national and European control, dissatisfaction with the curtailment of national fiscal discretion and fears that the social dimension will be neglected or that 'free-riding' and 'moral hazard' will become institutionalised (including through the ECB, the European Stability Mechanism or ESM, and any funds that may be established or filled, for example within the framework of the Banking Union).[5]

Ultimately, however, the debate on the future of the euro also revolves around dilemmas related to the production of public goods, as they are defined in this book. Normative considerations are often described in this context as reflections of the general interest ('the logic of appropriateness') and contrasted with considerations based on a cost-benefit analysis ('the logic of consequences'). It is from this perspective that the current chapter looks in greater depth at the specific policy dilemmas that define the debate on the future of the monetary union. The aim is to point out possible directions for strengthening the euro area in line with recent political and economic trends, based on the notion of variation. In doing so, it refrains from making detailed recommendations on the complex issues related to the future of the euro and EMU.

The problem of EMU has several different facets:

- a fiscal dimension (what do we do about out-of-control national debt and associated bailouts, and what does this mean in terms of risk-sharing?);
- an economic dimension (what are the consequences of differences in productivity, economic growth, exports, etc. between Member States?);
- a financial dimension (what do we do to mitigate the potentially destabilising effects of capital flows; what form of organisation is appropriate for the banking system?);
- a monetary dimension (what monetary policy allows for (major) differences between euro-area Member States?);
- and an institutional and political dimension (how can we improve the democratic legitimacy of the monetary union and euro governance?)

In this book, we discuss these dimensions as a whole, but puts greatest emphasis—within the limited scope of this chapter—on the fiscal dimension, because this is at the heart of emu and the euro as they have evolved since the Maastricht Treaty. That said, we also touch on the other four dimensions at various points in this chapter.

In a general sense, exploring the potential for variation in the euro and EMU is a highly complex exercise (more complex than in other policy domains). Readers should therefore regard this chapter as a general survey of how variation can help to safeguard the future of the euro beyond the crisis. As such, it serves to clarify the main message of this book (and is not a comprehensive, separate study into the causes of, and solutions to, the problems of the euro, or a general economic analysis of those problems). The starting point for this chapter is the (ad hoc) variation in the monetary union that arose at the outset and that has been amplified in many respects during the crises. The main focus, however, is on what variation can do to stabilise the monetary union within the existing Treaty frameworks, both in the medium term and in the steady state.

As we explore the potential to use variation to change and therefore improve the monetary union, it is essential to bear in mind the loss of confidence caused by the euro crisis. In other words, changes and solutions must contribute to restoring mutual trust (between Member States) and to rebuilding support for and the democratic legitimacy of the monetary union (in the Member States).

The critical question that then arises is: how can all euro-area Member States, from Greece to the Netherlands, become and remain credible participants in the euro? Inherent in the design of the monetary union as laid down in the Maastricht Treaty is that the euro-area Member States must take responsibility for themselves. The most visible evidence is the 3% of GDP ceiling (budget deficit) and the 60% of GDP ceiling (public debt) introduced since the Maastricht Treaty and as such fundamental to the monetary union.

Nevertheless, many of the plans proposing changes in the euro area tend to stress the responsibility of the EU's institutions—such as the European Council and the European Central Bank—and that of the Member States.[6] The question is, however, whether confidence can be restored by transferring more competences to the EU's institutions in an effort to boost the euro. Although proposed solutions to the euro's problems often involve the transfer of even more competences, supported by predominantly technocratic arguments, it is precisely there—in that technocracy and transfer of competences—that the road leading to restored confidence vanishes. How do we find it again? Before we can answer that question, we must go the heart of the current impasse.

Potential solutions within the existing frameworks are delimited by two extremes. At one end of the scale is the effort to boost the Stability and Growth Pact (SGP), the 3 and 60% ceilings mentioned above, with the Member States bearing maximum responsibility. At the other end are proposals to transfer as many euro-related powers as possible to the EC (with accountability to the EP), for example by installing a European 'Minister of Finance'. Both extremes soon lead to a widening gap with the national democracies (maintaining SGP through supranational mechanisms, institution-building). Both have their fervent proponents and opponents among the Member States. This is at the very heart of the impasse that is gripping the euro area.

Section 7.2 takes the current impasse as its starting point and places it against the backdrop of the history of the euro and the conflict between the 'logic of appropriateness' and the 'logic of consequences' that has coloured the euro's evolution in recent years. On that basis, it takes a new look at the question: where, given the current situation, are there opportunities for variation in EMU and the euro?

Section 7.3 answers this question by charting three possible routes for variation in EMU and the euro. They are routes in which variation (the co-existence of different arrangements) and unity (as formulated in the existing Treaties) can be recombined and can reinforce each other. We look in particular at the problems associated with the 'no-bailout clause'—which states that countries do not cover each other's debts when they are in trouble—owing to its de facto annulment in recent years. We also look closely at how IMF involvement might be continued, whether a European Monetary Fund (EMF) could resolve the current impasse, the importance of focusing on macroprudential policy, and whether all these elements can be combined by leaving more room for variation.

Section 7.4 presents a brief conclusion. In general, this chapter seeks solutions to the current EMU and euro problems in coordination or closer coordination within the existing institutional frameworks, as well as in some of the emergency arrangements rigged up during the euro crisis. This approach would allow the Netherlands to bring the euro and EMU more into line with its own political preferences, but notes at the same time that politicians and the public remain little aware of such opportunities.

7.2 The Two Logics and the Current Impasse

The positions at both the national and European extremes of the debate on the future of the euro are normatively charged. On the one hand, there are the 'Eurosceptics', who advocate for the primacy of the national state. On the other, there are the 'Europhiles', who are fighting for European primacy. The views of both groups are a matter of principle: depending on whether they support the national state or a federation, their arguments are dominated by either a national or a European 'logic of appropriateness' (although both groups often use the 'logic of consequences' to substantiate their positions). The views, plans and ideas positioned between these two extremes are predominantly pragmatic, i.e. aimed at reducing costs and maximising returns.

The tension between the logic of appropriateness and the logic of consequences has intensified in recent years. That tension is disruptive, all the more so because it is growing in a context in which Treaty law and institutions have only limited effect *and* in which the political support for changing the Treaties is inadequate.[7] In other words, the leeway for unifying solutions that reconcile both logics is limited.[8] As the current situation shows, moreover, the argument that the single currency is a 'logical' consequence of the internal market—the argument that underpinned the run-up to and establishment of EMU (see also Box 7.1)—is no longer conclusive. Powerful evidence can be found in the Greek sovereign debt crisis and the Brexit referendum.

In response to the Union's management of the euro crisis from 2011 onwards, which the United Kingdom (understandably) perceived as a move to border off the euro area, the British government warned that this would jeopardise the 'integrity of the European Single Market' and make its membership of the EU correspondingly more problematic.[9] British criticism of the euro echoed a broader, swelling chorus of doubt regarding the merits of the single currency.

At the time of its introduction, the euro was seen as an instrument for prosperity, growth and international influence. Progress in all those areas has been inadequate, however. In fact, in view of the euro crisis, the underperformance of the single currency has turned into a serious issue of multilateral coordination and political credibility in virtually every euro-area Member State.[10] At the same time, monetary union has also raised all sorts of problematic side effects, for example unfair tax competition, inadequate capacity for structural reforms, lack of fiscal discipline, the ECB's controversial policy of quantitative easing (QE), and distressing levels of unemployment and impoverishment.[11] These developments have put pressure on stability and prosperity growth, the main public tasks that the members of the euro area were attempting to fulfil through the single currency. A further question is whether the crisis management efforts of recent years have in fact strengthened the euro area. For example, the sovereign debt problem remains in many euro-area Member States and there is, as yet, no solution in sight for the broader crisis of confidence that has arisen between governments, EU institutions and citizens.

Even so, much has happened. Several adjustments have been made to EMU. There is closer surveillance of fiscal policy and macroeconomic imbalances, such as potentially harmful imbalances between the current account surpluses and deficits of euro-area members (Six-Pack 2011). Fiscal coordination has also been extended by boosting the budgetary competence of the European Commission (Two-Pack 2013), partly in the context of the 'European Semester' (2010), the cycle of economic and fiscal policy coordination within the EU.[12]

Efforts to set up a banking union are also under way, the ECB supervises system banks, there is a European directive on bank recovery and resolution, and a proposal for a European deposit guarantee scheme. On top of all this, an emergency fund has been set up for euro-area Member States that have experienced acute financial difficulties during the euro crisis, i.e. the European Stability Mechanism (ESM). There are also the Outright Monetary Transactions (OMT) for the Member States that have received ESM support—a programme in which the ECB figures as the de facto 'lender of last resort', even though the OMT mechanism has not been activated to date—as well as the ECB's (ultra-)low-interest-rate policy and its aforementioned programme of quantitative easing.[13]

Many of these EMU adaptations have bolstered the role of the EU's institutions vis-à-vis that of the governments of the Member States. For example, the ESM imposes far-reaching requirements on debtors, while the ECB, the 'daily' saviour of the euro, has gradually assumed a key role as the guardian of euro-area stability, for example by 'Europeanising' (banking) surveillance and expanding its balance sheet. These moves give the ECB much more influence in the governance of the single currency. They have, moreover, been accompanied by a certain 'shifting' of political responsibilities from the governments of the Member States to the EU's institutions, such as the ECB, the EC and the ESM, which are less subject to democratic control.

The euro's rescue, as it has evolved in recent years, has had far-reaching consequences. Political decisions concerning dilemmas of solidarity, reliability (e.g. with regard to fiscal discipline) and social cohesion are now 'hidden' to a greater or lesser extent in the policy-related techniques employed by the EU's institutions, for example in the ECB's balance sheets (TARGET2), in the ESM,[14] or in the zero risk weighting of government bonds on banks' balance sheets. This is not only increasing the power of the EU's institutions in the EMU, but also raising growing doubts about the independence of, for example, the ECB and concerns about monetary financing through the same ECB (which is prohibited).[15]

One of the most drastic crisis measures to stabilise the euro area was the creation of the ESM, an organisation that provides financial assistance to euro-area countries struggling with excessive government debt, subject to their undertaking a programme of reform. Where necessary, moreover, the ECB will buy government bonds from Member States participating in an ESM programme (through the OMT mechanism) to prevent destabilising speculation on sovereign debt. The OMT mechanism has not been activated to date. Measures such as the ESM and OMT are clearly a step towards more risk-sharing in the euro area,[16] and are politically controversial.

The controversies surrounding new moves towards greater risk-sharing reflect the current impasse (mentioned above). In other words, the tendency to shift responsibility in the euro area to the EU's institutions—such as the EC and the ECB—and away from the Member States is seemingly not the way to restore lost confidence. That is precisely why EMU and euro reform is so difficult and regarded with considerable suspicion and mistrust in the Member States.

The impasse has meant that, for the time being, the only progress being made concerns the proposals for completing a banking union. These proposals are meant to contribute to financial stability and to end the 'deadly embrace' between individual governments and 'their' banks. The problem, however, is that the plans establishing the banking union have not advanced far enough to actually navigate the euro into calmer waters.[17] It seems that more is required. This explains France's efforts to further 'deepen' and politicise the euro around the Franco-German axis, but these plans, in turn, have led to the political impasse described above. Whether they will, or will continue to, garner sufficient support and to what extent they serve the interests of the Netherlands is therefore hugely uncertain. In addition, the legitimacy of such plans remains problematic, in any case.

What we can conclude from the above is that there is a need for something else, a prospect that calls for a firmer commitment from euro-area Member States than at present. That prospect might also represent the only opportunity to genuinely reinforce the basis of support for the euro area and its democratic foundations. It must be sought in between the two extremes, i.e. bolstering the Stability and Growth Pact by placing maximum responsibility with the Member States on the one hand and further centralising euro governance by transferring as many competences as possible on the other.

Between these extremes are modalities of (greater) variation. In essence, they suggest a certain 'reversion' to the governments of the Member States, and therefore to their national parliaments. Instead of a stultifying focus on one or the other extreme, the idea would be to mark time so that preferences and expectations in each euro area Member State can become clear. A strategy of this kind would address the urgent need for more democratic legitimacy in the way the euro is managed.[18] The key question then is whether these different preferences can be expressed in (policy) variation between Member States, and, if so, in such a way that each Member State pursues a credible policy that is appropriate to monetary union. In short, can we allow differences between Member States that strengthen the unity behind the single currency at the same time?

There is no simple answer to the question of whether such variation is even possible within the monetary union. The pursuit of a stable monetary union between autonomous states is, by definition, a complex affair owing to the patently large interdependencies and externalities between Member States in the absence of an overarching (political) organisation that has democratic legitimacy and a basis of support among the inhabitants of those Member States. Nevertheless, that is the situation as it now stands, because that is how the single currency was formed (see box below).

Box 7.1 The Franco-German Deal and the Design of EMU and the Euro

Chancellor Helmut Kohl gave a new boost to the EMU project long before the fall of the Berlin Wall on 9 November 1989. The presentation of the Delors Report had made EMU the centre of attention that spring, but there were fears in Paris that events in Central and Eastern Europe would slow its momentum. It was the German Chancellor who took steps to allay French concerns.

Kohl carved out a place for European Political Union (EPU) in his projections of EMU, partly with a view to popular sentiment in his own country (EMU was not a popular topic in German domestic politics). EPU had broad support among West Germans at the time, especially because it implied giving the European Parliament (EP) more power. It also served to pacify the 'EMU-sceptic' Bundesbank. Frankfurt conceived of EMU merely as the culmination of a process of peremptory economic convergence, the 'crowning theory': first economic convergence and then EMU, and not the other way around. The rationale behind this position was as follows: EMU partners had to adopt German financial and economic best practices before there could be EMU. In terms of financial policy, EMU was to be 'German' or not happen at all. EPU fit right into this story. Something like an EPU would, after all, be essential to enforcing the sought-after economic convergence.[19]

France, however, looked unfavourably on this. In the eyes of President Francois Mitterrand, France had already made major concessions on two points. First, the EMU blueprint presented in the Delors Report was already very 'German'; it proposed an independent central bank, prioritised price stability and imposed strict convergence criteria concerning fiscal discipline and government debt. Second, in the 1980s France had reluctantly consented to the free movement of capital in the European Community, a prerequisite for further discussion of EMU put forward by Germany and the Netherlands.[20]

Moreover, a Europe that allowed the free movement of capital had to choose between a monetary union or floating exchange rates, but because exchange rate stability was vital for the internal market, the second option was not preferable. The concept of the monetary policy 'trilemma' states that it is impossible to have free capital flow, a fixed exchange rate and sovereign monetary policy at the same time. One of these policies always has to give way, and since capital had been liberalised, sovereign monetary policy would have to go.

After Mitterrand had agreed to the starting date of EMU negotiations, an important point in itself, Kohl promised at the Strasbourg Summit that EMU and German unification would be inextricably linked (December 1989). Economic and monetary objections to EMU, which were prevalent in Germany and in the Netherlands, were pushed to the background and German-Dutch concepts failed to prevail in the EMU's design. The crucial element in that design was the sequence: first monetary union, then economic convergence, and then perhaps EPU. Little or no attention was paid to problems that might accompany a monetary merger between very different national economies and the management of economic and financial interdependence—problems that could grow more serious as EMU expanded.

EMU was launched in 1999. The large group of Member States participating at the outset was contrary to expectations, at least those of the Germans and Dutch.[21] Prominent economists had also explicitly recommended starting out with a lead group, with Germany as its linchpin. They based their recommendation on Mundell's theory of 'optimum currency areas',[22] a system for sizing up the costs and benefits of a monetary union.

The major advantage of monetary union is that it eliminates exchange rate risks and shocks. This is particularly good news for the internal market, which becomes stronger thanks to lower transaction costs. In addition, the single currency also prevents governments from devaluing their currencies to improve the competitiveness of their businesses. Market distortions of this kind may be detrimental to the internal market and can trigger protectionist countermeasures, but a monetary union makes them impossible.

The costs of a monetary union stem from the loss of sovereign monetary policy instruments that can be deployed in response to country-specific shocks. Therein lies a fundamental contradiction between theory and emu practice. In general, the more countries trade with one another, the more benefits they gain by eliminating exchange rates between them and the lower the cost of abandoning sovereign monetary policy instruments. The latter is not always the case, however, because it depends largely on the production structure.

In the early 1990s, various studies indicated that the group of countries that had pegged their currencies to the German mark resembled an optimum currency area much more closely than the larger group in the single currency zone, which included the southern EU Member States.[23] The outcomes were inconclusive, however, and that is partly why the debate about optimum currency areas increasingly became a question of faith.

The question, ultimately, was whether exchange rates should be regarded as a source of potential distortions in the single market and should therefore be eliminated. Mundell and others were increasingly inclined to say yes, emphasising in particular the aforementioned benefits of monetary union.[24]

Consequently, Mundell and economists who supported his analysis encouraged a pro-EMU trend, which paved the way to a remarkable phenomenon: the accession criteria for EMU were *not* based on the theory of optimum currency areas.[25] Instead, they concerned macroeconomic policy indicators such as low inflation, small government deficits and exchange rate stability. They therefore did not acknowledge the core assumption of optimum currency theory as an argument for EMU, i.e. a sufficient degree of commercial integration. For example, they ignored the trade imbalances of potential Member States. In addition, countries with trade deficits were allowed to cover these with loans that could be raised on the recently liberalised European capital market, and the more likely an EU Member State was to join emu, the better the terms. The financial markets had already factored EMU membership into their interest rates and, for example, furnished countries such as Greece and Italy with generous amounts of capital on that basis.[26]

If anything became clear after the outbreak of the financial and economic crisis, it was that EMU in its present form and with its current members is not an 'optimum currency area', and that the European policy programme of the 1990s, which was based partly on this erroneous expectation, had diverted attention away from the risks that were taken in setting up EMU.

An imperfect understanding of the 'E' component meant that EMU was ill-equipped to commence with a large group of Member States, in other words a larger group than the core group pegged to Germany. Why, then, did it go ahead?

The Maastricht Treaty did not specify whether the third stage of EMU, the introduction of the single currency, would involve a smaller lead group of Member States or a whole pack. At the very last moment, France and Italy proposed including starting dates in the Treaty. If no majority of countries satisfied the emu criteria in 1997, then the third stage would commence in 1999 with the countries that did. That seemed to leave open the possibility of starting with a lead group with Germany as its core. That the group ultimately became a pack is due mainly to two factors.

First of all, the recession in 1991–1992 threw public finances in the EMU area off balance. Second, Germany's public finances suffered as a result of the high costs of unification. This made it impossible to launch EMU with a lead group in 1997, giving the southern Member States more time to meet the convergence criteria.

Italy's Amato government (1992–1993) did everything possible to exploit this opportunity, helped by the convergence game in the financial markets described above. Interest rates on public debt fell significantly across the whole area identified by the markets as the future euro area, which included Italy. The steady deterioration of Germany's public finances, which had to bear the costs of unification with the GDR, also meant that Berlin had to use every trick in the book to keep its budget deficit below 3% of GDP, although gross government debt rose above the 60% ceiling. This prevented Germany from playing any role in deciding which Member States would or would not advance to the third stage. In the end, both the Treaty *and* the markets forced EMU into a broad start in 1999. To understand 'the way of further strengthening EMU',[27] we need to know which strategic vision gained the upper hand in constructing the monetary union.

After the Maastricht Treaty (1992), it was mainly the German Bundesbank that stressed the importance of building a political union.[28] Its argument was inspired by the 'crowning theory', which held that EMU would ultimately be unsustainable without political union. In fact, monetary union could only be the 'crowning glory' of an existing political union. The 'crowning theory' is diametrically opposed to its reverse, the 'sequence' described above, which eventually gained the upper hand under pressure of the events in 1989–1991 and the momentum created by the Maastricht Treaty.[29,30]

Nevertheless, the ambiguous concept of 'an EPU' continues to hover over the market as a possible, but very controversial, panacea for the problems of the euro area. There has recently been a fundamental shift in the thinking about EPU, including viewing it as a possible solution to the current problems in the euro area. The origin of this shift can be traced back to 28 February 2013, when the then President of the European Council, Herman Van Rompuy, gave a speech in the City of London on the future of EMU and the euro area.

Van Rompuy was responding to the notorious speech by British Prime Minister David Cameron earlier that year, in which he openly expressed his doubts as to whether the United Kingdom should remain a member of the EU. Van Rompuy was clear about the way forward: 'We are not witnessing the birth pangs of a federal "Euroland". Changing the EU treaties is therefore not the priority.' Van Rompuy had a different 'top priority' in mind, i.e. 'deepening economic coordination', and in his view that meant '[e]volution, not revolution' in the subsequent development of the EMU.

Nevertheless, Van Rompuy *was* preaching 'revolution' because, despite his pragmatic modesty, he did nothing less than to write off the idea of an EPU as a realistic prospect or a solution to the acute crisis in which the euro area found itself at the time. The concept of political union that Van Rompuy described in London was an elaboration of the 'blueprint' for an integrated policy framework in the euro area and EMU that he had presented in the autumn of 2012 and that has been developed step by step ever since. That occurred in the following succession of documents: the Commission's 2012 blueprint for a 'deep and genuine' EMU, the aforementioned proposal by the President of the European Council in the same year, the 2015 *Five Presidents' Report*, and the proposals in the Commission's 2017 reflection paper referred to above. All these proposals recommend strengthening 'Europeanisation' in EMU and the euro area in the long run and greater solidarity between the Member States in the monetary union—including hints about debt mutualisation, with risks on public debt being shared.[31] This would not be on the basis of an EPU, but rather on the basis of Community policy coordination.

What is crucial to all these proposals is that they take shape within the existing Treaties. This is in line with Van Rompuy's implicit obstruction of the 'all-out EPU route' (by means of federalisation) in 2013, as described above. The point in all these proposals is to improve the existing mechanisms of policy coordination and their democratic legitimacy, not to change the Treaties or come up with new treaties and institutions.

7.3 Variation as a Possible Solution to Coordination Problems in the Euro Area: An Initial Exploration

Where, given the current situation, are there opportunities for variation in EMU and the euro? Opportunities in which variation (the co-existence of different arrangements) and unity (as formulated in the existing Treaties) can be combined and can reinforce each other? That is the question that we must answer if we are to break the current deadlock. This section explores specific variation options; it focuses on how to deal with situations in the euro area in which the members' fiscal policies have negative effects. Our discussion takes into account the three dimensions of variation described in Chap. 6.

A monetary union requires the advanced coordination of economic policies. The purpose of the single currency policy is to cushion the adverse impact of 'symmetrical shocks', for example a change in the global economy. 'Asymmetrical shocks' (which are country-specific) must be absorbed by labour market policies and national fiscal policies, but these are constrained by the conditions imposed on the size of the government's debt and budget deficit.[32] In the end, it is mainly adjustments in the labour market—including social security schemes—that must compensate for the absence of the exchange rate mechanism in this set-up.[33] This is, in short, the logic behind the emu's design, as laid down in the Maastricht Treaty. The 'no-bailout clause' was essential in this respect.

The logic behind the EMU's design as laid down in the Maastricht Treaty is that countries must have their own fiscal policies in proper order. The 'no-bailout' clause was critical in that countries would not come to one another's aid in the event of problems, making it pointless for the financial markets to speculate on a bailout. The purpose was to enforce sufficient fiscal discipline among the emu members. There was a good reason for this: large budget deficits and the ensuing public debt could jeopardise the value of the euro (and deposits in that currency).[34] By now, it has become clear that the no-bailout clause did not survive the euro area's collective response to the crisis. In that respect, the 'Maastricht order' has so far proved illusory (Box 7.2).

Box 7.2 The Problems of 'No Bailout' and SGP

If the dilemmas related to the production of such public goods as stability and prosperity growth have become apparent anywhere in recent years, it is in the no-bailout clause of the Maastricht Treaty. During the euro crisis, the basic principles underpinning the prescribed fiscal discipline of the euro area Member States and the ECB's mandate proved politically untenable, even though these principles were referred to explicitly in the Maastricht Treaty. They were also of huge importance in the Netherlands' decision to join EMU and the euro.

Much of what has happened in recent years, however, was already pre-ordained in the Maastricht Treaty. While the Treaty's 'excessive deficit procedure' (Article 104c, now Article 126 TFEU) was based on quantified reference values for Member States' budget deficits and debt quotas (3% and 60% of GDP respectively), these reference values were made 'dynamic' during the final phase of the Treaty negotiations. This means, for example, that budget deficits that exceed 3% of GDP are regarded as acceptable if they can be defined as 'temporary' or 'exceptional' deviations. It also means that it is the ECOFIN (Council of Finance Ministers) that determines this on a case-by-case basis, by qualified majority. Member States therefore do not have the right of veto. The Commission's role is limited to measuring the Member States' performance against the quantified criteria, and to monitoring the procedure. From the outset, then, the excessive deficit procedure, including the imposition of sanctions, was the subject of political decision-making between the Member States in ECOFIN. It has remained so, even though the Stability and Growth Pact (SGP) was added during the run-up to the Treaty of Amsterdam (1997) as extra inducement.

The conclusions of the Dublin European Council of 14 December 1996 were the prelude to the SGP: they announced that the excessive deficit procedure would be laid down in two directives and not in a supplementary treaty. In essence, Article 104C remained unchanged. At the Amsterdam Summit on 16 and 17 June 1997, the European Council adopted a Resolution establishing the SGP. In it, the EC pointed out the obligation under the Treaty to avoid excessive government deficits, but also noted that the 'Member States remain responsible' for meeting this obligation. The role of the Commission and ECOFIN remained as defined in the Maastricht Treaty. It was therefore still up to the Council of Ministers to take a final decision in accordance with the procedure laid down in the Treaty and to decide whether or not to impose the associated sanctions. ECOFIN may deviate from the procedure if a qualified majority in the Council determines that 'special circumstances' exist in the Member State that has exceeded the reference value, or if ECOFIN determines that the Member State has made sufficient efforts to address the deficit—although a decision 'not to act' on the Commission's recommendation must be supported by sound arguments.

At best, the SGP was a 'gentlemen's agreement' between euro area Finance ministers, based on the realisation that free riding at the expense of the single currency project—by taking advantage of the single currency's stability without linking it to national fiscal discipline—was unwise. There was, however, great confidence in the unifying power of the market as the foundation for monetary union.

The credibility of the SGP's quantitative reference values ultimately depended on a qualified majority. That changed dramatically in November 2003 when the German government under Chancellor Gerhard Schröder invoked the 'special circumstances' clause, referencing the ongoing costs of German unification (which had caused Germany's budget deficit to exceed the 3% of GDP ceiling). Germany managed to drum up a qualified majority in ECOFIN, partly thanks to the support of France, which had also exceeded the 3% threshold. The SGP was suspended temporarily and would later be made more flexible.[35] In euro area Member States such as the Netherlands, this turn of events was a blow to the credibility of the single currency as the key to long-term stability and prosperity growth, and to the credibility of the crucial no-bailout guarantee in the Maastricht Treaty. Doubts were further raised by the manner in which the euro had taken shape since the signing of the Maastricht Treaty, and in part by the large number of Member States that appeared to qualify for admission at the euro's introduction.

All these doubts were intensified by the course of events during the euro crisis. It turned out that it was impossible to adhere strictly to the no-bailout clause, that the rules for budgetary discipline were unfeasible, that the governance of the monetary union had less-than-perfect democratic legitimacy, and that yawning differences remained between the Member States. It became clear that the monetary union's design had certain consequences and involved certain responsibilities and budgetary risks, and that change and adaption would be unavoidable. That is where we are today. The general view is that the measures taken in recent years have considerably strengthened the institutional structure of EMU. At the same time, there is a widely shared awareness that the monetary union in its present form is 'unfinished' and a 'lack of consensus about how the EMU should develop further'.[36]

The problems surrounding the no-bailout clause clearly illustrate the dilemmas of collective action, for example the problem of 'moral hazard'. In essence, this means that when Member States can rely on assistance in the case of excessive debt, they may incur more debt. Another question is how to deal with debts incurred in the past. In other words, introducing debt sharing as a stabilisation measure could very well undermine the whole point of the single currency, namely (price) stability. This analysis helps us understand why euro-area Member States such as the Netherlands find using European debt mutualisation to prop up the euro area problematic.[37] Germany, the Netherlands and other Member States greatly prefer to bolster the single currency by restoring the credibility of the no-bailout clause in the Maastricht Treaty. This may not be impossible if the Union manages to make better use of its existing variation options.

The potential for more variation is inherent in the current set-up of the euro. It is, as it were, the 'flip side' of the Member States' own responsibility for fiscal discipline and structural reform. Variation in this sense requires different, co-existing arrangements. In exploring the actual potential for variation, we must briefly indicate which elements in the current governance of the euro might be included. There are at least three factors that need to be considered:

a. the extent to which euro-area Member States exercise market discipline;
b. whether the Member States want mutual insurance, and the status of a common monetary fund;
c. whether the IMF should be involved.

Using the terminology of the dimensions of variation introduced in Chap. 6, this list logically begins with variation in policy content, but it also considers variation in membership and decision-making.

What are the options that arise working with the above elements (on the understanding that we do not immediately assess their feasibility)? Below, we discuss potential routes to variation, by which we mean different arrangements that can co-exist. They are:

1. variation by means of market discipline and IMF involvement going forward;
2. variation by means of a European Monetary Fund (EMF).

Both forms of variation are geared primarily towards variation in policy content, i.e. the type of variation appropriate in situations in which the Member States concerned have the same motivation for collective action (in this case, reciprocity). However, they may have differing interpretations of the situation that drives this action, i.e. socio-economic goals versus price stability and structural reforms (see the concluding section of Chap. 4).

After surveying variation in policy content, i.e. creating leeway for national discretion based on framework or minimum agreements, we can then consider variation in decision-making and/or (sub)membership, for example with regard to the development of existing or the establishment of new institutions, such as the ESM or an EMF. What is the decision-making procedure on the appropriation of loans (supranational, Community, intergovernmental)? Who are the members of such funds and what does their membership consist of? In other words, is variation in membership possible?

This approach—variation in policy content first and then variation in decision-making and (sub)membership—forms the basis for our exploration of variation in the EMU and the euro by means of the two arrangements identified above.

There are, additionally, euro-related policy domains in which variation in policy content is already facilitated. One current and evolving example is macroprudential policy. We discuss this existing form of variation in more detail at the end of this section. We also identify ways of making this policy integral to efforts to strengthen EMU and the euro in the light of the arrangements that we will discuss first. The aim at all times is to consider the budgetary, economic, financial, monetary and institutional-political dimensions as a whole when taking further steps to strengthen EMU and the euro (see the introduction to this chapter).

1. **Variation by means of market discipline and IMF involvement going forward**

One option is for some Member States to exercise market discipline and submit to the IMF's recovery programmes in the event of difficulties while other Member States establish a common fund providing mutual insurance. In both cases, rules will be necessary, including the option of variation in decision-making and membership (of certain arrangements), the details of which are beyond the scope of this (exploratory) chapter. The existing euro architecture provides the necessary leeway for tightening up checks and balances through the exercise of market discipline and for reducing the technocratic complexion of policy-making. This is feasible without far-reaching politicisation at European level or Treaty amendments. Such leeway is the starting point for our discussion of this first route of variation.

The market discipline/IMF arrangement is appropriate for countries that are committed to taking responsibility for their own affairs. The fund arrangement, in turn, requires a large measure of trust between the Member States that choose to participate. In the toolkit of solutions for the dilemmas associated with bolstering the single currency, one element has garnered considerable attention recently: the creation of a European Monetary Fund (EMF), which is not provided for in the Treaty but is possible within its framework. An EMF may be of particular value as an emergency fund in the event of exceptional asymmetrical shocks and as an additional instrument alongside automatic stabilisers and temporary budget deficits.[38] In such cases, however, Article 122(2) TFEU already provides for the possibility of furnishing aid to Member States. As an interpretation of this clause, an EMF could take the form of an ex ante fund and/or (mutual) borrowing capacity.

In the case of mutual borrowing capacity, variation is possible in policy design (and possibly also in decision-making and degrees of participation). That would certainly be true if such organised borrowing capacity can be applied in tandem with pre-existing IMF funds (formed by euro-area countries). Moreover, the IMF has traditionally extended funds to ease pressure on the balance of payments caused by a policy of fixed exchange rates (of which the single currency is essentially a—specifically European—version).[39]

Specifically, this could mean, for example, that euro-area Member States whose government deficits regularly test the boundaries of the rules and agreements would be more likely to request assistance from an EMF and/or the IMF, or do so more frequently, than other euro-area Member States. This makes it possible to build variation into the architecture of an EMF for example pegging risk premiums to such fiscal behaviour by applying SGP criteria (as proposed on several occasions; see, for example, CEPR 2018).[40]

Another option is to make the establishment of the emergency fund optional for Member States. Those that want to arrange joint coverage contribute to the fund (and can rely on it in crisis situations). Those that do not want such an arrangement do not contribute and must rely on themselves (and the IMF) in crisis situations. As a result, the basic fund, in which everyone participates, may be limited or very limited. The Member States that do not participate in the fund will no longer receive assistance if they get into financial difficulties but will instead be forced to restructure their debt, with the expense then being borne by the private sector.

Variation in this sense implies less integration, for example with regard to fiscal rules.[41] In the latter case, that would mean a reshuffle of the responsibilities in the monetary union by devolving responsibility (to the national parliaments), a move that so far has seldom been considered. This could provide a more effective way of addressing a key dilemma of policy coordination within EMU: on the one hand, there seems to be a need for more coordinated action (to better guarantee resilience, balance and growth, including bridging the investment gap[42]), while on the other such action is at odds with the decentralised nature of EMU, as structured in the Maastricht Treaty, and with the aim of minimising pressure on national and European budgets on account of the euro.

The Dutch Council of State [*Raad van State*] has examined this approach in information furnished at the request of the Dutch House of Representatives in November 2017[43] and noted that if this more 'decentralised' trend were to be continued, three elements would be important: (1) completion of the banking union, (2) certain financial safety nets, (3) European enforcement of fiscal and economic rules in special circumstances.[44] This corresponds with the main outlines of our examination in this section and the rest of the chapter in this book.

2. **Variation by means of an EMF**

An EMF is another way to deal with the dilemma of stabilisation versus decentralisation. It differs from the 'variation by means of market discipline' discussed above (particularly in terms of (fund) membership), in which an EMF can be combined with existing IMF instruments. As discussed in this section, 'variation by means of an EMF' primarily involves creating a fund that could act as an additional stability mechanism for the single currency, alongside market discipline. This approach fits in with the history of European integration, which features an array of 'fund structures' meant to compensate for market frictions and to act as a buffer in crises.[45] It is driven by the ongoing quest to strike the right balance between European intergovernmental or supranational buffers on the one hand and market incentives that are deployed optimally to induce national responsibility on the other. That quest requires a certain amount of institutional agility.

Institutional agility can be achieved by allowing variation in policy content and (fund) membership. The single currency as it now stands offers starting points for a move in that direction. For example, the European Stability Mechanism could form the basis for a permanent stabilisation fund. The set-up of the fund can remain intergovernmental in nature. At least as important, however, is that an EMF offers certain advantages: (1) it would take some of the pressure off the debate about the need for an EPU, and (2) it would create new scope for a stricter interpretation of the ECB's mandate (because the fund could serve as a 'lender of last resort') Moreover, both of these would be consistent with the Dutch position on the future of the euro in recent years.

There have already been various suggestions as to the form that such a fund might take, some involving the installation of a 'European Minister of Finance'. Other suggestions include a European system of investment protection, a European system of national unemployment insurance, or a 'rainy day fund' for euro-area Member States in the event of major economic shocks.[46] In the case of the latter two options, all sorts of alternatives are certainly conceivable (variation in policy content).[47] In addition, they carve out more scope for democratic control and/or economic 'conditionality' as prerequisites for such a fund. This can be intergovernmental in nature or involve a hybrid blend of intergovernmental and Community elements (variation in decision-making). It is also important to decide between ex ante funding or the institutionalisation of ex post borrowing capacity.

An EMF can chart an alternative route to strengthening monetary union, namely through variation in short, medium and long-term measures, as well as in overarching conditions of democratic control and economic robustness. In particular, the existing European Semester (which is essentially a policy dialogue between EU institutions and Member States) could be used to achieve temporal variation in policy content and variation in the overarching conditions of economic robustness (and their application). The European Semester already involves a dialogue with *individual* Member States, a country-specific approach (shown, for example, by the country-specific recommendations that are central to this cycle). There is therefore already considerable potential for (further) variation here.

We can elaborate on this reality in relation to an EMF. For example, the set-up of an EMF could be patterned on whether or not certain Member States implement economic reforms. The EMF can thus assist the IMF by customising the IMF's instruments for the euro. It would exploit what is already a visible pattern of variation between Member States by permitting those that are facing major structural economic reforms to derogate from the reference values.

It could also mean that euro-area Member States whose government deficits regularly test the boundaries of the rules and agreements would be more likely to request assistance from an EMF or the IMF, whereas others would not have to. It then becomes possible to build variation into the architecture of an EMF, for example by charging different premiums on high-risk fiscal behaviour. This could also be reflected in the risk weighting of government-issued securities on banks' balance sheets (to loosen the galling bonds between government debt and national banks).

In addition, an EMF also clears a path to addressing the problem of the no-bailout requirement. That path has already been described, in tentative terms, by the Dutch Council of State in information that it provided at the request of the Dutch House of Representatives in November 2017.[48] The path mapped out by the Council of State and the routes described in this chapter (in particular the first two), which have the potential to co-exist, are very similar:

> One possible way of further strengthening the emu is to place responsibility for policy and for complying with agreements more firmly at the level of the Member States, along with greater market discipline through the credible reinstatement of the no-bailout clause. This would allow more scope for policy competition based on national preferences, placing accountability for their performance within the emu squarely with the Member States.[49]

This is in line with the variation in policy content that occupies a central place in the present report.

Like the present report, the Council of State also describes a variation route involving an EMF:

> At the same time, however, it would be necessary to increase a number of European responsibilities so that it becomes possible to transfer more responsibilities to the national level in other domains without jeopardising the survival of EMU… First of all, a new division of responsibilities requires that Member States be goaded into complying with agreements by other means than centralised enforcement (alone). This would require greater market discipline through strict application of the no-bailout clause. That will only be credible if financial markets are convinced that there are mechanisms in place that affect them directly and that will be applied as soon as a Member State encounters difficulties. Otherwise, financial markets will continue to speculate in the belief that other Member States will eventually help out.

This could be a 'European mechanism' for 'orderly debt restructuring',[50] in which the Council of State notes that 'one obvious option is to transfer this mechanism to the ESM (by means of an amendment to the ESM Treaty) and transform it into an EMF'.[51] An important advantage of variation through an EMF is that it could serve as a unifying factor in the euro area.

A European Monetary Fund would be an outgrowth of the European Stability Mechanism that is already in place. It would align with the institutional paths trodden in response to the euro crisis: excluding Treaty amendments but including the structural involvement of the IMF. After all, the ESM was created to support vulnerable euro-area Member States and as such replaced the European Financial Stability Facility (EFSF). It functions as a permanent defensive wall of euro 700 billion to fund bailout loans to euro-area Member States in the event of a solvency crisis, provided that the Member State in question implements a programme of economic reforms. It is important that the creation of an EMF complements the IMF (which is often already the case when IMF support is supplemented by additional support, e.g. from neighbouring countries); duplication of funds through the IMF and an EMF must be avoided.

Facilitating long-term stability through the ESM could take the form of an EMF. In certain respects, this would also fit in with the next phase of the programme to strengthen the euro area—following the acute crisis management of recent years—which will have to focus on reassessing national and European responsibilities for the single currency going forward.

Macroprudential policy as an example of variation in policy content

For some time now, blueprints of what is known as the 'fourfold union' have circulated in the French Ministry of Finance and various Brussels think tanks, for example. This depiction elaborates on the path taken since the introduction of Van Rompuy's blueprint (see Box 7.1) by proposing four pillars that would shape the monetary union going forward[52]:

1. financial integration (banking union, capital market union);
2. fiscal integration (funds, euro-area budget);
3. economic integration (macroeconomic balance, structural reforms);
4. political integration (European Minister of Finance, euro-area parliament, Eurogroup as co-legislator).

These plans call for coherence between the four pillars, implying that they must be created jointly. The components of the different pillars vary in terms of scope, feasibility and degree of change, however. On the one hand, there are the 'no regret' measures identified by the Council of State,[53] which mainly involve completing what has begun, such as the banking union. On the other, there are measures so far-reaching—for example setting up a euro-area parliament—that they in any case imply a Treaty change. In between these two extremes are suggestions for reforms within the current institutional frameworks, such as the creation of an EMF.

In the light of the above, it is important to consider the dimension of timing with regard to the 'fourfold union'. In other words, which suggestions can be prepared now and which should be planned for the future? This makes it possible to size up the various elements and, possibly, decide on their sequencing and conditions.

One option that merits further discussion in this book is to continue refining the existing 'macroprudential policy', which is largely decentralised.[54] In its current form, this is already a policy area in which a conscious choice has been made to allow national authorities to chart their own course (variation in policy content), given that financial cycles can vary widely between Member States, making a one-size-fits-all policy undesirable. It would be better, however, to position this policy alongside the existing macroeconomic imbalances procedure and the enforcement of price stability, a task entrusted to the ECB. In addition, a clearer distinction could be made between country-specific macroprudential policy (designed to address country-specific shocks when monetary policy is ineffective) and Union-wide macroprudential policy. The first has been elaborated in all sorts of ways, the second much less so.

Neither the Maastricht Treaty nor the theory of optimum currency areas gave much thought to this. The forces of global financial development and integration have made them much more important, however. In addition, the greater importance of financial markets in the monetary union is creating new problems with regard to managing the deeper financial and economic interdependencies. All these factors have indisputable consequences for the ways in which the single currency can be strengthened in the future[55]—ways that require further examination.

7.4 Conclusion: Ways Forward for Variations in Policy

It is already complicated enough to coordinate monetary, fiscal, financial and labour market policies in a single country, let alone between different countries. In reality, the quest to boost prosperity through common measures has proved to be very difficult and has resulted in lengthy negotiations about how to distribute prosperity gains, especially since some Member States 'lose' and others 'win', for example in terms of trade surpluses or (emergency) loans. Matters are further complicated by the fact that the shocks to emu only become apparent after the fact.[56]

At the same time, however, it is clear that the euro area needs to be strengthened. How this should happen, however, remains far from clear (see also the information provided by the Council of State on 7 November 2017). Some potential solutions, such as far-reaching debt mutualisation or major leaps forward in centralisation and federalisation, also entail consequences that will be interpreted as unfeasible or contrary to Dutch interests. Nevertheless, it must be said that the euro's current situation leaves plenty of room for improvement.

The existing euro architecture and EMU offer scope for tightening up the system of checks and balances without resorting to a Treaty change. That requires us to view the conflicting short- and long-term considerations associated with the 'logic of appropriateness' and the 'logic of consequences', but also with individual, national and European interests, from a longer-term perspective: beyond the crisis, even, if possible, including the dismantling of a crisis policy that has stretched EMU to the limit, in particular with regard to the no-bailout rule and the ban on monetary financing through the ECB.[57] The basis for this approach could well be the aforementioned 'no regret measures' meant to strengthen the monetary union.[58]

The institutional and political framework for a more gradual path of this kind took shape following the introduction of initiatives based on Van Rompuy's 'blueprint' (2012), which ruled out any 'quantum leap' in federalisation. This framework creates leeway both for more centralisation and for more decentralisation (by enhancing the role of the national parliaments), as well as for refining existing instruments, policy coordination and democratic accountability, including through variation. The present report offers a frame of reference for constructing such scenarios, including possible sub-variations in membership/members (of which the euro area itself offers the most detailed example). Such scenarios can give the Netherlands a better understanding of the opportunities and risks intrinsic to the future of the euro area and allow it to anticipate them.

In the approach sketched above, an EMF (with the ESM as its possible basis) merits more study (with regard to the scope for variation), for example by comparing it with alternatives such as continuing the current regime of ongoing IMF involvement. There may be an additional advantage for the Netherlands in that setting up an EMF would create scope for enforcing a stricter interpretation of both the ECB's mandate and the no-bailout rule (if the fund can be linked to market discipline in varying arrangements that allow for the differing preferences of the Member States).

We can conceive of all sorts of variations on an EMF, including mechanisms for reallocating funds between Member States based on prearranged formulas, more discretionary powers of assessment—which may imply more politicisation—and linking disbursements from the fund to criteria, for example macroeconomic 'conditionality'. All this implies seeking to strengthen the single currency along a route which may not have been provided for in the Treaty, but which appears to be possible under the Treaty in the current situation.

This route also offers new variation options, for example by establishing framework conditions for democratic control per country and for financial, economic and macroeconomic robustness and convergence (e.g. through variation in risk premiums). One potential advantage is that this route may well create new opportunities to use variation as a means of building closer ties to the national democracies.

The euro and EMU need to change, but effectuating such change by making a quantum leap in federalisation or by shattering the existing monetary union seems neither realistic nor desirable. In other words, neither the straightjacket of federation nor the straitjacket of the national state can drive the necessary change in the euro area and EMU. There is another way, however, which involves making use of the opportunities for variation offered by the current Treaty frameworks. This chapter has outlined a few of these opportunities.

Notes

1. Bara et al. (2017: 6), AIV (2017: 15–21).
2. Boot and van Riel (2014).
3. Fabbrini et al. (2015).
4. For a good and complete overview see: Boot and van Riel (2014).
5. The resulting tensions can be detected in several key documents that form part of the ongoing debate on the future of the euro, such as the European Commission's reflection paper, the German Federal Constitutional Court's referral to the ECJ of a case against the Expanded Asset Purchase Programme (EAPP), and in particular the Public Sector Purchase Programme (PSPP), but also the ECB's motivations for its existing interest rate and quantitative easing policies.
6. Schmidt (2016: 5).
7. Leonard (2017: 46–48).
8. See Raad van State (2017a: 54).
9. In the run-up to the referendum and during negotiations on the 'Better deal for Britain' (the Cameron Government's 'Bremain' campaign before the referendum), the British Government made it crystal clear why it considered EU membership to be increasingly problematic. The main reason was that in the UK's eyes, the euro area was becoming a locked fortress at the heart of the single market (particularly with respect to financial services and economic and financial policy). That put non-euro members at a disadvantage, according to the British Government (George Osborne, *Speech to the BDI conference in Berlin*, 3 November 2015).
10. See Enderlein et al. (2016).
11. Fabbrini et al. (2015: VI).
12. The macroeconomic imbalance procedure (IMP) is one of the Six-Pack measures aimed at broadening economic policy coordination in an attempt to correct existing differences in the euro-area members' balance of payments.
13. Centraal Planbureau (2017), Bara et al. (2017).
14. Armbruster (2017: 16).
15. See Press release No. 17/2017 of 15 August 2017, 'Proceedings on the European Central Bank's Expanded Asset Purchase Programme are stayed—Referral to the Court of Justice of the European Union', which states, among other things, that: '… significant reasons indicate that the ECB decisions governing the asset purchase programme violate the prohibition of monetary financing and exceed the monetary policy mandate of the European Central Bank, thus encroaching upon the competences of the Member States'; available at https://www.bundesverfassungsgericht.de/SharedDocs/Pressemitteilungen/EN/2017/bvg17-070.html.
16. Centraal Planbureau (2017).
17. While it is clearly useful to improve the supervision of banking and make it more objective (and while this has reasonable support; i.e. it is less controversial an issue in the Member States themselves), the financial system remains

intertwined with the individual Member States and a systematic separation between their financial systems and their socio-economic systems is unlikely. That is in part why initiatives such as the Capital Market Union (CMU) may be useful, for example because it can reduce the dependence on bank financing.
18. Boot and van Riel (2014: 742–745).
19. Segers and van Esch (2007: 1101).
20. Dokumente zur Deutchlandpolitik (1998: 475, 565–567 and 597), Bakker (1996: 187 and 253), Delors (2004: 385).
21. Metten et al. (2000: 27), Janssen (2012).
22. Mundell (1961).
23. See de Grauwe (2003: 82–85).
24. Mundell (1997: 214–216).
25. See Raad van State (2017a: 53).
26. Jones (2012).
27. Raad van State (2017a: 51)
28. Deutsche Bundesbank (1992).
29. Segers and van Esch (2007: 1096–1098).
30. The agreements reached between Mitterrand and Kohl in Evian in June 1988 are what drove the EMU momentum. Mitterrand had conceded the free movement of capital to the Germans in exchange for their support for an ambitious EMU agenda (which had led to the Delors Report) and Delors' reappointment as President of the Commission. As a result, they could no longer keep EMU at bay by arguing that political union was a necessary prerequisite (Segers 2013, 234–41).
31. See Raad van State (2017a: 52).
32. See, for example, Bayoumi and Eichengreen (1992), Verhoef (2003).
33. A good example is the Wassenaar Agreement of 1982, in which unions and employers agreed to wage restraint to help restore the competitiveness of the Dutch economy. Wage restraint is sometimes referred to as internal devaluation, because production becomes cheaper than in the rest of the world without an exchange rate adjustment.
34. However, the Maastricht Treaty's rules on the excessive deficit procedure (Article 104, now Article 126 TFEU) are not strictly quantitative and binding, and are highly intergovernmental in nature (Metten et al. 2000, p. 59).
35. Tietmeyer (1994), Segers and van Esch (2007: 1102).
36. Raad van State (2017a: 51).
37. See Centraal Planbureau (2017: 3)
38. See Wyplosz (2017).
39. This policy route—mutual borrowing capacity in the event of an emergency paired with IMF assistance—could even render ex ante funding superfluous, or limit it to ad hoc contributions by neighbouring Member States in the event of IMF support. Such an arrangement involves maintaining a permanent (borrowing) capacity so that Member States can quickly borrow money made available (in part) through the IMF (which also avoids an unwanted replication of funds).

40. This assumes that the base situation is sustainable (and healthy). One could think in terms of packages—some countries purchase more insurance to give themselves more budgetary leeway. And the higher the level of (necessary) insurance, the higher the premium.
41. Raad van State (2017b: 53, 68–69, 92–93), Sandbu (2015).
42. See also the Report of 31 October 2017 on combating inequalities as a lever to boost job creation and growth (2016/2269(INI)), published by the European Parliament's Committee on Employment and Social Affairs.
43. Kamerstuk 34 387, nr. 6; here: Raad van State (2017b).
44. Raad van State (2017b: 93).
45. One of the first detailed examples of this is the 'readaptation fund' that the Dutch Minister of Foreign Affairs Johan-Willem Beyen included in his influential 1952 plan for a stable common market of 'the Six' (Segers 2013).
46. See Raad van State (2017a: 54).
47. By way of illustration, in its recent advisory report *De staat van de euro*, the Council of State mentions three versions of a rainy day fund: 'funds could automatically be redistributed between member states on the basis of pre-arranged formulas (e.g. via fixed ex ante formulas based on economic indicators), but more discretionary powers of assessment are also conceivable, as well as the possibility of linking disbursements to other criteria such as [for example] certain reforms' (Raad van State 2017a: 54).
48. See Raad van State (2017b).
49. Raad van State (2017b: 68).
50. See Raad van State (2017b: 69).
51. See Raad van State (2017b: 69–73); here too, the Council of State provides a clarifying and detailed assessment of the socio-economic, political, institutional and legal aspects of this route, although its conclusions are largely tentative.
52. See Trésor-Economics (2017: No. 190).
53. Raad van State (2017a: 85–89).
54. A European macroprudential policy framework is already in place. The Capital Requirements Directive (CRD) IV and the Capital Requirements Regulation (CRR) provide for explicit macroprudential instruments that can be activated. These are policy instruments in the banking sector: macroprudential authorities may activate them to address systemic risks. In the Netherlands, for example, they have been used to impose additional capital requirements on the ing, Rabo and ABN AMRO banks. The European Systemic Risk Board (ESRB)—formally part of the ECB—is authorised to issue warnings on systemic risks and to advise macroprudential authorities in this area. Article 5 of the SSM Framework Regulation (Banking Union) gives the ECB certain powers in the domain of macroprudential policy, allowing it to 'top-up' national macroprudential policy measures. If the ECB believes that systemic risk is accruing in certain countries, it may impose additional requirements on institutions in those countries.

55. *ESB* (2017: 41).
56. See de Grauwe and Costa Storti (2005), Beetsma and Bovenberg (2001).
57. See Schmidt (2016: 5).
58. See also Raad van State (2017a: 85–89).

Chapter 8
Variation in Asylum, Migration and Border Control

8.1 Introduction

Human migration is an outstanding example of a policy domain in which the links between European countries and their surroundings are revealed. The policy domains of asylum, migration and border control touch on international mobility, the protection of fundamental human rights, and international security all around Europe and within it. They also provoke intense debate among populations. These are policy domains where unexpected changes may arise (such as the sharp increase in refugees and migrants from conflict zones since 2014), where cooperation within Europe is clearly of added value (as in the case of joint surveillance of external borders), but where policy harmonisation may also prove extremely complicated (as in the case of asylum applications). Moreover, national politics may have an enormous influence in these domains, such as the German decision in 2015 to suspend a protocol that obliged Syrian refugees to apply for asylum in the EU Member State where they had first arrived (if that could be determined at all), and Prime Minister Viktor Orbán's decision in the same year to close the southern and eastern borders of Hungary.

International cooperation on migration is often undermined by obstructions, a lack of solidarity, and an unwillingness to face problems.[1] That is no different in the EU.[2] At the same time, policies in this domain give the EU an opportunity to make its geopolitical position clearer, for example by using mobility management to try to influence neighbouring regions.

International migration is a complex phenomenon, however, involving complex relationships; simple push-pull models are inadequate.[3] Migration is usually the result of multiple factors, for example inequalities, conflicts, demographic trends, scarcity and climate change, but very often also of a very human tendency to seek out and explore opportunities and move on when prospects change. Moreover, migration is not only exogenous to Europe; political choices made in the past also influence people's motives.

E. Hirsch Ballin et al., *European Variations as a Key to Cooperation*, Research for Policy, https://doi.org/10.1007/978-3-030-32893-1_8

The challenges are considerable and overlap with other issues, such as security, human rights, foreign policy and the functioning of the internal market. The purpose of this chapter is to describe how the different policy domains of asylum, borders and migration are related, to survey the main trends and events, and to analyse which topical issues merit attention in terms of harmonisation, integration and policy variation. The focus here is on the movement of persons, not goods (although that is obviously another important aspect of border control). As in the previous chapter, we analyse variation in the issues of migration and in the positions and responses of the Member States, and explore other possible variations in European cooperation. We also identify the conditions and limits of variation.

8.2 History of the Policy Domain

The history of Europe is one of individuals, groups and peoples moving across the continent. Empire-building, the Great Migration, countless wars and, in the twentieth century, the two world wars that erupted from European conflicts caused people to drift from place to place, again and again. After the Second World War, millions of people were forced to move elsewhere.[4] Suppression of the uprisings in Hungary in late 1956 and in Czechoslovakia in 1968 led to the displacement of hundreds of thousands of people in each case.[5] The Yugoslav Civil War once again displaced millions of people, with some 2.4 million fleeing to other countries.

As the European Communities and the European Union took shape, migration gradually became a main focus of interest and (controversial) point of decision-making. The free movement of workers provided for in the Treaty establishing the European Economic Community (now Article 45 TFEU) was transformed in the Single European Act of 1986[6] into the free movement of persons (now Article 3(2) TEU). It is important to note that from 1986 to 1995, the European Communities consisted of nine territorially contiguous Member States, namely the six original Member States as well as Denmark, Portugal and Spain, and three Member States separated from the others by seas, namely the United Kingdom, Ireland and Greece. Although there were usually border controls between these states, there were no fences or walls preventing border crossings (unlike in the case of the Iron Curtain). Enforcement of admission and residence rules depended to a large extent on domestic supervision of aliens. The continental part of the European Communities had the most to gain from the free movement of persons and therefore gave it the greatest level of support.

In 1995, the original Member States, with the exception of Italy, agreed to abolish internal border controls while simultaneously introducing a common visa system, closer cooperation in law enforcement, and external border checks (Schengen Agreement). The system did not enter into force until 1995 and required an Implementing Convention and a variety of practical facilities, such as separate areas at international airports for intra-Schengen and extra-Schengen flights. In the meantime, the other continental Member States had joined the system, although implementation in Italy was delayed until 1997. Greece had to wait until 2000, pending the implementation of satisfactory measures at the external borders,[7] and the Scandinavian Member States until 2011, when the other states in the Nordic Passport Union became part of the Schengen Area.

Parallel to implementing the Schengen system, all EU Member States agreed in the 1990 Dublin Convention that, in principle, the Member State of first entry would be responsible for examining asylum applications. This protocol was meant to discourage asylum seekers from travelling on to those countries where they expected to have better prospects. The Convention eased the workload for countries such as the Netherlands and Germany, even though many asylum seekers continued to arrive at airports. In the Netherlands, political opponents to the Convention mainly argued that some of the asylum seekers who had passed through the country should be taken in. The Convention entered into force on 1 September 1997.

The Schengen and Dublin systems were thus established in separate treaties, outside the structure of the European Communities. The Maastricht Treaty (1992), which became effective in 1993, merged police, judicial and migration cooperation into a Third Pillar under the auspices of the European Union. The Treaty of Amsterdam (1997), which became effective in 1999, subsequently integrated asylum and migration into the Community structures so that the matters covered under the Schengen Agreement and the Dublin Convention could henceforth be governed by EC regulations, supplemented by treaties with non-Member States. Initially, the Schengen and Dublin systems were applied mainly by a socially and economically convergent group of Member States, along with Sweden, Finland and Austria from 1995 onwards.

The situation changed dramatically when a total of 13 Central and Eastern European states joined the EU in 2004, 2007 and 2013. Socio-economic convergence programmes were established for these new members, but their reorientation in terms of the rule of law and citizenship required a cultural change that proved difficult to organise. In their accession (although the three states that acceded most recently were, temporarily, not accepted into the Schengen Area), uniformity was prioritised over variation without considering the public tasks that needed to be fulfilled in this case.

8.3 Tensions

The tensions associated with the policy domain of asylum, migration and border control arose long before 2015, when large numbers of people arrived from the Eastern Mediterranean and Africa. Ever since the EU's major enlargement in 2004, a discrepancy has been visible between the Community arrangements and the reality of this policy domain. Internal and external changes have played a role in this. *Internally*, the free movement of persons—not only of workers, but also of (quasi) self-employed service providers—sparked an increase in migration, especially from Poland. From a legal standpoint this was strictly a matter related to the functioning of the internal market, but in the Member States' official statistics and in the eyes of many of their people, these fellow European citizens were aliens. *Externally*, the end of repression-induced stability in North Africa and the Middle East had huge consequences. Against the background of terror caused by al-Qaeda's attacks, many people fled to Europe after the invasion of Iraq in 2003, the 'Arab Spring' in 2010–2011 and, in particular, the Syrian civil war from 2011 onwards, seeking refuge in particular in the older part of the EU, where conditions for their reception and integration were more favourable than in the Member States that had acceded since 2004. The stream of refugees reached its climax 2015–2016, aggravated by migration from Sub-Saharan Africa and the Horn of Africa. These events were all the more dramatic because many of the refugees had taken huge risks crossing dangerous regions and seas and exposing themselves to exploitation by human traffickers.

Western Europe thus quickly became part of a worldwide pattern of refugeeism, migration and urbanisation that had been noticeable for much longer. In the public's view and in statistics used in policymaking, these very different groups of migrants became one 'flow'. The common area that was the aim of the Schengen Agreement and the Dublin Convention was, in fact, divided into countries on the external border struggling to cope with the many arrivals (mainly Italy, Spain, Malta and Greece, which was also in the throes of a disruptive budgetary crisis), countries in Central and Eastern Europe that were averse to immigration and that offered few prospects to the refugees who came anyway, and countries in Western and Northern Europe (in particular Germany), which absorbed the lion's share of the refugees.

The European Union tried to stabilise this situation mainly by harmonising procedures and criteria for admission and residence, building on the 'acquis' of the Schengen and Dublin regulations. The European Asylum System, introduced in 1999, includes guidelines on asylum procedures and the reception, recognition and return of asylum seekers that have gradually been clarified. Since the revised Asylum Procedures Directive (2013/32/EU) became effective, stricter requirements have also been imposed on the quality of the judicial procedure. In addition, a relocation and quota policy was instituted; although it was rejected by some Central European Member States, it has now been approved by the Court of Justice (6 September 2017, ECLI:EU:C:2017:631). Surveillance of the external borders is regulated in a series of European directives; some are implemented by the FRONTEX, formerly the European Agency for the Management of Operational Cooperation at the External Borders of the European Union, which in 2016 became the European Border and Coast Guard Agency.

8.4 Intractable Realities

The Common Asylum System has smoothed out many of the differences in the way Member States assess asylum applications and enforce decisions. Nevertheless, discrepancies remain. Some of these are related to the effective implementation of the system. Without assistance from other EU states, it is impossible for Greece, with its many islands, to carry out effective border surveillance involving the registration of country of entry. Other Mediterranean Member States face similar problems. And as long as registration does not take place, it is equally impossible for the other EU Member States to invoke the Dublin protocol allowing them to transfer asylum seekers to the country of entry.

More important, however, are the actual circumstances of reception, accommodation and integration into society. For many asylum seekers, these are the deciding factors in their choice of destination, leading to a very uneven distribution of refugees among the Member States. Council decisions in 2015 and 2016 concerning the redistribution of asylum seekers, adopted on a proposal by the Commission and with the advice of the European Parliament, were meant to reaffirm solidarity between Member States at a time when vast numbers of asylum seekers were arriving in Europe. A follow-up is a proposed revision of the Dublin Regulation, now under negotiation after discussion by the European Parliament. Instead of each Member State being responsible for reception and processing, a pan-EU approach is to be taken to the issue, with implementation tasks being divided between the countries.

The past two decades have raised serious doubts as to whether the system as it stands is tenable. After all, the Member States have such differing attitudes to asylum and migration that there is little prospect that a policy based on harmonising procedures and on redistribution will succeed. These differences are both external and internal in nature. Asylum seekers want to arrive in a country that not only protects them from bombing and torture but that also allows them to start afresh. That is why they want desperately to escape from the hopelessness of local refugee camps or reception centres in Greece and other border countries. At the same time, migrants have become less welcome in Western Europe, partly because social cohesion based on traditional patterns has eroded, but also because in the same period, neoliberalism undermined the protections afforded by the social democratic state.[8] The change in the political and social climate has been even more pronounced in Central and Eastern Europe.[9] An overly hasty transition from a nationally motivated struggle against Marxism to a (hyper)liberal economic system has raised acute fears of a loss of national 'identity' in the Member States that acceded in 2004 and afterwards, making them even less willing to accept asylum seekers.

8.5 Solidarity in Migration Policy?

The task of coordinating asylum and migration policy and European and international law raises the necessary questions. Much of the current policy ignores the fact that the group of irregular migrants from Libya, for example, is mixed. Although the majority of people who cross over are economic migrants who do not qualify for asylum status, some are refugees entitled to international protection.

Recognising variation in legal status is essential to guaranteeing fundamental human rights, both in European and African territory. This approach requires policies that allow for an internationally legitimate assessment of individuals on African territory, and not only after refugees have made the dangerous crossing into EU territory. Legal access channels to Europe are important in this respect. There must be further discussion of establishing external hotspots where asylum applications can be submitted, so that Europe can meet its international obligations.[10] The policy for regulating the influx of economic migrants is also inadequate. They constitute the vast majority of migrants arriving on European territory and do not have the right to residence status. At present, the return policy of many EU Member States is weak, despite the Return Directive (2008/115/EC). This means that the majority of asylum seekers who have exhausted all the legal procedures do not actually return to their country of origin, stoking public dissatisfaction and chipping away at any public goodwill towards migrants who are entitled to asylum status.[11]

The issues facing the EU and the Member States are numerous: from the future of Schengen and a possible Dublin IV or V to the geopolitics of international migration management by means of mobility partnerships, and from the future of the ceas and the EU Blue Card to the mandate given to the European Border and Coast Guard and the design of data information systems. Instead of evaluating each component, the aim of this section is to understand issues as 'public goods', with a balance continuously being struck between the logic of appropriateness and the logic of consequences.

A logic of appropriateness could be based on solidarity. Article 80 of Chap. 2 of the Treaty on the Functioning of the European Union, entitled 'Policies on Border Checks, Asylum and Immigration', explicitly refers to the notion of solidarity.

> The policies of the Union set out in this Chapter and their implementation shall be governed by the principle of solidarity and fair sharing of responsibility, including its financial implications, between the Member States. Whenever necessary, the Union acts adopted pursuant to this Chapter shall contain appropriate measures to give effect to this principle.

Does this provide a legal basis? Not necessarily. The concept of solidarity as laid out in the Treaty also raises questions. Solidarity between whom? Commentators have pointed out that the point here is not solidarity between the EU and other countries, nor with or between individuals, but solidarity between Member States.[12] Moreover, as the EU's foreign policy with regard to border control has intensified, there is the question of whether such solidarity can be limited to the EU. After all, the logic of appropriateness and the logic of consequences extend to countries to the east and south of the EU, far into Africa and the Middle East. There must be a certain measure of solidarity in migration deals too if they are to last.

When solidarity has only limited usefulness as a starting point for policy, the most sensible approach is to shift to strengthening the institutional basis for that policy, as a mitigated logic of consequences. Examples include the transformation of FRONTEX into a European Border and Coast Guard Agency, the endorsement by the Court of Justice of the quota policy, and the Commission's mandate to continue building mobility partnerships.

The question, however, is whether the rationality of the internal market—such as setting quotas for the admission of asylum seekers—provides sufficient grounds for an asylum and migration system that is sustainable in the longer term. In a keynote address delivered on 20 March 2015, Prof. Guy Goodwin-Gill pointed out the possibility of establishing an agency to oversee Member States' compliance with international obligations related to refugees and migrants. Such an institution may be the answer to the 'how' of policy. But the 'how' in this case addresses the balance between the two logics, of appropriateness and consequences. According to Guild,[13] such an institution's most important contribution would be to improve international solidarity within and outside the EU. And improvement is necessary in that respect, despite there being a European Asylum Support Office (EASO) and the Fundamental Rights Agency (FRA). The proposed institution should have more far-reaching powers without being 'coercive', something that would not promote solidarity.

This approach has received theoretical support from Rossi (2017), who, inspired by a 'public goods approach', outlines a quota system, reinforced by binding criteria for the rights of asylum seekers.[14] Rossi[15] described the European asylum system as a 'non-cooperative game'. Although the EU does have some of the features of game theory and all its associated dilemmas when it comes to burden-sharing, it is nevertheless based primarily on the 'games real actors play'.[16] This means that the playing field is ample and mobile: Member States that refuse to participate in one round of negotiations, for example on the distribution of refugees, may feel the effects later in another round on a completely different subject, for example the distribution of agricultural subsidies. As a result, game theory does not always apply in full to the practice of politics and policymaking.

Whereas institutionalisation points down a narrow path in navigating between the two logics, the 'public goods approach' emphasises the content of the issues at stake: protection of people and borders, national sovereignty and identity, security and geopolitics. Institutionalisation should not lead to an instrumental management approach to policymaking, in any event. As one Dutch commentator stated in a now-famous essay, 'A refugee is not a cod'.[17] Quotas, distribution keys and relocation mechanisms are internal market instruments that work very well in certain policy domains, but their effectiveness is severely limited when they are applied without further ado in the area of migration. Policy in that area must be based on a certain measure of solidarity. The 'trade-offs' and 'distribution mechanisms' that may subsequently prove necessary must in some way or another be sensitive to the public goods at stake in this case: international mobility, security, and the protection of people and borders.

8.6 Conclusion: Ways Forward for Variations in Policy

Migration is a critical factor in Europe's geopolitical position because controlling international mobility is important to the exercise of sovereignty vis-à-vis non-EU countries. The policy on asylum, migration and border control allows us to observe just how far cooperation can go and at what point national preferences make a difference. It should be noted, first and foremost, that issues of migration must be considered from a variety of different perspectives: that of the migrant, that of the citizens of the host community, and that of international economic and political relations. The fundamental guarantees laid down in the Geneva Convention on Refugees, Article 3 of the ECHR, and Article 18 of the Charter of Fundamental Rights of the European Union establish a legal minimum for the treatment of asylum seekers: expulsion must not expose them to persecution or degrading treatment. These obligations are incumbent on both the Member States and the Union as a whole. In all further questions of policy and legislation, the point is to assess the most appropriate model of action.

The policy domains of asylum, migration and border control already provide several examples of variation that can be broken down into the different forms discussed in this book (variation in policy content, decision-making method, and membership). 'Flexible solidarity' with regard to the resettlement of asylum seekers qualifies as an example of variation in policy content. The EU-Turkey Statement of 18 March 2016 (the 'deal') is an example of variation in the decision-making method, as it takes the place of a Treaty and does not adhere to the usual procedure[18] Instead of the Community method, intergovernmental decision-making was applied within the European Council to reach this agreement. Similar variations in decision-making method could be helpful in the event of future refugee crises. Schengen is an example of variation in membership: not all EU Member States are part of the Schengen Area, while some non-EU Member States are part of it.

Arguments derived from the logic of appropriateness (such as encouraging meaningful participation in society) and from the logic of consequences both play a role in all these forms and examples, and they are not mutually exclusive. It would be difficult to consider questions of border surveillance and admission as anything other than shared questions, at least as far as the continental Member States are concerned. By contrast, there is still a great deal of discretion for national labour market policy, while matters of public order concerning foreign nationals who have neither been legally admitted nor expelled tend to come up more at the local level. Such considerations could lead to multiple variations in future migration policy, possibly including a range of different choices as to the Member States covered by the policy.

The concept of collective appropriateness is defined by Article 18 of the Charter of Fundamental Rights of the European Union, which incorporates the asylum guarantees of the Geneva Convention on refugees into European law. However, this human rights standard does not necessarily imply a uniform migration policy and even leaves scope for variation in the way in which asylum is ensured; only *refoulement* (forcibly returning people to a country where they are likely to be persecuted) is in any case unlawful. However, there is also a *need* for European unity stemming directly from the requirements of the internal market and its open borders. In addition, certain dimensions of this policy belong more to the national political domain, for example labour market policy and the integration of newcomers. The latter dimension influences the destination favoured by asylum seekers and migrants, who prefer to go where they and their families have the opportunity to make a fresh start.

There is an urgent need to review the objectives and patterns of migration policy. Public acceptance of current policies is eroding, while at the same time events in Africa and, even more so, the longer-term effects of climate change will drive up the pressure to admit migrants, whether or not as asylum seekers. The legal distinction between refugees and other migrants is debatable if we consider migration driven by exploitation and climate change[19] and it requires that asylum procedures should be assessed on a case-by-case basis. The question is whether and how the EU and its Member States will cope with these developments, and also whether the EU can itself survive disruptive conflicts between Member States.

We must further assess any variation in fulfilling these European public tasks with a view to strengthening democratic support for migration policy. Social and political differences between the Member States suggest less unity, but the nature of the problems may in fact require more. In terms of this book's analytical framework, this means that the choice of institutional order will be influenced in part by different opinions concerning the motivations for collective action.

Variation can take many different forms. Migration policies are so closely intertwined with other public tasks that different forms of variation may be required, depending on the subject In 2016, the Advisory Council on International Affairs (AIV) recommended creating more scope for variation in migration policy within the circle of Schengen countries.[20] The AIV drew attention to the possibility of closer cooperation as defined in the EU Treaty (Article 20 TEU) between Member States wishing to implement the Schengen Agreement *within the framework* of a fully functioning common asylum system, including similar forms of reception and integration, the acceptance of distribution keys, sharing information on abuses, coordination with the UNHCR on resettlement, and agreements with safe countries outside the EU regarding the return of migrants. Other Schengen countries would maintain open internal borders under normal circumstances and share responsibility for external borders and the common visa policy, *provided* that they agree to share costs, jointly manage external borders and perform selective checks at internal borders (for example verification of travel documents at airports and key sea ports). This proposal allows for societal differences between Member States. After all, there is little point in forcibly transferring a refugee to a Member State that does not want to take in asylum seekers. In terms of the EU's own development, it is important that this variation does not jeopardise the socio-economically valuable single market.

The EU has placed restrictions on migration and border crossings from outside Europe, which are meant to regain control of mobility, but has not yet moved to give specific groups of people extra opportunities for migration. There has also been little headway in setting up systems for commencing the asylum application procedure outside the EU's borders. The embassies of EU Member States could play a more active role in this respect ('diplomatic missions policy').

Labour market policy associated with migration and the policy on knowledge migrants enrolled in study programmes are not fully harmonised within the context of the internal market. This discrepancy must be considered when the inevitable follow-up question arises: can we prevent the asylum procedure being used for economic reasons by lowering the threshold to legal labour migration? Such a move would be advantageous for only a few Member States, among them the Netherlands and Germany. Here too there may be an opportunity for variation at a fundamental level: Member States would be offered the option of permitting 'circular migration' under an agreement concluded with other countries. The fourth Balkenende government had already experimented with this possibility in a pilot project. Admission would be temporary, but upon returning to his or her country of origin, the labour migrant would have gained enough experience and accrued enough start-up capital to participate in economic life there. States that agree to such arrangements would be expected to cooperate with the return policy.

One of the major issues in the EU's foreign and security policy is how to prevent an unmanageable flow of people to other countries and continents. It is an issue that has been given little notice in migration policy to date, with the exception of controversial attempts to conclude agreements with countries on the other side of the Mediterranean that are tantamount to the obstruction of migration. Betts and Collier[21] came up with more sweeping proposals. They recommend putting more emphasis on training and employing for the millions of people currently living in refugee camps, as part of a coherent refugee policy. Their assertion is that participation in the host country's economy creates opportunities for refugees, whether they gain long-term refugee status or return to their country of origin. The final step for refugees who have no meaningful prospects would be a programme of resettlement in EU Member States or elsewhere.

Fijnaut[22] has also highlighted the importance of a 'transnational political deal' to 'reimburse' third countries that tighten up surveillance of their borders with Europe by investing in their economies and setting up legal migration programmes. This idea has been elaborated in the proposals published by the Centre for European Policy Studies (CEPS) (12 October 2017). It advocates a 'trade-off' in that European countries can fast-track the processing of asylum applications and permit a broader, but targeted, work permit policy in exchange for African countries, in particular, doing more to take in those whose asylum applications have been rejected. To some extent, this idea is in line with Dutch proposals aimed at circular migration as part of an overhaul of migration policy. The Commission's European Agenda on Migration already acknowledges the importance of returning migrants to third countries and linking this to the need for legal migration channels that permit temporary labour migration.

The two logics, of appropriateness and of consequences, go hand in hand—but never without friction. Even considerations of solidarity are thus subject to an inevitable cost-benefit trade-off and can be supported by greater institutionalisation. Policy based on the two logics is not limited to the Member States, but also affects non-EU countries with which the EU has established partnerships. These ideas can be incorporated into an overhaul of migration policy that is no longer buckling under the pressure of maintaining an appearance of unity. At the same time, they preserve what the European Asylum System *can* achieve, i.e. unity in terms of procedures and policy content pursuant to the basic prohibition against *refoulement* as set out in the Geneva Convention. Finally, it is important to recognise that any serious preventive policy can only be the work of a European Union that presents a united front on the international stage. The Union must pursue a common policy on country of origin and take proactive measures to avert fresh crises.

Notes

1. de Haas (2016).
2. International migration as a percentage of the world's population has remained fairly constant since the Second World War. In a world population of 7.4 billion people, around 3% are international migrants (excluding refugees). The percentage of refugees has been less stable. At the moment, approximately 0.3% of the world's population are refugees. The vast majority of these (about 85%) remain in developing countries; about 15% reach more prosperous countries (Haas de 2016).
3. Jennissen et al. (2007), Geddes and Scholten (2016: 4–5).
4. Oltmer (2016: 101).
5. Oltmer (2016: 103).
6. On that occasion, Article 7a was inserted into the EEC Treaty, charging the Community with the task of establishing the internal market, an area without internal frontiers in which the free movement of goods, persons, services and capital is ensured, by 31 December 1992 at the latest.
7. The extent to which Greece can effectively meet these requirements remains to be seen; this is not a question of unwillingness, but of the geographical reality of a vast archipelago with external borders.
8. Supiot (2010).
9. AIV (2017a).
10. Palm (2017).
11. Barslund and Ludolph (2017).
12. Farcy et al. (2016).
13. Guild et al. (2016: 586).
14. Rossi (2017: 57).
15. Rossi (2017).
16. Scharpf (1997).
17. van Middelaar (2016).

18. Idriz (2017).
19. Sassen (2014).
20. AIV (2016).
21. Betts and Collier (2017: 227–236).
22. Fijnaut (2017: 200).

Chapter 9
Conclusions

9.1 Variation as a Guiding Perspective

The European Union seems to lurch from one crisis to the next in the past decade, from the financial crisis to the euro crises and from the refugee crisis to Brexit, not to mention pressure on the democratic rule of law in some Member States themselves. Opinions vary widely as to how best to respond to these push-pull forces: some argue that the answer lies in closer European integration,[1] while others suggest that it is time for Europe to invest in an exit strategy and to develop a disintegration policy.[2]

The choice between deeper integration and hard disintegration is misleading, however. European variation is a reality whose worth remains underappreciated or underexploited. It is not a question of everything or nothing. Cooperation within the European Union allows for a number of different approaches. Only rarely do the Member States move simultaneously in the same direction in every policy domain; very often, they differ. That is usually regarded as a problem, but in our opinion, that view is unjustified. Just because their positions diverge does not mean that cooperation between them can only be suboptimal at best. What it *does* mean is that cooperation demands more conscious and proactive variation than a stark choice between a uniform Community alliance in which *all* Member States work together and a selective alliance in which obstructionists necessitate opt-outs or multiple speeds. There is enormous diversity in Member States, challenges, issues, policy domains, procedures and institutions. Contrary to what the choice between integration and disintegration suggests, it is such diversity that is the appropriate motto.

Options allowing for greater diversity can be found both within and outside the current Treaty frameworks. The aim is to make the current quest for an optimal form of cooperation both proactive and more conscious, so as to provide a basis for a more constructive process. That requires us to place the debate on the future of the EU in a broader context. At the moment, the focus of discussion tends to be on the form of the institutional order. That focus, however, is based on a straightforward

E. Hirsch Ballin et al., *European Variations as a Key to Cooperation*,
Research for Policy, https://doi.org/10.1007/978-3-030-32893-1_9

contrast between 'more' or 'less' EU. By looking more specifically at the relationship between the nature of the problems, the differing goals, public interests and motivations, and possible forms of cooperation, we will gain a clearer idea of the forms of variation available.

This final chapter elaborates on the main message of our book. To support that message, we also review the variation options discussed in the chapters on the internal market, the euro area, and asylum, migration and border control. Our purpose is not to identify specific policy choices, but rather to illustrate possible directions for policymaking that could lead to greater variation. While our discussion covers the institutional structure, we do not make any specific recommendations in that regard. If more scope for variation is created in terms of which Member States are involved in legislation and policymaking in a given domain, then it is obvious that provision will also be made for non-participation in decision-making by representatives of other Member States. As in the case of the European Monetary Union, only representatives of the Member States involved will be able to take part in the decision-making process.

As this book explains, what variation is *not* is the consequence of an attempt at integration that has stranded halfway. There is no specified end point to cooperation in the European Union. Cooperation is always open-ended, because the nature of future relationships can never be clear. The emphasis should therefore be on the fundamentally open-ended nature of the destination to which the Member States and the EU are headed. That is why we have developed guidelines that we believe will help the European Union respond more effectively to the needs and legitimate expectations of its citizens. We recommend approaching the further development of the European Union with variation in mind. What this means is:

- accepting that not all tasks for which governments are responsible need to be based on the same relationship between European, national and regional or local policy (leaving room for variation in policy content), and
- recognising the value of different patterns of European cooperation between Member States (which may manifest themselves in different decision-making methodologies and/or different forms of membership).

Unlike the existing differentiation by means of opt-outs and deviations, variation is not a concession intended to resolve impasses in negotiations; it is, rather, a different structuring principle that takes differences in needs and in democratically expressed convictions seriously.

Variation cannot be accepted or pursued in every policy domain or everywhere to the same extent. A common core remains necessary for the European Union as a whole, specifically concerning the basic principles of democracy, rule of law, fundamental rights and freedoms, and the common market.

Article 2 of the TEU states that the Union is founded on the values of respect for human dignity, freedom, democracy, equality, the rule of law and respect for human rights, including the rights of persons belonging to minorities. The Member States share these values and they have asserted and committed themselves to upholding them. Their societies endorse pluralism, non-discrimination, tolerance, justice, solidarity and gender equality values that should be reflected explicitly in the EU's political communications and institutional design. This is crucial for the credibility of European integration.[3] We therefore back the AIV's recommendation (in its report *The will of the people? The erosion of democracy under the rule of law in Europe*) that respect for diversity in states' democratic functioning should be paired with efforts to prevent the erosion of the rule of law.

We expect that elaborating on variation as a guiding perspective will nurture the critical political and policy-related imagination, so that it can also be declared applicable in other domains in which European public tasks have an impact.

This could have significant consequences in terms of the EU's institutional structure. Where variation implies that not all Member States participate, and that European legislation therefore does not apply in all Member States, then it must also be possible to vary the composition of EU institutions. In the future, for example, this could mean that the Council and Parliament meet in differing configurations depending on the subject matter and territorial scope.

Because variation allows the relationship between European, national and sub-national bodies to differ depending on the issue at hand, it also creates leeway to root the fulfilment of public tasks more firmly in the political basis of the Member States. The institutional design may be altered in certain respects, but what is most important is to regard the EU less in terms of a state-like institutional design; instead, it should be viewed as a system of dispersed and shared principles and responsibilities, with democratic roots both in the Member States and in the European Union thus clearing the way for the concept of *demoicracy*.

This book further explores the variation perspective in the domains of the internal market, EMU and the euro, and asylum and migration. It can, obviously, also apply in many other policy domains, and in fact it already does so. Our final chapter outlines the dimensions in which variation can occur (Sect. 9.2). We follow up with an overview of our findings in a number of policy domains (Sect. 9.3) and a description of the prospects for variation in the ongoing development of the European Union (Sect. 9.4). We conclude our book by describing how the Netherlands can contribute to further consultations on the future the European Union (Sect. 9.5).

9.2 The Dimensions of Variation

The EU's current situation has forced the debate on variation as a tool for change in the EUout into the open. The Treaties and the reality on the ground already offer myriad examples of what could be seen as steps towards variation, pushed even further by the turbulence in the euro area. Perhaps, in the years ahead, variation will gain political acceptance as a desirable feature of the fulfilment of public tasks in the context of the European Union. This book sees an opportunity here to align the European Union more closely with its existing political and social diversity, but it is not blind to the risks associated with too much variation. Coherence between different policy domains could be undermined, and Member States might engage in cherry-picking. All this raises questions concerning the appropriate relationship between socio-economic stability, human rights, security, and the four freedoms that define the internal market.

This book reveals a whole range of possibilities for variation within the European Union. It discusses forms of variation that fall both within and outside the current framework of European Union Treaty law. As we stated earlier, variation has three dimensions: (1) policy content, (2) decision methodology, and (3) the Member States. The options for variation can be represented as a three-dimensional continuum whereby the degree of uniformity in each dimension runs from minimum to maximum.

Variation in policy content

The first dimension concerns the scope for variation within the content of policy, i.e. the leeway that each Member State has to interpret how certain public interests, objectives and values are to be achieved. This means that Member States can have different interpretations of policy but continue to participate in decision-making and show support for a political form of solidarity. More specifically, they are given more policy discretion in directives involving minimum harmonisation or open standards. Such directives employ concepts that allow the Member States more leeway to shape national policy as they see fit. At the other extreme are regulations that apply directly at national level and that limit national policy discretion.

The room for manoeuvre created for the Member States in this manner prevents the tensions caused by diverging aims from resulting in opt-outs, for example (variation in membership). Variation in policy content makes it possible to incorporate the Member States' diverse motivations for collective action or diverse interpretations of the same into the process of European integration without compromising unity in participation. The process of policymaking must then reveal, time and again, how much room for manoeuvre there actually is.

Trade-offs are also possible within a policy area. One example of this is 'flexible solidarity' within the context of migration, asylum and borders. Variation in this domain is not meant to ignore the basic principle of solidarity, but it does require paying greater attention to geographical and political differences between the Member States.

Variation in the decision-making method

This dimension concerns the way in which policy and legislative decisions must be taken: in an intergovernmental context, via the Community method, or entirely at supranational level.

Within an intergovernmental framework, there is no interference from institutions to which the cooperating states are subordinate; competences are not surrendered and are thus retained at the national level. Decision-making thus requires unanimity. States have the right to veto any policy measure or legislative act, guaranteeing that their policy autonomy is preserved. The open method of coordination (OMC), which does not involve legislative competences and in which decisions are taken on the basis of unanimity, is one example of this form of variation.

Policies and legislation developed according to the Community method apply equally to all participating Member States and are based on (1) supranational institutions as initiators and guardians of the Treaty order, (2) qualified majority voting in the Council and (3) co-decision-making by the European Parliament (ordinary legislative procedure). The difference between this and a fully supranational decision-making framework is that, in the Community method, qualified majority voting makes it possible to form blocking minorities, for example in the Council. This means that, unlike in the supranational method, enough Member States must cooperate to reach a decision.

Variation in membership/members

The third dimension concerns membership. If the Member States' motivations for collective action differ too much to fulfil public tasks by means of the Community method or variation in policy content, the Member States can switch to the most extreme form of variation, i.e. variation in membership/members. In this form of variation, the Member States do not see sufficient reason to undertake collective action and must pursue a different type of relationship with one another. Examples include opt-outs, lead groups, multiple speeds, and closer cooperation. When new Member States accede to the Union, this form of variation allows for a more realistic and less constrained approach to situations where a state is not ready to accept all aspects of the Union's total body of laws and rules (the 'acquis').

To apply the variation options in actual practice, however, the Union must keep an open mind to the opportunities afforded by the existing Treaties by (1) considering the relationship between motivations for collective action and the possible institutional orders, and thus (2) relinquishing its fixation on regulations and directives, the Community method and participation by all the Member States, and on the resulting compulsion to rely on certain motivations for collective action.

The normative and actual evolution of the relationship between socio-economic stability, human rights, security and the four freedoms determines whether and, if so, what variation in European integration is appropriate and necessary. Variation in the internal market for goods is scarcely feasible (although some Member State regions are excluded territorially) because unimpeded trade is only possible when products are subject to the same requirements. In the initial decades of the European Communities, differences in place of establishment still played an important role: the free movement of persons was still closely linked to the frameworks of the national labour market and mainly concerned effective participation in this market.

That changed quite suddenly when the free movement of services was implemented in full. The free movement of services could then be used to circumvent the frameworks of the national labour market and weaken the associated protection. In response—and in addition to tightening up the Services Directive and the Posting of Workers Directive—there were calls for closer harmonisation of socio-economic policy. That is an obvious next step, but since there is little inclination to do, greater variation may offer an alternative.

While membership of the current Member States is regarded as a given, it is possible to reassess, in dialogue with and between Member States, which policy domains require the EU to fulfil public tasks. The conclusions may differ from one Member State to the next. Variation not only means 'which Member States cooperate in which domains and in which form'. As indicated, it can also mean a change in the design of the institutions of the European Union, for example by allowing them to operate in different configurations depending on which Member States are involved or their relationship with national parliaments. It can also mean reassessing the relationship between the four freedoms and important public tasks associated with stability, security, prosperity and social protection.

9.3 Variation (Options) Within the Internal Market, Emu and Asylum, Migration and Border Control

In this final chapter, we elaborate on the main message of this book and illustrates the options for variation. This section looks at the options described earlier for the internal market (Chap. 5), the euro area (Chap. 7), and asylum, migration and border control (Chap. 8). More specifically, these are options for exploring and analysing opportunities for variation, not concrete policy options or policy recommendations.

Variation is not an end in itself, but a path ripe for exploration. It offers solutions whenever stalemates threaten cooperation and it creates opportunities that take existing differences between the Member States and their populations into account. The main question is: How can variation serve as a starting point for European cooperation? Variation is certainly not the answer in all cases, and not all issues allow the same degree of variation. Nevertheless, there are myriad opportunities for making further use of variation, and it can serve as a guiding perspective in many policy domains.

9.4 Variation and the Internal Market

In Chap. 5, we considered which options are currently available in each of the three dimensions of variation. Within the internal market, variation in policy content currently consists of minimum harmonisation, open standards, and higher levels of protection in certain Member States. Regarding the second dimension, variation in decision-making, the internal market illustrates how the special legislative procedure (in the form of the open method of coordination) concerns not the harmonisation of national legislation but rather the coordination of national policies (without mandatory standards). Member States cannot be outvoted in this decision-making method because decisions are only taken unanimously.

The internal market's legal framework is so flexible that both the legislator and the Court can weigh economic market interests against other public interests, the former from a political and the latter from a legal standpoint. That is because the organisation of the internal market reflects the explicit pursuit of a social market economy and the view that fundamental rights and the principles of solidarity, proportionality and 'mainstreaming' (which mirror public interests) are important principles of market organisation under the Treaty. Moreover, the Treaties assume that the functioning of the internal market will contribute positively to the public's well-being and standard of living.

There are also objections to variation. Variation between the guiding principles of the internal market and closely associated policy domains raises problems when it comes to establishing a social market economy. Variation in the way the Member States interpret the four freedoms could also pose a major risk not only to the economic completion of the internal market but also to the safeguards afforded to the associated social and public interests. The general principles of Union loyalty and effectiveness of Union law limit such variation, in any event. At the same time, however, we also see that the broad spectrum of principles underpinning the internal market does, in fact, offer more scope for national variation, especially where no EU legislation applies. These principles allow for variation by permitting Member States to apply certain rules and practices that protect certain public interests in preference to the interests of the internal market.

Existing variations within the internal market inspire variation options within other policy domains, such as EMU and asylum, migration and border control, two controversial and divisive topics within the European Union. We discuss these below.

9.5 Variation in EMU and the Euro

Chapter 7 on variation in EMU and the euro outlined various possibilities for variation. Here, variation requires different, co-existing arrangements. Elements of the current governance of the euro that can be included in variation without further ado are:

- the extent to which euro-area Member States exercise market discipline;
- whether the Member States want mutual insurance, and the status of a common monetary fund;
- whether the IMF should be involved.

This list begins with the option of variation in policy content, but that does not exclude the possibility of variation in membership and decision-making.

What are the options that arise working with the above elements (on the understanding that we do not immediately assess their feasibility)? Below, we discuss two potential routes to variation, by which we mean different arrangements that can co-exist. They are:

1. variation by means of market discipline and IMF involvement going forward;
2. variation by means of a European Monetary Fund (EMF).

In addition, we discuss variation as a form of macroprudential policy as it currently exists and as explained in Chap. 7.

Re 1. Variation by means of market discipline and IMF involvement going forward

One option is for some Member States to exercise market discipline and submit to the IMF's recovery programmes in the event of difficulties while other Member States establish a common fund providing mutual insurance. The market discipline/ IMF arrangement is appropriate for countries that are committed to taking responsibility for their own affairs. The fund arrangement, in turn, requires a large measure of trust between the Member States that choose to participate (e.g. in an EMF). An EMF may be of particular value as an emergency fund, but Article 122 (2) of the Treaty already provides for the possibility of financial assistance to Member States in such cases. As an interpretation of this clause, an EMF could take the form of an ex ante fund and/or (mutual) borrowing capacity.

In the case of mutual borrowing capacity, variation is possible in policy design (and possibly also in decision-making and degrees of participation). That would certainly be true if such organised borrowing capacity can be applied in tandem with pre-existing IMF funds (formed by euro-area countries). Specifically, this could mean, for example, that euro-area Member States whose government deficits regularly test the boundaries of the rules and agreements would be more likely to request assistance from an EMF and/or the IMF, and do so more frequently, than other euro-area Member States.

Variation can be built in by pegging risk premiums to this fiscal behaviour, for example by applying SGP criteria. Another option would be to make the establishment of an emergency fund optional for Member States: those that want to arrange joint coverage contribute to the fund (and can rely on it in crisis situations); those that do not, do not contribute and must rely on themselves (and the IMF) in crisis situations. As a result, the basic fund, in which everyone participates, may be limited or very limited. Variation in this sense may also imply less integration, for example with regard to fiscal rules.

The Dutch Council of State has also examined this approach, noting that if this more 'decentralised' trend were to be continued, three elements would be important: (1) completion of the banking union, (2) certain financial safety nets, (3) European enforcement of fiscal and economic rules in special circumstances.[4] This is in keeping with the main thrust of the analyses in this section and the previous chapter of this book.

Re 2. Variation by means of an EMF

An EMF could function as a stabilisation mechanism for the monetary union. The single currency as it now stands offers starting points for a move in that direction. For example, the European Stability Mechanism could form the basis for a permanent stabilisation fund. The set-up of the fund can remain intergovernmental in nature. Within that set-up, all sorts of variation options are conceivable (in policy content), and more scope can be created for democratic control and/or economic 'conditionality' as prerequisites for such a fund. The latter can be intergovernmental in nature or involve a hybrid blend of intergovernmental and Community elements (variation in decision-making).

An EMF could bolster the monetary union by allowing for variation in short, medium and long-term measures, as well as in overarching conditions of democratic control and economic robustness. It could also mean that euro-area Member States whose government deficits regularly test the boundaries of the rules would be more likely to request assistance from an EMF or the IMF, whereas others would not have to. It then becomes possible to build variation into the architecture of an emf, for example by charging different premiums on such fiscal behaviour.

An EMF would be an outgrowth of the ESM that is already in place, and would align with the institutional paths trodden in response to the euro crisis: excluding Treaty amendments but including the structural involvement of the IMF. In certain respects, this would also fit in with the next phase of the programme to strengthen the euro area—following the acute crisis management of recent years—which will need to focus on reassessing national and European responsibilities for the single currency going forward. This will be part of a broader approach to the underlying problems that stem largely from the lack of appropriate coordination mechanisms for dealing with major differences between economies.

Variation in the form of macroprudential policy

Finally, with reference to EMU and the euro, this book briefly mentioned an existing example of variation in the form of macroprudential policy. As it now stands, a conscious choice has already been made to let national authorities chart their own course in this policy area, given that financial cycles can vary widely between Member States. This policy should be positioned alongside the existing macro-economic imbalances procedure and the enforcement of price stability, a task entrusted to the ECB. The case for developing a macroprudential policy of this kind stems from the increasingly decisive role that financial factors play in the functioning of EMU and the euro. The options for institutional design range from intergovernmental to supranational.

9.6 Variation in Asylum, Migration and Border Control

Chapter 8 on asylum, migration and border control outlined several examples of existing variation and also described other options. The statutory provisions concerning the treatment of asylum seekers laid down in the Geneva Convention on Refugees, Article 3 of the ECHR, and Article 18 of the Charter of Fundamental Rights of the European Union establish a clear-cut minimum level of uniformity in European asylum policy. Only *refoulement*—forcibly returning people to a country where they are likely to be exposed to persecution or degrading treatment—is in any case prohibited. This obligation is incumbent on both the Member States and the Union as a whole. Even so, this human rights standard need not lead to a completely uniform asylum policy; in fact, it even allows scope for variation in the way in which asylum is ensured. In other words, in all further questions of policy and legislation, the point is to assess the most appropriate model of action.

We can assess variation in the fulfilment of European public tasks concerning asylum and migration in part by considering whether such variation strengthens democratic support for migration policy. Social and political differences between the Member States suggest less unity, but the nature of the problems may in fact require more.

In 2016, the Advisory Council on International Affairs recommended creating more scope for variation in migration policy within the circle of Schengen countries.[5] The AIV drew attention to the possibility of closer cooperation as defined in the EU Treaty (Article 20 TEU) between Member States wishing to implement the Schengen Agreement within the framework of a fully functioning common asylum system, including similar forms of reception and integration, the acceptance of distribution keys, sharing information on abuses, coordination with the UNHCR on resettlement, and agreements with safe countries outside the EU regarding the return of migrants. This is an example of variation in membership. Other Schengen countries would maintain open internal borders under normal circumstances and share responsibility for external borders and the common visa policy, provided that they agree to share costs, jointly manage external borders and perform selective checks at internal borders, all of which points to 'flexible solidarity' towards the resettlement of asylum seekers, as suggested by a number of Central European Member States. This proposal allows for societal differences between Member States and includes trade-offs within a policy domain—in other words, variation in policy content. After all, there is little point in forcibly transferring a refugee to a Member State that does not want to take in asylum seekers. In terms of the EU's own development, it is important that this variation does not jeopardise the socio-economically valuable single market.

Variation in the decision-making method is conceivable, for example when treaties are concluded by departing from the usual decision-making procedure (e.g. by means of intergovernmental decision-making within the European Council). It is crucial that minimum thresholds, such as the principle of *non-refoulement* reaffirmed in the Charter of Fundamental Rights of the European Union, are fully respected. Anticipatory policy must set the stage for what follows in all cases. That can only be entrusted to a European Union that pursues international policy towards countries of origin and takes action to prevent new crises.

9.7 Perspective on Change

The capacity for change and adaptation has always been a critical force behind European integration. It is vital that we rediscover that capacity, because if the EU itself cannot change, then circumstances will at some point force inevitable changes upon it. The main objective is not to amend the Treaty, but rather to adopt a different attitude towards the Treaties and their application. This will also lighten the burden on new Member States that are caught between the political will to accede to the Union and the real obstacles to their immediate and equal participation in all areas. Nor is it necessary to make a binary distinction between Member States and non-Member States in relation to associated countries and territories. The same applies to the distinction between overseas countries and territories, including the Caribbean parts of the Kingdom of the Netherlands, and the 'outermost regions'.

The functional rationality that has long been a powerful driver of European integration is not inviolable. History has made that more than evident. The (1) unique momentum of market integration, (2) spill-overs between sectors, i.e. the 'dissemination' of integration practices from one policy domain to another, and (3) their consolidation by supranational institutions that uphold the supranational rule of law, are, moreover, processes that cannot be maintained under altered circumstances. European cooperation and integration have often been the result of negotiations or major external events that required a response. To forge a covenant between peoples is not to narrow that covenant down to an institutional narrative.

How can the Member States continue to chart a course on the basis of self-determination? The notion of 'demoicracy' put forward in this book is based on the assumption that the 'demoi', the *political* peoples of Europe, should be regarded in plural. This would, for example, be possible if national parliaments not only had negative powers, such as the yellow card procedure, but also the right to initiate European policy and legislation, including variations in that policy. What we are emphasising here is that there are no hierarchical but rather cooperative relationships between EU and national institutions. The EU's current system is in fact not modelled on the structure of the national state. In that context, legislative, policy-making, administrative and judicial competences are derived from the power structure shaped by history. The exact opposite is true in the European Communities and now in the EU: the need for a partly common legal order led to the creation of institutions by treaty.

What this implies is that, at European level, the principle of democracy takes on a different meaning. The European order is a legal order, an economic order and, in a certain sense, a political order, but it is not a democracy in the same manner as a state. The EU provides a structure for cooperation, to offer protection and build a future lived in freedom; based on those goals and the common values in which they are rooted, however, it is also a structure for taking and overseeing joint decisions. In this European context, citizens exercise their influence primarily through their national elections, and it is there that the EU must seek its basis of support.

In addition, by being more self-aware and proactive in its approach to variation, the EU can better reflect the diversity of 'demoi', and the different interests and aspirations arising from it, in legislation and policy. To involve the 'peoples' more closely in the EU, it must have a closer relationship with the national parliaments. It should also be more aware that each and every parliament represents a people who want space and protection for their life plans and those of future generations. The Charter of Fundamental Rights of the European Union can serve as a guideline in this respect. The Charter does not refer specifically to the division of tasks between European and national governments, but it does identify and protect the fulfilment of public tasks as indispensable to the pursuits of citizens, their organisations and businesses.

The 'logic of consequences', i.e. the question of what costs and benefits are at stake, is inextricably bound up with the 'logic of appropriateness', i.e. the question of what moral considerations play a role. After all, cooperation within the Union is always based on the principles of democracy, the rule of law and fundamental rights and freedoms, including social rights and the right to protection against persecution.

These requirements are particularly important when it comes to the protection of the rule of law, democracy and human rights. If we accept variations as a feature of the European Union, we must face up to the question of what the Union's essential common features are. Only then will it be possible to appreciate differences while maintaining sufficient cohesion. Too often, the European Union stands accused of straightjacketing its Member States and showing no regard for their individuality. Such dissatisfaction indicates a fundamental cross-border appreciation for individuality in diversity. Respecting this means seeing people not as separate individuals, but as persons who engage with others on the basis of their culture, beliefs and traditions. That is the view of humanity that underpins the notion of human rights.

The scope for variation sought in this book and recommended with a view to future developments must not endanger the above vision of human society; in fact, it is precisely this vision that has inspired our call to abandon the forced pursuit of uniformity. Respect for individuality is manifest—or, indeed, lacking—at various levels. In each case, what is at stake is the rights and responsibilities of people as citizens: as citizens of their town or village, as citizens of their country, and as European citizens. No variation in the allocation and fulfilment of public tasks should lose sight of that. It is expressed in the scope of application of the Charter of Fundamental Rights of the European Union (Article 51 as interpreted in the case law of the European Court of Justice).

The variations that we have recommended therefore do not limit the fundamental values set out in Article 2 of the EU Treaty, let alone cast them aside. Only by recognising that these values—which include democracy, the rule of law and human rights—are closely bound up with the EU and European citizenship can an EU of variation maintain and act upon its vision of a shared future. While the effect may vary depending on local and national circumstances, the democratic rule of law must be regarded as inviolable. We therefore endorses the AIV's recommendation[6] in its report *The will of the people? The erosion of democracy under the rule of law in Europe* that respect for diversity in states' democratic functioning should be paired with efforts to prevent the erosion of the rule of law.

Another important aspect of the perspective offered in this book is that, regardless of the level of policy diversity or uniformity, the EU's internal relationships must be equal to the challenges posed by the outside world. The EU and its Member States are dealing with external forces, forces that affect international trade, security, data transmissions and even the integrity of democratic procedures. The nature and intensity of European integration must be able to adapt constantly to these forces.

9.8 The Dutch View of the European Union

What is the significance of the variation perspective for the Netherlands? The main purpose of this book is to consider a particular approach to European cooperation. The options put forward in different policy domains in the previous chapters provide examples. However, our most important message here is that the fundamental openness of the European project should be perceived as a space for creativity and imagination. In other words, variation should not be a mere last resort when compromise is required and differences are simply unavoidable.

Variation does not offer *carte blanche* to Member States, including the Netherlands. The significance of the 'variation' perspective for the Netherlands is evident in two areas, namely the area of interests and the area of values. This distinction—which is rife with interdependencies in the real world—corresponds to the logic of consequences (interests, cost-benefit) and the logic of appropriateness (normative perspective), discussed earlier.

The 'logic of consequences' has become even more important for the Netherlands, in part because Brexit has brought about an intensification in Franco-German cooperation. The economic, cultural and technical evolution of the Netherlands is inextricably bound up with that of these important neighbouring states. In its relationship with these and other Member States, the Netherlands must regard its place in the European Union as a given, but alterable, reality. To deny this would lead to further democratic alienation and involve portraying matters as if nothing could be changed about European integration.

It is therefore necessary for the Netherlands to express its political commitment to Europe in words and deeds, and it is equally necessary for this commitment to be reflected in the form of the EU at the same time. Both manifestations of political commitment are essential, all the more so because the political organisation of the EU is highly specific and its democratic embeddedness is extremely complex.

In today's reality, we see this in the position of the prime minister, for example, who has increasingly also taken on the role of 'Minister for European Affairs', partly owing to his or her position as a member of the European Council—a role that can go to improve the visibility of European affairs.

Public tasks are not merely the outcome of a process of give and take, of wheeling and dealing. They are fundamental because they arise against the backdrop of shared history, geographical proximity, trade, and political ideals. The creation of the European Communities and, later, of the European Union was, of course, the result of negotiations and agreement reached between states as sovereign actors, but this particular process of international coordination differed from ordinary negotiations in two respects. It was compelled by the insight that the governments of Europe, and the peoples they represented, had more to gain than a mere trade-off of interests: the experience of destruction that preceded the coordination process taught them that they shared an important interest in the relatively small continent of Western Europe, where close relationships had always abounded. That meant finding an arrangement on which citizens and their organisations and businesses could depend across national borders. That is the essential feature of the European Union.

A parallel can be drawn in this sense between the discussions on the future of 'the Netherlands' and those on the future of 'Europe'. Both in the European context and in the Netherlands, there is a need to flesh out the 'big words' that are needed so that the outcomes of cooperation are not reduced to a trade-off of interests. Those outcomes may be better than expected or disappointing, which is why they are always debatable. In that sense, the debate on the Netherlands and the EU is the same: it requires a discussion about long-term reliability in the fulfilment of public tasks.

The 'logic of consequences', i.e. the question of what costs and benefits are at stake, is inextricably bound up with the 'logic of appropriateness', i.e. the question of what moral considerations play a role. Cooperation within the Union is always based on the principles of democracy, the rule of law and fundamental rights and freedoms, including social rights and the right to protection against persecution.

If we accept variation as a feature of the European Union, we must, time and again, face up to the question of what the Union's essential shared features are. The common foundations are set out in the Treaties and in the Charter of Fundamental Rights of the European Union. Cooperation within the Union is always based on the principles of democracy, the rule of law and fundamental rights and freedoms, including social rights and the right to protection against persecution, and the principles of subsidiarity and solidarity. Respect for individuality is manifest—or, indeed, lacking—at various levels of organisation. At each level, what is at stake is the rights and responsibilities of people as citizens: as citizens of their town or village, as citizens of their country, and as European citizens. Variation in fulfilment is crucially important because the desire for personal responsibility is something that connects people across borders.

Notes

1. Guérot (2017).
2. Jones (2018); Zielonka (2012).
3. AIV (2017c).
4. Raad van State (2017a: 93).
5. AIV (2016).
6. AIV (2017c).

Appendix A
Applying the Matrix

Possibilities and Impossibilities of European Public Tasks

In this appendix, we apply the matrix described in Chap. 4 to some recently proposed policy instruments. Our examples illustrate the centrifugal forces now at work in European cooperation. They are: the quota system for relocating asylum seekers among the Member States, adopted by the Council in 2015 on a proposal from the European Commission, (Decision (EU) 2015/1601); the establishment of the European Border and Coast Guard Agency (Regulation (EU) 2016/1624), which succeeded FRONTEX; and a controversial proposal in 2016 to revise the 1996 Posting of Workers Directive (com(2016)0128—Proposal for a Directive amending Directive 96/71/EC concerning the posting of workers in the framework of the provision of services) in accordance with the principle of 'equal pay for equal work in the same place'.

Our discussion proceeds as follows:

1. We illustrate the background to each policy instrument by explaining the European Commission's original initiative.
2. We assign the proposal a position in the matrix that mirrors the motivation for collective action combined with the institutional order. This is the combination envisaged in the Commission's proposal. These proposals illustrate both the straitjacket of reciprocity and Community cooperation and the (functionalist-Community) 'policy rationality', which increasingly invokes normatively charged motivations for collective action, such as 'calculation based on European interest' and 'solidarity'.
3. By way of explanation, we position some of the more notable political positions of a number of EU Member States in the matrix. Their motivation for collective action (vertical axis) determines their preference in terms of institutional order (horizontal axis). Their views also reveal differences in public interests or the

E. Hirsch Ballin et al., *European Variations as a Key to Cooperation*,
Research for Policy, https://doi.org/10.1007/978-3-030-32893-1

prioritisation of the same. It thus becomes clear why the fulfilment of European public tasks has become so difficult, but we also see new opportunities emerge.

Tensions Associated with the Influx of Refugees: Relocation of Asylum Seekers by Means of a Quota System

Background and content

The changing geopolitical landscape and the many 'hotspots' along European border regions have driven large groups of migrants across the Mediterranean and Aegean to the European continent since early 2015. In that year alone, more than a million migrants arrived in the EU, many fleeing persecution and war, some also to escape bleak economic prospects. A significant proportion of these migrants applied for asylum in the hope of obtaining refugee status or secondary protection. This had a disruptive impact on the Common European Asylum System (CEAS). Combined with the closing of the Balkan route by national measures, the Dublin Regulation led to large numbers of asylum seekers being detained in the first country of arrival (Greece or Italy), but also to some of them moving on to Western Europe, in particular to Germany.

To manage the flow of refugees and to alleviate the pressure on Greece and Italy and their already shaky asylum systems, the European Commission announced a plan in 2015 to relocate 120,000 asylum seekers from these two countries to the other EU Member States in a two-year period.[1] Germany was particularly supportive of this plan. The Council of Ministers voted in favour of the proposal by qualified majority. Hungary, Slovakia, the Czech Republic and Romania voted against it. This was noteworthy, as the Council usually seeks consensus for sensitive decisions.

The asylum quotas established on the basis of a distribution key were mandatory. For the Netherlands, this meant receiving approximately 7,000 asylum seekers who would be obliged to go through the asylum application procedure there. The four Member States that had voted against the proposal were also allocated a number of asylum seekers. An appeal against this decision was rejected by the Court of Justice on 6 September 2017.[2]

Position of the relocation decision in the matrix

The asylum quotas are meant to get all the Member States to share the considerable burden bearing down on the southern Member States. The relocation mechanism also forces the Member States to share responsibility for safeguarding the fundamental rights of asylum seekers, based on Article 78(1) of the Treaty on the Functioning of the European Union. This obligation is also in line with Article 18 of the Charter of Fundamental Rights of the European Union and also applies to all Member States individually by virtue of international conventions.[3]

At the very least, the relocation of asylum seekers requires 'calculation based on European interest' as a basis for collective action. For this proposal to function in the longer term, however, recourse to the principle of interstate solidarity may also be necessary. The Commission's proposal reflects this. It means that Member States share the responsibility and absorb individual losses in pursuit of a higher intangible goal, namely to safeguard human rights and the fair sharing of burdens. This does not imply, however, that it is impossible for the objective of relocation to be based on other motivations for collective action, for example reciprocity (see Sect. 3.1).

Given the critical circumstances and the existing institutional order applicable in this policy area, including opt-outs for the uk, Ireland and Denmark, the final Commission proposal was designed as a flexible arrangement, in line with the CEAS within which the quota plan had been proposed.

In the relocation decision, the 'logic of appropriateness' provides the decisive arguments for cooperation, with the asylum quota plan being based on normative considerations of interstate solidarity. The decision is therefore politically charged, increasing the risk that some Member States will regard the relocation of asylum seekers as coercive and undemocratic.[4] It is therefore not inconceivable that cooperation with like-minded Member States can be raised to a higher level. First, however, it is necessary to explore the opponents' motivations and whether a compromise is possible that gets everyone on board: can a form of variation be conceived that does not immediately lead to variation in membership, including new opt-outs and lead groups (Fig. 1)?

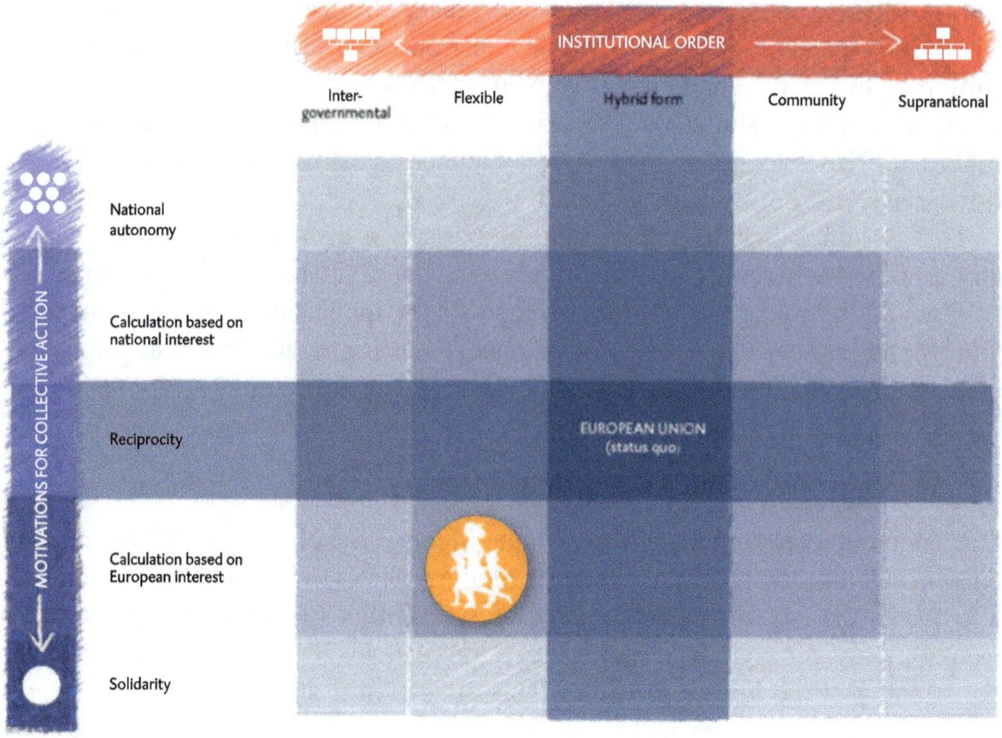

Fig. 1 Position of Commission's asylum quota proposal

Notable political positions of some EU Member States

The asylum quotas quickly met with fierce resistance from a number of Central European Member States that did not wish to implement the decision. Partly as a result, the plan soon ran aground. Hungary and Slovakia even took their case to the Court of Justice to challenge the mandatory relocation. In their petition asking the Court to annul the relocation mechanism, they argued as follows:

1. The content of the decision took the form of a legislative act, which should have only been adopted under a legislative procedure, whereas the Treaty on the Functioning of the European Union did not provide for any legislative powers to this end. This violated Article 78(3) of the TFEU and the rights of the national parliaments and the European Parliament.
2. The national parliaments and the European Parliament were not consulted sufficiently during the procedure.
3. The Council's amendments and additions to the Commission's proposal were not properly made, as the European Parliament was not involved and the amendments and additions were not adopted unanimously by the Council.[5]

These arguments can be read as a demand for respect for the autonomy of the Member States. The Court of Justice ruled that Hungary and Slovakia should comply with the Council Decision adopted on the basis of the Commission's proposal.[6] The fact that these Member States, together with Poland and the Czech Republic, nevertheless refuse to implement the decision places them in the 'autonomy'/'intergovernmental' cell in the matrix.

In defending the relocation mechanism, the southern Member States Italy and Greece invoke the 'principle of solidarity and fair sharing of responsibility … between Member States' as set out in Article 80 of the TFEU. Countries such as Germany and the Netherlands argue the issue mainly by referring to the fair distribution of costs. On that basis, and recognising the uk, Ireland and Denmark opt-outs, Italy and Greece are positioned in the 'solidarity/flexibility' cell, while the Netherlands and Germany are in the 'calculation based on European interest/flexibility' cell (Fig. 2).

The European Border and Coast Guard Agency (Formerly FRONTEX): 'Flexible Solidarity'?

Background and content

In December 2015, the Commission presented a proposal to create a European Border and Coast Guard Agency, giving new impetus to the existing agency, FRONTEX, which had proved inadequate to managing the refugee crisis. After brief resistance from Hungary and Poland, the regulation was adopted on 14 September 2016 and the new agency became operational the following month. The

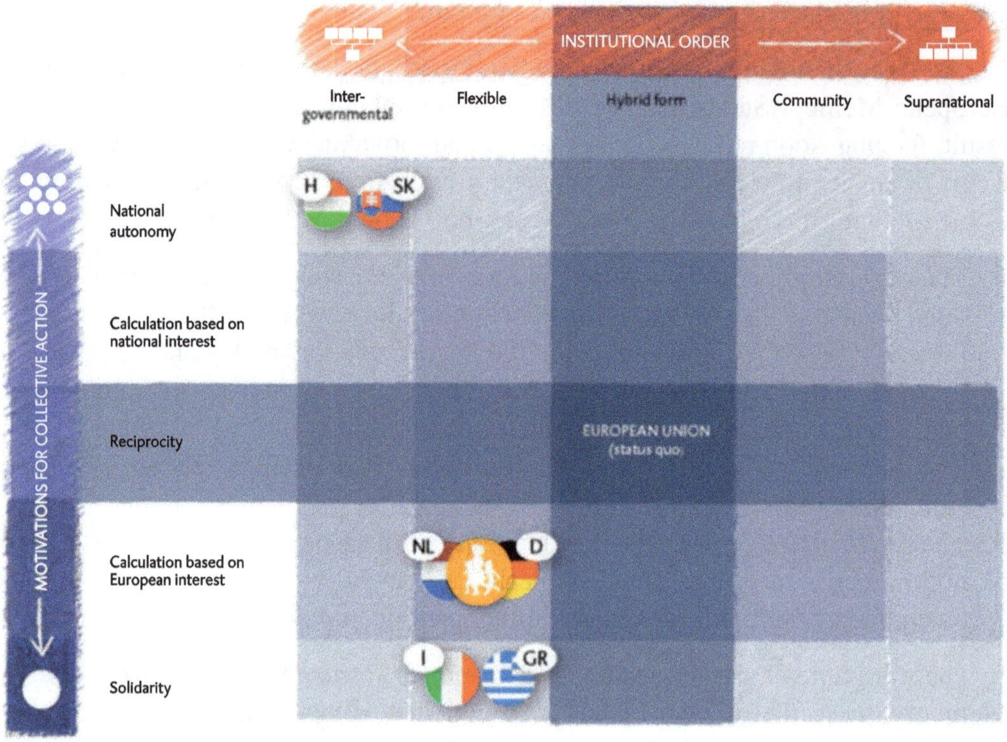

Fig. 2 Commission's asylum quota proposal, position of Member States

implication was that the Member States and the EU would need to cooperate more closely to secure the EU's external borders.[7]

The new regulation significantly increased the powers and tasks of the European border and coast guard. For example, the agency sees to it that EU legislation on border management is implemented correctly. It is notable that it is allowed to intervene even when not requested to do so by the relevant EU Member State, in any event when the proper functioning of the Schengen area is at risk. In other words, the agency has become more supranational in nature, and the borders of Member States situated on the EU's external borders have since become the external borders of *all* EU Member States. The policy autonomy of the EU Member States located on the EU's external borders has thus been further reduced.

The joint securing and protection of the EU's external borders is a critical component of the EU's political response to the tensions surrounding the influx of refugees. It is an attempt to join forces in controlling migration, improve the EU's internal security, and restore the Schengen system of free movement of persons. It is further regarded as a move towards the Member States and the EU sharing responsibility and towards a more inclusive European asylum system.

Position of the establishment of the European Border and Coast Guard Agency in the matrix

Both FRONTEX in its old form and the new European Border and Coast Guard Agency are organisations that deliver collective benefits to the EU through the

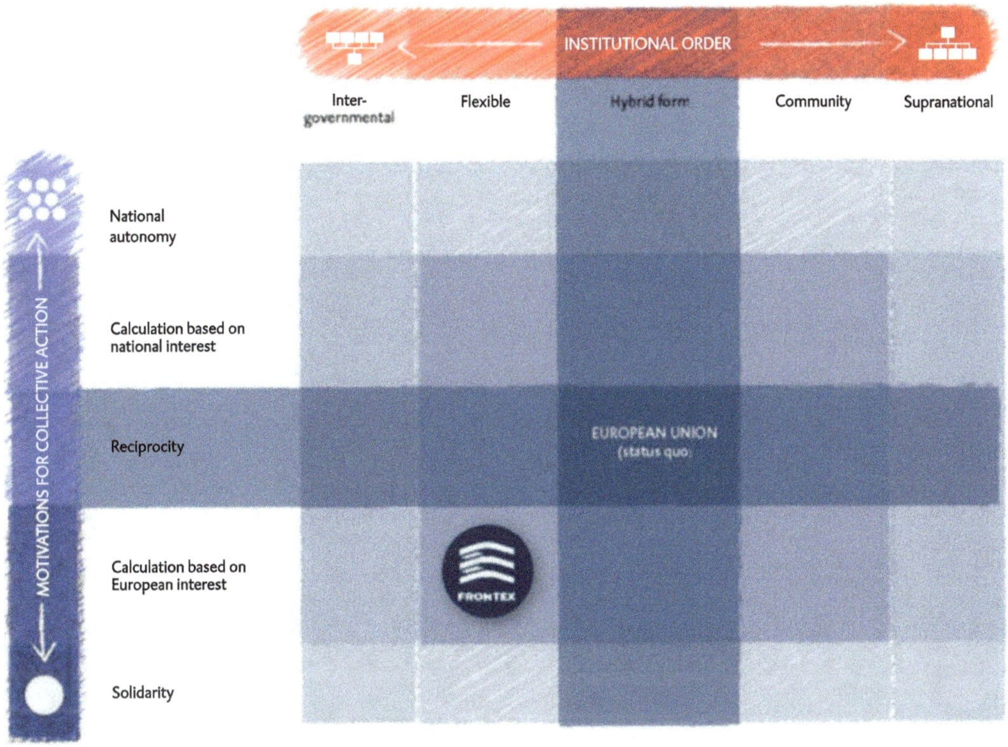

Fig. 3 Position of Commission's European Border and Coast Guard Proposal

pooling of forces. The basis for collective action is therefore the prospect that such cooperation will serve the greater good of the Union as a whole, i.e. internal security and the free movement of goods and persons. Since the creation of the European Border and Coast Guard Agency, individual Member States situated at the EU's external borders, such as Poland and Hungary, have lost out by surrendering their autonomy over their national border controls.

Whereas FRONTEX was a non-binding intergovernmental alliance, the new agency is much more supranational in nature because it can intervene in exceptional situations without being asked to do so by the Member State in question. It can also recommend the reintroduction of internal borders if a Member State refuses to cooperate. Like other policy instruments in the domain of migration and asylum, this instrument is flexible. There are opt-outs for directives and regulations under the CEAS, which is based on reciprocity and the convergence of different asylum systems within the EU (Figs. 3 and 4).

Notable political positions of some EU Member States

In May 2016, the Commission put forward a controversial proposal to impose a 'solidarity contribution' on Member States that refused to implement the asylum seekers relocation plan. The fine could mount to as much as 250,000 euros per refused asylum seeker and would be spent on the reception of refugees in those Member States that *did* respect the asylum quota. The Commission's idea was to prevent Member States such as Hungary and Slovakia from blocking an asylum

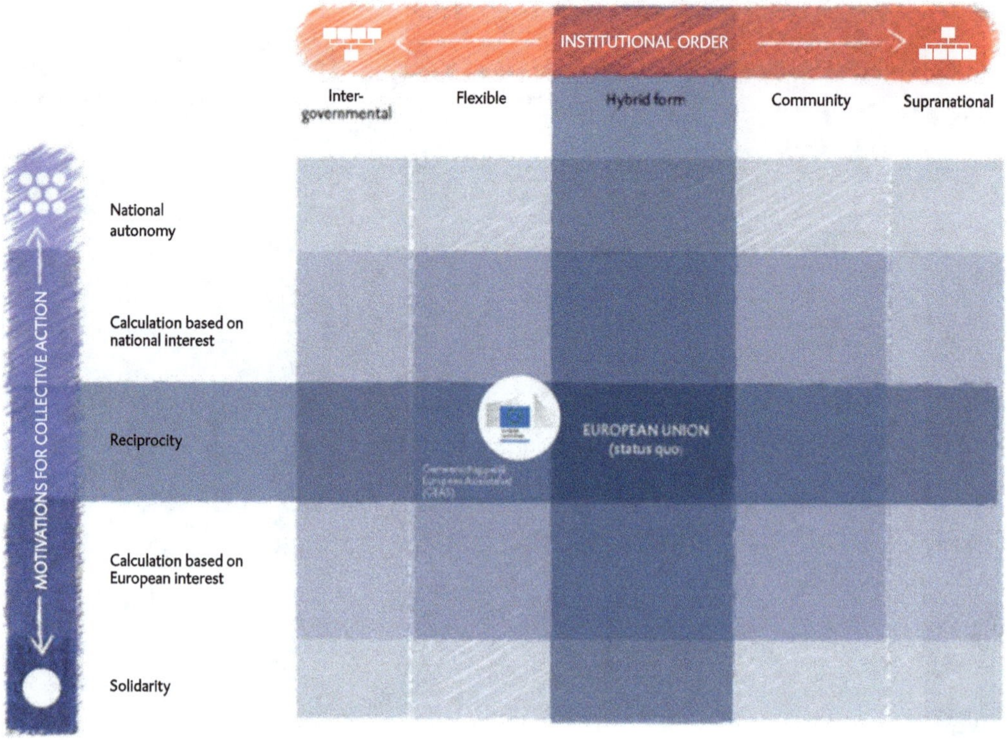

Fig. 4 Position of CEAS

policy based on solidarity. This opened the door to the idea of 'flexible solidarity', which the Central European Member States used to introduce a new perspective on both flexibility and solidarity in October 2016 (in the sense of 'trade-offs' within or between policy areas).

The principle of 'flexible solidarity' included new forms of solidarity as an alternative to the relocation mechanism for asylum seekers. One specific example is the deal between Austria and Slovakia whereby the latter temporarily receives migrants who, under the Dublin Regulation, must ultimately apply for asylum in Austria. Reinforcing the European Border and Coast Guard or freeing up more development funding also fall under 'flexible solidarity'. Central European Member States add their support to such trade-offs by arguing that security should take precedence as a European public interest. As a result, Slovakia and Hungary have shifted to the same position on the matrix as Germany and the Netherlands, namely 'calculation based on European interest'/'flexibility' (see Fig. 5). European ministers, but also the Commissioner for Migration, Home Affairs and Citizenship, Dimitris Avramopoulos, took this idea on board, recognising that flexibility was needed in this instance to reach a compromise. The result was variation in cooperation by permitting trade-offs within the asylum policy domain, with Member States being allowed to decide for themselves which public interest was most important to them.

The European Commission has reconsidered this issue since then and, bolstered by the Court's ruling, has demanded that the Central European Member States also

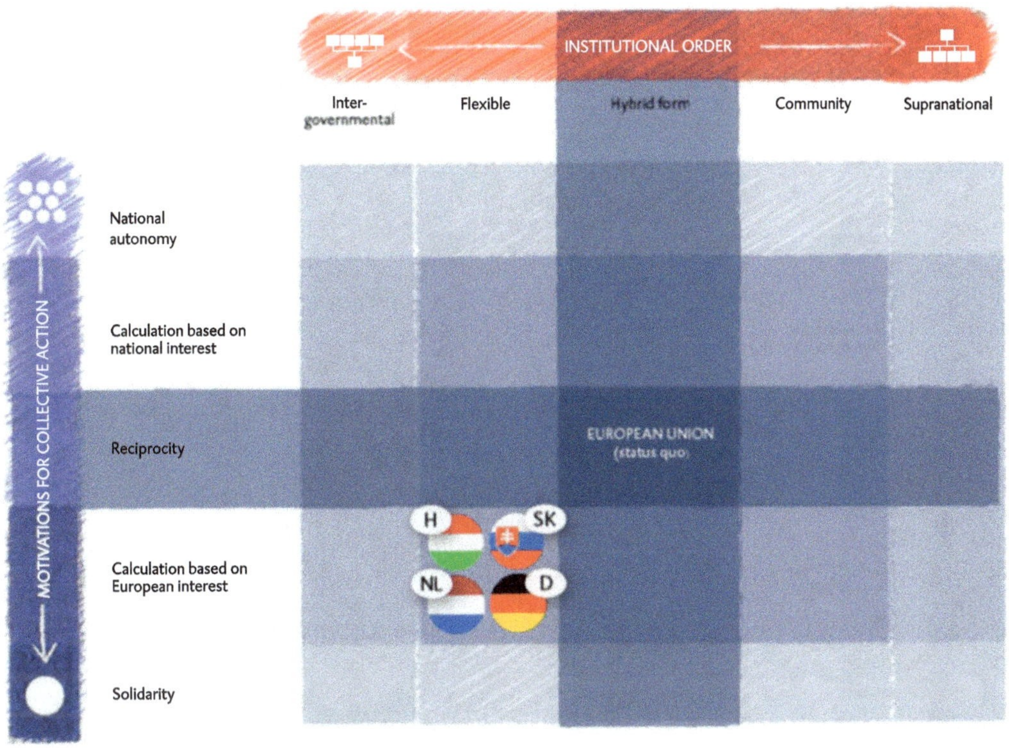

Fig. 5 Shift in Position of Hungary and Slovakia on Asylum Quotas

participate in the relocation mechanism. The President of the European Council, Donald Tusk, then asked that greater understanding be shown towards the Central European Member States and called for the mandatory asylum quotas to be withdrawn. Estonia, which held the Presidency of the EU in the second half of 2017, presented a compromise proposal based on quotas but allowing exceptions. As tensions mount in response, the question is what forms of variation within the asylum policy domain can help the parties involved reach a compromise. It is a question that has become more relevant, emphasised by the fact that, by accepting 'flexible solidarity', the different Member States and the Commission are moving towards the same cell of the matrix (Fig. 6).

Revision of the Posting of Workers Directive According to the Principle 'Equal Pay for Equal Work in the Same Place'

Background and content[8]

In March 2016, the European Commission submitted a proposal to revise the Posting of Workers Directive 96/71/EC. The directive lays down rules on the posting of workers when providing services in another EU Member State. The

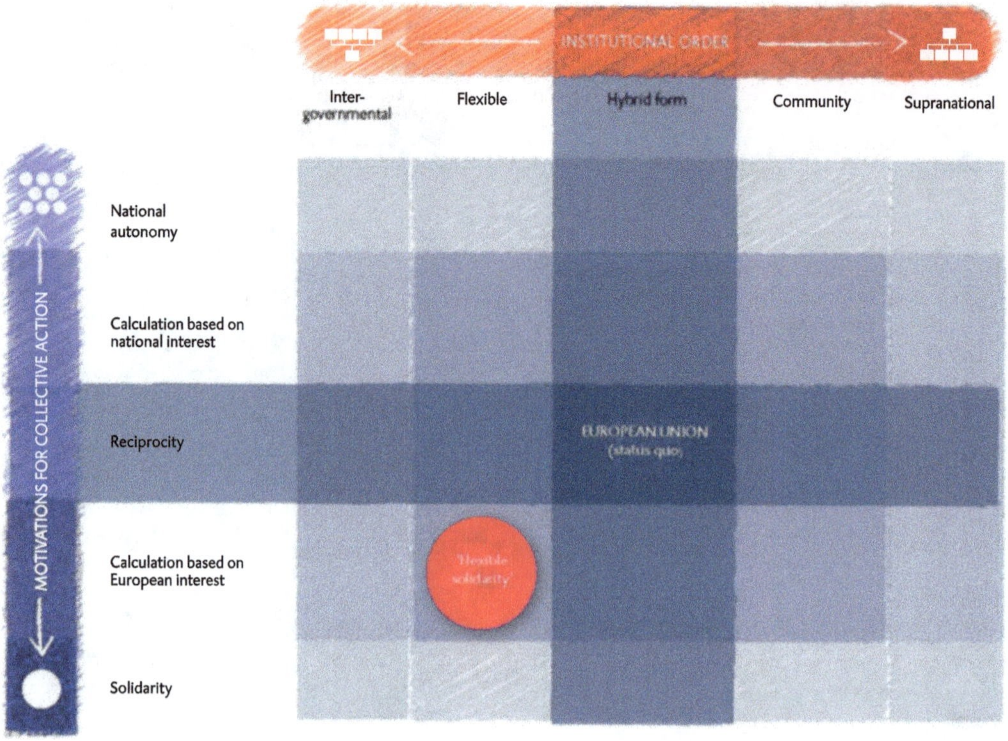

Fig. 6 Position of 'flexible solidarity'

Commission's aim in proposing the revision is to promote a level playing field, that is to say fair competition. It argues that in a competitive internal market, competition should be based not on labour costs but on quality of service, productivity and innovation. The proposed amendment aims to promote the free movement of services by clarifying the applicable terms and conditions of employment.

After two years of intensive debate, the Member States and the European Parliament reached an agreement in principle on the Commission's proposal in March 2018. The agreement stipulates that the same collective agreement will apply to posted workers as to workers in the host country in question. Previously this was the case only in the construction sector, but the rule is now to be extended to all other sectors (except transport). It has also been agreed that a secondment may last for a maximum of 12 months, with a possible six-month extension. Once this period has elapsed, the host Member State's employment law also becomes effective. Social security contributions may still be paid in the home country for up to 24 months, however.

Position of the Commission's proposal in the matrix

The revised version of the Posting of Workers Directive mainly aims to create a level playing field by harmonising labour costs. The motivation for collective action is therefore reciprocity. This position can also be presented as 'calculation based on European interest', since it can be argued that all EU employees benefit in this way.

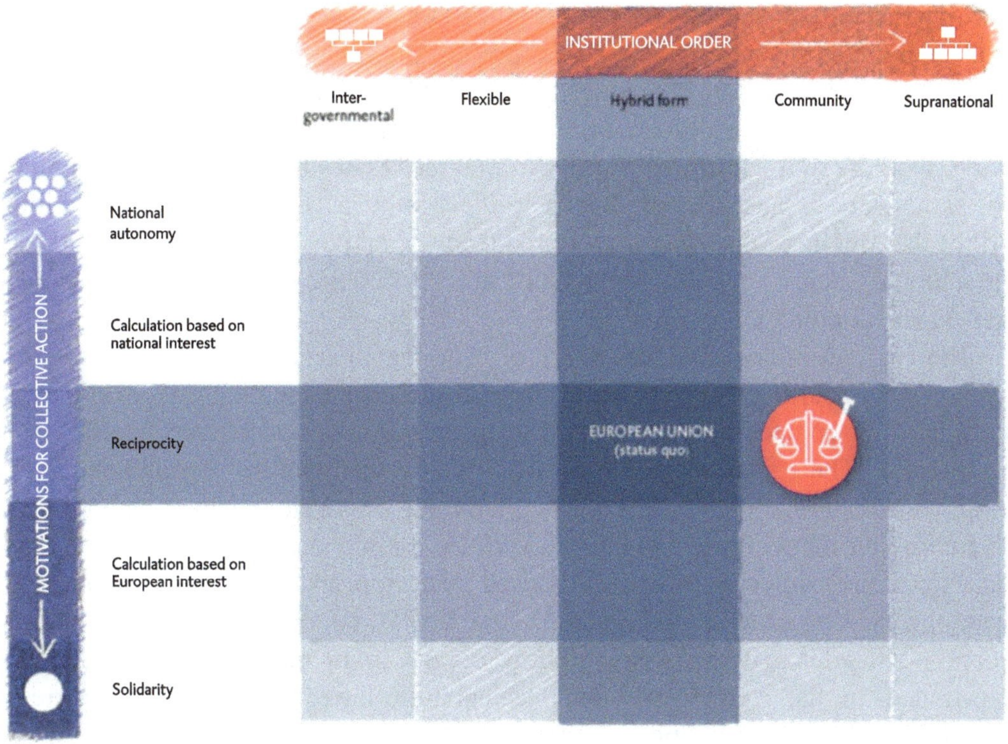

Fig. 7 Position of the Commission's proposal for a Posting of Workers Directive

The overall objective of the revision is to stimulate the internal market through better management of the free movement of services. In the current EU system—in which the integrity of the internal market is a shared general principle—Community cooperation is the obvious course of action. Legislation can be produced within the framework of the internal market that weighs free movement against other interests, but this would then apply to all members. Structural invalidation of the four freedoms would make free-rider behaviour possible. After the 'Better Deal for Britain', however, this became an increasingly distinct possibility; after all, the EU showed itself prepared to negotiate with the uk about the social security entitlements of EU migrants (Fig. 7).

Notable political positions of some EU Member States

From the outset, the Netherlands was in favour of revising the Posting of Workers Directive. To encourage the Commission to take the initiative, the Netherlands and six other like-minded Member States—France, Germany, Sweden, Belgium, Luxembourg and Austria—wrote a letter to the European Commissioner for Employment, Social Affairs, Skills and Labour Mobility in June 2015 in which their ministers of Social Affairs argued in favour of reforming the Posting of Workers Directive. In response, Poland, the Czech Republic, Hungary, Slovakia, Estonia, Latvia, Lithuania, Romania and Bulgaria sent a letter opposing the revision. These Member States were initially against further harmonisation of posting policies in the EU.

In essence, both sides are standing up for their own employees. Some countries oppose more stringent requirements for posted workers because this would deprive them of their competitive advantage. After all, Central and East European workers benefit by offering cheaper labour than workers in the host country. On the other hand, workers from Northwest European Member States benefit from equal pay for the same work because they are then less likely to be driven out by the competition. All of the Member States have therefore taken up the position of 'calculation based on national interest', albeit in defence of different public interests (free movement versus social policy).

The two sides have different ways of bringing their views to bear. The main proponents, including the Netherlands, are calling for the creation of a level playing field and fair competition within the European internal market and the associated reciprocity. Their approach to reciprocity takes the working conditions of EU employees as its starting point. They regularly pay lip service to the social objective of improving the working conditions of *all* EU employees (in that case, the rationale for their position is 'calculation based on European interest'). The opponents want the existing situation to continue. They invoke the optimal functioning of the economic freedoms, in the sense of mutual access. In the matrix, the proponents are positioned in the 'reciprocity' and 'calculation based on European interest'/ 'Community' cell. The opponents, on the other hand, are positioned in the 'reciprocity/Community' cell (Fig. 8).

Member States' Different Positions

This appendix analyses some recent policy instruments related to two major European issues (i.e. the future of the free movement of persons and services, and the tensions surrounding the influx of refugees) using the matrix introduced in Chap. 4. The instruments analysed are the Decision to relocate asylum seekers according to established quotas, the European Border and Coast Guard Agency (the successor of FRONTEX) launched in 2016, and a proposal in 2016 to revise the 1996 Posting of Workers Directive.

We see that the Commission's proposal on asylum quotas follows the 'policy rationality' described in Chap. 2, which often tends towards deeper European integration to deal with problems and which increasingly invokes motivations for collective action that are normative in nature, such as 'calculation based on European interest' and 'solidarity'. Because the refugee issue is politically charged, the relocation mechanism is a divisive force in European politics. It is therefore a prime example of the politicisation of European public tasks, and it is no surprise that the decision itself reflects contrary trends in the EU, i.e. 'policy rationality' versus 'democratic alienation'. The establishment of the European Border and Coast Guard Agency also calls for deeper European cooperation with supranational aspects, to which 'the logic of consequences' is admittedly more applicable. The EU straitjacket of reciprocity and Community cooperation—as described in

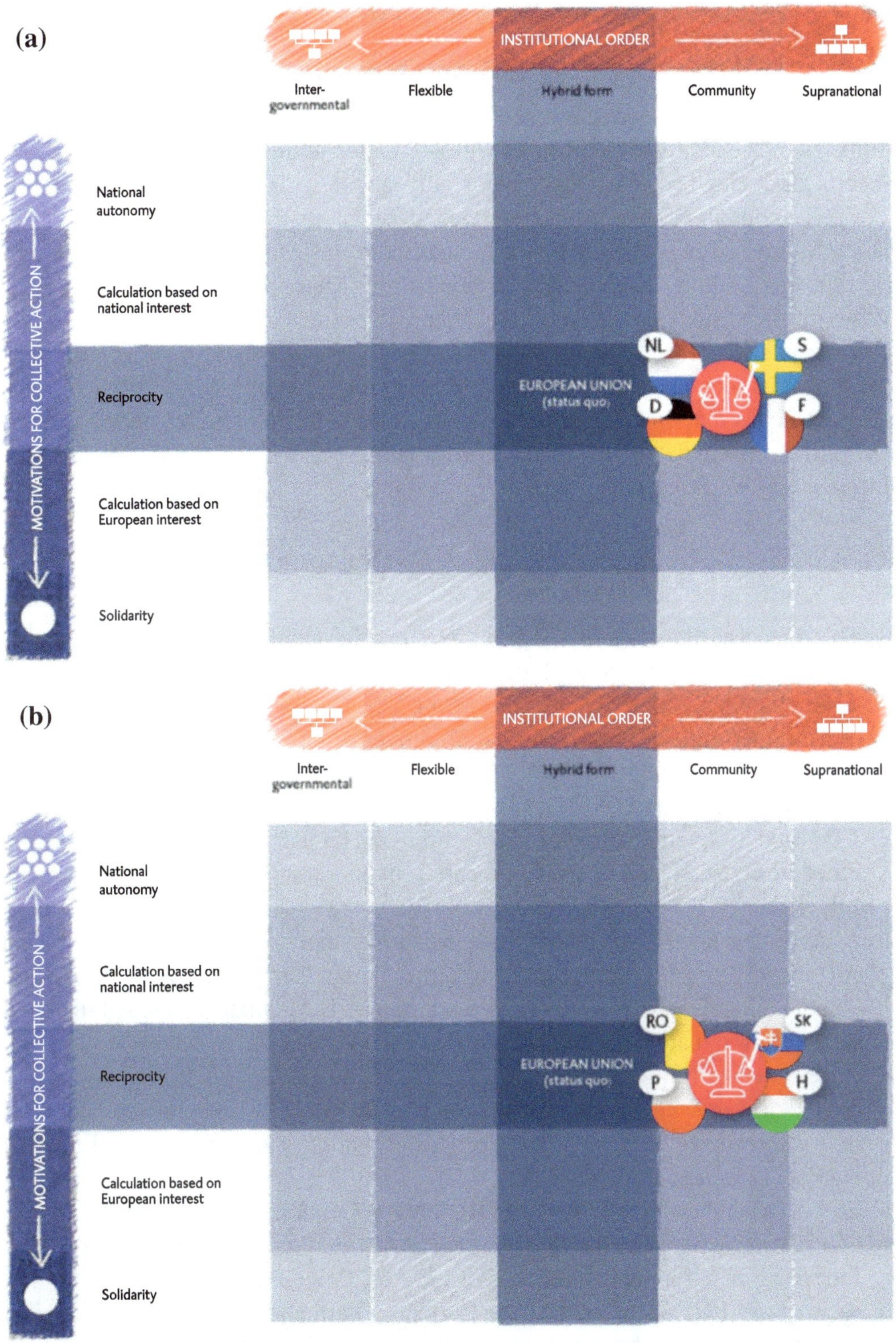

Fig. 8 **a** A position of the member states on the posting of workers directive. **b** B position of the member states on the posting of workers directive

Chap. 2—is clearly in evidence in the proposed reform of the Posting of Workers Directive.

There is variation, however, in the position of the EU Member States. A demand for more variation is emerging, most explicitly in the demand for 'flexible solidarity', which encourages a different way of looking at the EU and what is possible. Specifically, 'flexible solidarity' is not only about variation in form, where discussions about flexibility often get bogged down in the traditional question of which Member States will or will not participate. Instead, variation here concerns the question of how much policy discretion the Member States can be given to weigh up the various European public interests, values and objectives themselves. The matrix shows that, as long as we continue to look solely at the form, based on institutional order and the number of participating Member States, the different Member States may indeed appear to view an issue from a similar perspective but will still not be able to resolve it, and no progress will be made on designing European public tasks.

Notes

1. This breaches the 'Dublin system' because the Dublin Regulation makes the Member State where the asylum seeker first entered the EU responsible for the asylum application procedure. As a result, Greece and Italy in particular are now bearing the brunt of processing large numbers of asylum seekers.
2. ECLI:EU:C:2017:631.
3. United Nations Convention relating to the Status of Refugees, Geneva, 28 July 1951 and Convention for the Protection of Human Rights and Fundamental Freedoms (also known as the European Convention on Human Rights), Rome, 4 July 1950.
4. A study by the Bertelsmann Stiftung shows that the majority of European citizens want a fair distribution of refugees within Europe. There is, however, a notable difference between the 'old' and 'new' EU Member States. All in all, the study shows that EU citizens want a European solution. See https://www.bertelsmann-stiftung.de/en/topics/aktuelle-meldungen/2016/februar/majority-of-the-eu-citizens-wants-a-fair-distribution-of-refugees/.
5. ECJ 2 December 2015 C-643/15 (Slovak Republic V Council of the European Union), ECLI:EU:C:2016:038/55.
   ECJ 3 December 2015 C-647/15 (Hungary v Council of the European Union), ECLI:EU:C: 2016:038/56.
6. Judgment of 6 September 2017, ECLI:EU:C:2017:631.
7. Regulation (EU) 2016/1624 of the European Parliament and of the Council of 14 September 2016 on the European Border and Coast Guard.
8. This section is based on the BNC-fiche Wijziging detacheringsrichtlijn and https://www.europa-nu.nl/id/vk2aqy964tui/herziening_detacheringsrichtlijn#p5.

Appendix B
List of Interviewees

A. Agotha, European Commission
S. Alonso, *NRC Handelsblad*
H. Benink, Tilburg University
A. Brenninkmeijer, European Court of Auditors
M. Boots, Dutch Ministry of General Affairs
B. Borgman, VNO-NCW
M. Bos, Social and Economic Council of the Netherlands
T. van den Brink, Utrecht University
Chr. Calliess, European Commission and Freie Universität Berlin
V. Cramer, Dutch Ministry of Justice and Security
E. Dame, Dutch Ministry of Infrastructure and the Environment
M. Dekker, Dutch Ministry of Economic Affairs and Climate
R. Dekker, Permanent Representation of the Netherlands to the EU
F. Duijn, Dutch Ministry of Foreign Affairs
J. Dijsselbloem, former Dutch Minister of Finance and President of the Eurogroup
B. Eickhout, Member of the European Parliament representing GroenLinks
M. Emmelkamp, Embassy of the Kingdom of the Netherlands in Baghdad
F. Fabbrini, Dublin City University Brexit Institute
E. Faber, Permanent Representation of the Netherlands to the EU
W. Geurts, Dutch Ministry of Foreign Affairs
P. de Gooijer, Embassy of the Kingdom of the Netherlands in Paris
M. de Grave, Permanent Representation of the Netherlands to the EU
D. Grimm, Humboldt Universität Berlin
B. Hassing, Permanent Representation of the Netherlands to the EU
E. Jones, Johns Hopkins School of Advanced International Studies
M. van Keulen, Hague University of Applied Sciences
C. Lobbezoo, Permanent Representation of the Netherlands to the EU
H. von Meijenfeldt, Dutch Ministry of Foreign Affairs
J. Morijn, Permanent Representation of the Netherlands to the EU and University of Groningen

E. Hirsch Ballin et al., *European Variations as a Key to Cooperation*,
Research for Policy, https://doi.org/10.1007/978-3-030-32893-1

E. Mulders, Dutch Ministry of Infrastructure and the Environment
C. Noland, Dutch Ministry of Foreign Affairs
J. Pelkmans, Centre for European Policy Studies
K. Piri, Member of the European Parliament representing Partij van de Arbeid
M. de Ridder, Dutch Ministry of Foreign Affairs
B. van Riel, Social and Economic Council of the Netherlands
F. Ronkes Agerbeek, European Commission
J. Rood, Clingendael Institute and Leiden University
A. Schout, Clingendael Institute
L. Senden, Utrecht University
B. Smulders, European Commission and Free University of Brussels
M. Sie Dhian Ho, Clingendael Institute
A. Sorel, European Asylum Support Office
J. Terstegen, Dutch Ministry of Justice and Security
T. Vanheste, *De Correspondent*
S. Vanthournout, Sense about Science EU
S. de Vries, Utrecht University
J. Waanders, Dutch Ministry of Defence
J. Wiers, Dutch Ministry of Foreign Affairs and University of Groningen

Bibliography

Advisory Council on International Affairs (aiv). (2015). *Differentiated integration: Different routes to EU cooperation*. AIV: The Hague.

Advisory Council on International Affairs (aiv). (2016). *The future of Schengen*. AIV: The Hague.

Advisory Council on International Affairs (aiv). (2017). *Is the Eurozone stormproof? On deepening and strengthening the EMU*. AIV: The Hague.

Advisory Council on International Affairs (aiv). (2017). *The will of the people? The erosion of democracy under the rule of law in Europe*. AIV: The Hague.

Advisory Council on International Affairs (aiv). (2017). *Towards a new relationship with the uk*. AIV: The Hague.

American Chamber of Commerce to the EU. (2017). *The EU single market: Impact on member states*. www.amchameu.eu/sites/default/files/publications/files/amcham_eu_single_market_web.pdf.

Anderson, P. (2009). *The new old world*. London: Verso.

Armbruster, A. (2017). Der 'optimale' Währungsraum. Gibt es eine Theorie hinter dem Euro? *Frankfurter Allgemeine Zeitung, 56*.

Bakker, A. (1996). *The liberalization of capital movements in Europe: The monetary committee and financial integration 1958–1994*. Dordrecht: Kluwer.

Bara, Y. et al., Ministère de l'Économie et des Finances, Trésor-Economics. (2017). 'A contribution to the work on the strengthening of the euro area'. www.tresor.economie.gouv.fr/Ressources/File/440712.

Barendrecht, E. & Wijffelaars, M. (2017). 'De interne markt is een onvoltooid succes'. *ESB* 3 November.

Barnard, C. (2008). Unravelling the services directive. *Common Market Law Review, 45*, 323–394.

Barnard, C. (2010). *The substantive law of the EU. The four freedoms*. Oxford: Oxford University Press.

Barnard, C., & Peers, S. (2014). *European Union law*. Oxford: Oxford University Press.

Barslund, M. & Ludolph, L. (2017). *Migrants in the Mediterranean: Easy and difficult solutions*. www.ceps.eu/publications/migrants-mediterranean.

Bauman, Z. (2004). *Europe: An unfinished adventure*. Cambridge: Polity Press.

Bayoumi, T., & Eichengreen, B. (1992). Shocking aspects of European monetary integration. *NBER Working Paper* 3949.

Beck, U., & Grande, E. (2007). *Cosmopolitan: Europe's way out of crisis*. Wiley.

Beetsma, R. M. W. J., & Bovenberg, A. L. (2001). The optimality of a monetary union without a fiscal union. *Journal of Money, Credit and Banking, 33*(2), 179–204.

E. Hirsch Ballin et al., *European Variations as a Key to Cooperation*, Research for Policy, https://doi.org/10.1007/978-3-030-32893-1

Benz, A. (2015). Multilevel governance in the European Union: Loosely coupled arenas of representation, participation, and accountability. In S. Piattoni (Ed.). (pp. 1201–1218).

Betts, A., & Collier, P. (2017). *Refuge—Rethinking refugee policy in a changing world*. New York: Oxford University Press.

Bialasiewicz, L. (2011). *Europe in the world: EU geopolitcs and the making of European space*. Farnham: Ashgate.

Bitterlich, J. (1998). *Schwierige Nachbarschaft am Rhein*. Bonn: Bouvier.

Blanke, H.-J., & Mangiameli, S. (Eds.). (2012). *The European union after Lisbon: Constitutional basis, economic order and external action*. Heidelberg: Springer.

Bogdandy, A. von (2017). *Von der technokratischen Rechtsgemeinschaft zum politisierten Rechtsraum. Probleme und Entwicklungslinien in der Grundbegrifflichkeit des Europarechts*. Max Planck Institute for Comparartive Public Law and International Law, MPIL Research Paper Series 12. SSRN 2971097.

Bohman, J. (2007). *Democracy across border: From Demos to Demoi*. Cambridge, MA: MIT Press.

Boot, A. W. A., & Riel, A. van (2014). De politieke speelruimte voor de euro. In: *Economische Statistische Berichten (4699–4700/99)* (pp. 742–745).

Boudewijn, R. (2009). Vijf jaar Europees Nabuurschapsbeleid. *Openbaar Bestuur, 5*, 28–31.

Brink, T. van den, Jaremba, U., Senden, L., & Vries, S. de (2019) *Variatie en de interne markt*. WRR-Working Paper no. 32. The Hague: Wetenschappelijke Raad voor het regeringsbeleid.

Brink, T. van den, Bijl, Y., Hübner, M. (2019a). *Differentiatie en uniformiteit in EU-wetgeving: detachering en gegevensbescherming*, WRR-Working Paper no. 31, The Hague: Wetenschappelijke Raad voor het regeringsbeleid.

Brink, T. van den (2017). Refining the division of competences in the EU. National discretion in EU legislation. In S. Garben & I. Govaere (Eds.), *The division of competences between the EU and the member states* (pp. 251–275). Oxford: Hart Publishing.

Brink, T. van den (2015). Towards an ever clearer division of authority between the European Union and the member states? In T. van den Brink, M. Luchtman, & M. Scholten (Eds.), *Sovereignty in the shared legal order of the EU* (pp. 217–248). Cambridge: Intersentia.

Bronk, R. & Jacoby, W. (2013). Avoiding monocultures in the European Union: The case for the mutual recognition of difference in conditions of uncertainty. *LSE 'Europe in Question' Discussion Paper Series* 67.

Brown, W. (2011). *Walled states, waning sovereignty*. Cambridge, Mass.: The MIT Press.

Brsakoska Bazerkoska, J. (2011). The European union and the world trade organization: Problems and challenges. *Croation Yearbook of European Law Policy, 7*, 277–290.

Bungenberg, M. (2010). Going global? The EU common commercial policy after Lisbon. *European Yearbook of International Economic Law, 1*, 123–151.

Centraal, P. (2008). *The internal market and the impact on the Dutch economy. Implications for trade and economic growth*.

Centraal, P. (2017). *Discussienota Europese Commissie over EMU*.

Cini, M., & Perez-Solorzano Borragan, N. (2016). *European Union politics*. Oxford: Oxford University Press.

Claassen, R., & Gerbrandy, A. (2016). Rethinking European competition law: From consumer welfare to a capability approach. *Utrecht Law Review, 12*(1), 1–15.

Cremona, M. (2001). A policy of bits and pieces? The common commercial policy after nice. *Cambridge Yearbook of European Legal Studies, 4*, 61–91.

Cremona, M. (2017). The internal market and external economic relations. In P. Koutrakos & J. Snell (Eds.), *Research handbook of the law of the EU's internal market* (pp. 479–499). Cheltenham: Edward Elgar.

Dagmar, S., Oliver, L., Forde, C. & Alberti, G. (2015). *EU social and labour rights and EU internal market law*. www.europarl.europa.eu/RegData/etudes/STUD/2015/563457/IPOL_STU%282015%29563457_EN.pdf.

Davies, N. (1997). *Europe: A history*. London: Pimlico.

Dekker, P. (2017). Niet van harte en onzeker: de publieke stemming over de EU. *Internationale Spectator, 71*(2), 4–8.

Delors, J. (1985). *Speech IGC*. Luxemburg.

Delors, J. (2004). *Erinnerungen eines Europäers*. Berlin: Parthas.

Deutsche Bundesbank. (1992). *The Maastricht decisions on EMU. Monatsberichte der Deutsche Bundesban*. February 1992.

Dijkhuizen, B. (2014). *Geen verdere liberalisering EU-transportmarkt*. www.logistiek.nl/distributie/nieuws/2014/04/geen-verdere-liberalisering-eu-transportmarkt-10146201.

Dimopoulos, A. (2010). The effects of the Lisbon treaty on the principles and objectives of the common commercial policy. *European Foreign Affairs Review, 15,* 153–170.

Dokumente zur Deutschlandpolitik. (1998). *Deutsche Einheit*. Munich: Oldenbourg.

Domurath, I. (2013). The three dimensions of solidarity in the EU legal order: Limits of the judicial and legal approach. *Journal of European Integration, 35*(4), 459–475.

Dougan, M. (2000). Minimum harmonization and the internal market. *Common Market Law Review, 37,* 853–885.

Dyson, K., & Sepos, A. (Eds.). (2010). *Which Europe? The politics of differentiated integration*. Hampshire: Palgrave Macmillan.

Editorial Comments. (2006). The services directive proposal: Striking a balance between the promotion of the internal market and preserving the European social model? *Common Market Law Review, 43*(2), 307–311.

Enderlein, H., Letta, E. et al. (2016). *Repair and prepare: Growth and the Euro after Brexit*. Gütersloh: Bertelsmann Stiftung, Jacques Delors Institut. www.institutdelors.eu/wp-content/uploads/2018/01/repair-and-prepare-growth-and-the-euro-after-brexit.pdf?pdf=ok.

European Commission. (1997). *Actieplan voor de interne market*. eur-lex.europa.eu/legal-content/NL/TXT/HTML/?uri=LEGISSUM:l70002&from=NL.

European Commission. (2006). *Global Europe competing in the world. A Contribution to the* EU*'s growth and jobs strategy*. trade.ec.europa.eu/doclib/docs/2006/october/tradoc_130376.pdf.

European Commission. (2010). *Trade, growth and world affairs. Trade policy as a core component of the* EU*'s 2020 strategy*. trade.ec.europa.eu/doclib/docs/2010/november/tradoc_146955.pdf.

European Commission. (2016). *Het sociaal acquis, swd* (2016)50 draft.

European Commission. (2017a). *Discussienota over de sociale dimensie van Europa*. ec.europa.eu/commission/sites/beta-political/files/reflection-paper-social-dimension-europe_nl.pdf.

European Commission. (2017b). *Informatieblad ceta—een nieuwe maatstaf voor de wereldhandel*. europa.eu/rapid/press-release_MEMO-17-271_nl.htm.

European Commission. (2017c). Persbericht. *Staat van de Unie 2017*—Commissie presenteert volgende stappen naar krachtiger, doeltreffender en eerlijker migratie- en asielbeleid van de EU Brussels. europa.eu/rapid/press-release_IP-17-3406_nl.htm.

European Commission. (2017d). *State of the Union 2017*. ec.europa.eu/commission/sites/beta-political/files/state-union-2017-brochure_en.pdf.

European Commission. (2017e). *Witboek over de toekomst van Europa. Beschouwingen en scenario's voor de eu-27 tegen 2025*. ec.europa.eu/commission/sites/beta-political/files/witboek_over_de_toekomst_van_europa_nl.pdf.

European Commission. (2018). *Negotiations and agreements*. ec.europa.eu/trade/policy/countries-and-regions/negotiations-and-agreements/.

European Council. (2016). *eu-Turkey statement, 18 March 2016*. www.consilium.europa.eu/en/press/press-releases/2016/03/18/eu-turkey-statement/#.

European Council. (2017). *Leaders' Agenda: Migration: way forward on the external and internal dimension*. www.consilium.europa.eu//media/32083/en_leaders-agenda-note-on-migration_.pdf.

ESB-Redactie. (2017). Keuzes voor Europa: Eenwording, samenwerking of ontvlechting. *ESB Dossier* 4754S/102.

Fabbrini, F., Hirsch Ballin, E., & Somsen, H. (Eds.). (2015). *What form of government for the European Union and for the Eurozone?*. Oxford: Hart Publishing.

Fabbrini, S. (2015). Alternative views of the European Union: Which institutional architecture for a political union? In S. Piattoni (Ed.), *The European Union: Democratic principles and institutional architectures in times of crisis* (pp. 184–200). Oxford: Oxford University Press.

Fabbrini, F. (2016). *Economic governance in Europe: Comparative paradoxes and constitutional challenges*. Oxford: Oxford University Press.

Farcy, J., O'Neill, E., & Watt, D. (2016). *Desperately searching for solidarity: The* EU *asylum saga continues*. eumigrationlawblog.eu/desperately-searching-for-solidarity-the-eu-asylum-saga-continues/.

Fijnaut, C. (2017). De 'voorwaartse bewaking' van de zuidelijke EU-buitengrenzen. In M. Sie Dhian Ho, R. Cuperus, A. Pilon (Eds.), *Over de grens: De vluchtelingencrisis als reality test.* Amsterdam: Van Gennep.

Fioretos, O. (2011). *Creative reconstructions: Multilateralism and European varieties of capitalism after 1950*. Ithaca, London: Cornell University Press.

Geddes, A., & Scholten, P. (2016). *The politics of migration and immigration in Europe*. London: Sage.

Garben, S. (2017). The Constitutional (Im)balance between 'the market' and 'the social' in the European Union. *European Constitutional Law Review, 13*(1), 23–61.

Geiger, M. (2016). Policy outsourcing and remote management: The present and future of border and migration policies. In R. Zaiotti (Ed.), *Externalizing migration management: Europe, North America and the spread of 'remore control' practices*. New York: Routledge.

Gerbrandy, A. (2016). Toekomstbestendig mededingingsrecht. *Markt & Mededinging, 3,* 102–112.

Gerbrandy, A. (2017). Regeerakkoord vergeet EU bij voorstellen mededingingsrecht. NRC, 20 oktober. www.nrc.nl/nieuws/2017/10/20/regeerakkoord-vergeet-eu-bij-voorstellen-over-mededingingsrecht-a1578024.

Goodwin-Gill, G., & McAdam, J. (2007). *The refugee in international law*. Oxford: Oxford University Press.

Goodwin-Gill, G. (2015). Regulating "irregular" migration: International obligations and international responsibilities. Keynote Address to the International Workshop. National and Kapodistrian University of Athens Faculty of Law.

Grauwe, P. de (2003). *Economics of monetary union*. Oxford: Oxford University Press.

Grauwe, P. de & Costa Storti, C. (2005). Is monetary policy in the Eurozone less effective than in the us? *CESIFO Working Paper* 1606.

Grimm, D. (2016). *Europa ja—aber welches? Zur Verfassung der europäischen Demokratie*. München: C.H. Beck.

Gronden, J. W. van de, & Mortelmans, K. J. M. (Eds.). (2001). *Mededinging en niet-economische belangen*. Deventer: Kluwer.

Guérot, U. (2017). *Warum Europa eine Republik werden muss!: Eine politische Utopie*. Bonn: Die Deutsche Nationalbibliothek.

Guild, E. et al. (2016). *An analysis of the working of the Schengen area in the wake of recent developments*. www.ceps.eu/publications/analysis-schengen-area-wake-recent-developments.

Haas, E. B. (1958). The challenge of regionalism. *International Organization, 12*(4), 440–458.

Haas, H. de (2016). Refugees: A small and relatively stable proportion of world migration. https://heindehaas.blogspot.com/2016/08/refugees-small-and-relatively-stable.html.

Haas, H. de, Natter, K., & Vezzoli, S. (2016). Growing restrictiveness or changing selection? The nature and evolution of migration policies. *International Migration Review* 1–44.

Habermas, J. (2011). *Zur Verfassung Europas: Ein Essay*. Berlin: Suhrkamp.

Habermas, J. (2015). *The lure of technocracy*. Cambridge: Polity Press.

Hei, L. van de, Rabobank. (2017). *De EU en de Nederlandse transportsector: winnaars en verliezers*. https://economie.rabobank.com/publicaties/2017/maart/de-eu-en-de-nederlandse-transportsector-winnaars-en-verliezers/.

Heijer, M. den, Rijpma, J., & Spijkerboer, T. (2016). Dwang, verbod en grootse verwachtingen: Over het falende Europese asielbeleid. *Nederlands Juristenblad, 24,* 1672–1682.

Hoeven, R. van den (2016). *Dani Rodrik: We moeten de globalisering redden. De Groene Amsterdammer* 23 November. www.groene.nl/artikel/we-moeten-de-globalisering-redden.

Hoffmann, I. (2016). *Majority of the EU citizens wants a fair distribution of refugees.* www.bertelsmann-stiftung.de/en/topics/aktuelle-meldungen/2016/februar/majority-of-the-eu-citizens-wants-a-fair-distribution-of-refugees/.

Idriz, N. (2017). The EU-Turkey statement or the 'refugee deal': The extra-legal deal of extraordinary times? In D. Siegel, V. Nagy (Eds.), *The migration crisis? Criminalization, security and survival* (Eleven Publishing); T.M.C. Asser Institute for International & European Law Research Paper no. 2017-06. SSRN: 3080881.

Janssen, R. (2012). *De Euro: Twintig jaar na het Verdrag van Maastricht.* Amsterdam: De Bezige Bij.

Jabko, N. (1999). In the name of the market: How the European Commission paved the way for monetary union. *Journal of European Public Policy, 6*(3), 475–495.

Jennissen, R. P. W. (2007). Causality chains in the international migration systems approach. *Population Research and Policy Review, 26*(4), 411–436.

Jennissen, R. P. W. (2015). Asielzoekers in Europa: de geopolitieke context. *Justitiële verkenningen: Vluchtelingen in Europa, 41*(3), 9–29.

Joas, H. (2001). *The genesis of values.* Chicago: University of Chicago Press.

Joas, H. (2008). *Cultural values of Europe.* Liverpool: Liverpool University Press.

Joas, H. (2013). *The sacredness of the person: A new genealogy of human rights.* Washington: Georgetown University.

Joerges, C., & Rodl, F. (2009). Informal politics, formalised law and the 'social deficit' of European integration: Reflections after the judgments of the ECJ in Viking and Laval. *European Law Journal, 15*(1), 1–19.

Jones, E. (2012). *Efficient markets won't prevent the next crisis.* www.eurointelligence.com.

Jones, E. (2018). Towards a theory of disintegration. *Journal of European Public Policy, 25*(3), 440–451.

Kapteyn, P., & VerLoren van Themaat, P. (2003). *Het recht van de Europese Unie en van de Europese Gemeenschappen.* Deventer: Kluwer.

Kaunert, C., & Léonard, S. (2012). The development of the EU asylum policy: Venue-shopping in perspective. *Journal of European Public Policy, 19*(9), 1396–1413.

Klamert, M. (2015). Services liberalization in the EU and the WTO: Concepts, standards and regulatory approaches. *Yearbook of European Law, 34*(1), 361–365.

Krajewski, M. (2008). Of modes and sectors—External relations, internal debates and the special case of (trade in) services. In M. Cremona (Ed.), *Developments in EU external relations law.* Oxford: Oxford University Press.

Krajewski, M. (2012). The reform of the common commercial policy. In A. Biondi, P. Eeckhout, & S. Ripley (Eds.), *European Union law after the treaty of Lisbon.* Oxford: Oxford University Press.

Larik, J. (2011). Much more than trade: The common commercial policy in a global context. In M. Evans & P. Koutrakos (Eds.), *Beyond established legal orders. Policy interconnections between the EU and the rest of the world.* Oxford: Hart Publishing.

Leonard, M. (2017). Brave new Europe. *The New York review of books* (pp. 46–48) 9 November.

Lindseth, P. L. (2010). *Power and legitimacy: Reconciling Europe and the nation state.* Oxford: Oxford University Press.

Lindseth, P. (2014). Equilibrium, Demoi-cracy, and delegation in the crisis of European integration. *German Law Journal, 15*(4), 529–567.

Lindstrom, N. (2010). Service liberalization in the Enlarged EU: A race tot he bottom or the emergence of transnational political conflict. *Journal of Common Market Studies, 48,* 1307–1327.

Majone, G. (1993). Deregulation or re-regulation? Policy-making in the European community since the single act. *EUI Working Papers in political and social sciences* 93(2).

Majone, G. (2014). *Rethinking the Union of Europe post-crisis: Has integration gone too far?*. Cambridge: Cambridge University Press.

March, J., & Olson, J. (1995). *Democratic governance*. New York: The Free Press.

Martinico, G. (2012). *The tangled complexity of the EU constitutional process. The frustrating knot of Europe*. London: Routledge.

Mazower, M. (2013). *Governing the world. The history of an idea*. London: Penguin Books.

Mestmäcker, E.-J. (Ed.). (2006). *Wirtschaft und Verfassung in der Europäischen Union: Beiträge zu Recht, Theorie und Politik der europäischen Integration*. Baden-Baden: Nomos.

Metten, A., van Riel, B., Loren, Ver, & van Themaat, P. (2000). *De keuzes van Maastricht*. Assen: Van Gorcum.

Middelaar, L. van (2016). Een vluchteling is geen kabeljauw. *De Groene Amsterdammer* (28 September) www.groene.nl/artikel/een-vluchteling-is-geen-kabeljauw.

Middelaar, L. van (2016). The return of politics: The European Union after the crises in the Eurozone and Ukraine. *Journal of Common Market Studies, 54*(3), 495–507.

Middelaar, L. van (2017). *De nieuwe politiek van Europa*. Groningen: Historische Uitgeverij.

Milward, A. S., Brennan, G., & Romero, F. (1994). *The European rescue of the nation-state*. London: Routledge.

Ministerie van Buitenlandse Zaken, Expertisecentrum Europees Recht (n.d.) *Economisch en monetair beleid*. www.minbuza.nl/ecer/verdrag-lissabon/repertorium-verdrag-van-lissabon/beleidsvelden/economisch-en-monetair-beleid.html.

Ministerie van Buitenlandse Zaken. (2015). *Vluchtelingencrisis vereist new deal met Afrika*. www.rijksoverheid.nl/actueel/nieuws/2015/11/07/vluchtelingencrisis-vereist-new-deal-met-afrika.

Ministerie van Buitenlandse Zaken. (2016). *BNC-fiche Wijziging detacheringsrichtlijn*. www.rijksoverheid.nl/documenten/richtlijnen/2016/04/04/voorstel-herziening-detacheringsrichtlijn.

Moerel, E. (2014). *Big data protection: How to make the draft EU regulation on data protection future proof*. Tilburg: Universiteit van Tilburg.

Moravcsik, A. (1998). *The choice for Europe: Social purpose and state power from Messina to Maastricht*. New York: Cornell University Press.

Mortelmans, K. J. M. (1985). *Ordenend en sturend beleid en economisch publiekrecht*. Deventer: Kluwer.

Mortelmans, K. (1998). The common market, the internal market and the single market, what's in a market? *Common Market Law Review, 35,* 101–136.

Mundell, R. A. (1961). A theory of optimal currency areas. *The American Economic Review, 51* (4), 657–665.

National Board of Trade. (2012). *The internal market in a global context*. www.kommers.se/Documents/dokumentarkiv/publikationer/2012/rapporter/report-internal-market-in-a-global-context.pdf.

National Board of Trade. (2015). *Economic effects of the* EU *single market. Review of the empirical literature*. www.kommers.se/Documents/dokumentarkiv/publikationer/2015/Publ-economic-effects-of-the-european-single-market.pdf.

National Board of Trade. (2015). *Single market, four freedoms, sixteen facts—Economic effects in the* EU. www.kommers.se/Documents/dokumentarkiv/publikationer/2015/Publ-single-market-4-freedoms-16-facts.pdf.

Newdick, C. (2006). Citizenship, free movement and health care: cementing individual rights by corroding social solidarity. *Common Market Law Review, 43,* 1645–1668.

Net, J. van der (2017). *Aan de Europese natie*. Utrecht: Klement.

Nicolaïdis, K. (2003). Our European demoï-racy: Is this constitution a third way for Europe? In K. Nicolaidis, S. Weatherill, (Eds.), *Whose Europe? National models and the constitution of the European Union*. European Studies at Oxford Series. Oxford University Press.

Nicolaïdis, K. (2004). We the peoples of Europe. *Foreign Affairs*, 1 November. www.foreignaffairs.com/articles/europe/2004-11-01/we-peoples-europe.

Nicolaïdis, K. (2012). The idea of European demoicracy. In J. Dickson & P. Eleftheriadis (Eds.), *Philosophical foundations of* EU *Law* (pp. 247–274). Oxford: Oxford University Press.

Nicolaïdis, K. (2013). European demoicracy and its crisis. *Journal of Common Market Studies, 51* (2), 315–369.

Nicolaïdis, K. (2015). Demoicratic theory and Europe's institutional architecture in times of crisis. In S. Piattoni (Ed.), *The European Union: Democratic principles and institutional architectures in times of crisis* (pp. 137–173). Oxford: Oxford University Press.

Nic Shuibhne, N. (2013). *The coherence of EU free movement law*. Oxford: Oxford University Press.

Niemann, A. (2006). *Explaining decisions in the European Union*. Cambridge: Cambridge University Press.

Nugent, N. (2006). *The government and politics of the European Union*. Basingstoke: Palgrave Macmillan.

Olson, M. (1965). *The logic of collective action. Public goods and theory of groups*. Cambridge: Harvard University Press.

Osborne, G. (2015). *Speech to Germany's* BDI *on trade*. Berlin. www.ft.com/content/3d629e00-821c-11e5-a01c-8650859a4767.

Ostrom, E. (2009). A general framework for analyzing sustainability of social-ecological systems. *Science, 325*(5939), 419–422.

Ostrom, E. (2010). Beyond markets and states: Polycentric governance of complex economic systems. *American Economic Review, 100*(3), 641–672.

Oltmer, J. (2016). *Globale migration. Geschichte und Gegenwart*. München: C.H. Beck.

Palm, A. (2017) The Italy-Libya memorandum of understanding: The baseline of a policy approach aimed at closing all doors to Europe? EU *Immigration and Asylum Law and Policy*. http://eumigrationlawblog.eu/the-italy-libya-memorandum-of-understanding-the-baseline-of-a-policy-approach-aimed-at-closing-all-doors-to-europe/.

Pennings, F., & Manunza, E. R. (2015). The room for social policy conditions in public procurement law. In T. Brink, M. van den, M. Luchtman, M. Scholten (Eds.), *Sovereignty in the shared legal order of the* EU. *Core values of Regulation and Enforcement* (pp. 163–195). Cambridge: Intersentia.

Piattoni, S. (2010). *The theory of multi-level governance. Conceptual, empirical and normative challenges*. Oxford: Oxford University Press.

Piattoni, S. (Ed.). (2015). *The European Union. Democratic principles and institutional architectures in times of crisis*. Oxford: Oxford University Press.

Pierson, P. (1996). The path to European integration: A historical institutionalist analysis. *Comparative Political Studies, 29*(2), 123–163.

Piris, J.-C. (2010). *The Lisbon treaty: A legal and political analysis*. Cambridge: Cambridge University Press.

Piris, J.-C. (2012). *The future of Europe: Towards a two-speed EU?*. Cambridge: Cambridge University Press.

Prechal, S. (2006). *Juridisch cement voor de Europese Unie*. Amsterdam: Europa Law Publishing (inaugural lecture Utrecht University).

Prechal, A., & de Vries, S. A. (2009). Seamless web of judicial protection in the internal market? *European Law Review, 34,* 5–24.

Prechal, S., de Vries, S., & van Doorn, F. (2012). The implementation of the services directive in the Netherlands. In U. Stelkens, W. Weiss, & M. Mirschberger (Eds.), *The implementation of the EU services directive: Transposition, problems and strategies* (pp. 435–474). The Hague: T.M.C. Asser Press.

President of the European Council. (2012). Towards a Genuine economic and monetary union. EUCO 120/12. www.consilium.europa.eu/media/21570/131201.pdf.

President of the European Council. (2013). Britain in Europe: Channelling change together. *Annual Conference of Policy Network* EUCO 56/13.

Prins, C., & Moerel, L. (2017). Discussie over gegevensbescherming en de 'homo digitalis': Repliek. *Nederlands Tijdschrift voor de Mensenrechten, 42*(2), 169–173.

van State, R. (2013). *Voorlichting inzake de verankering van de democratische controle bij de hervormingen in het economische bestuur in Europa ter bestrijding van de economische en financiële crisis*. The Hague: Raad van State.

Raad van State. (2017a). *De staat van de euro*. Voorlichting van de afdeling advisering van de Raad van State.

Raad van State. (2017b). *Burgerinitiatief 'Peuro'.* Voorlichting van de afdeling advisering van de Raad van State, Kamerstuk 34 387 Nr. 6.

Rood, J. (2016). Meer, minder, anders: de toekomst van de EU-27. *Internationale Spectator* 3. https://spectator.clingendael.org/pub/2016/3/de_toekomst_van_de_eu27/.

Ross, M. G., & Borgmann-Prebil, Y. (Eds.). (2010). *Promoting solidarity in the European Union*. Oxford: Oxford University Press.

Rossi, E. (2017). Superseding Dublin: The European asylum system as anon-cooperative game. *International Review of Law and Economics, 51,* 50–59.

Ruggie, J. (1982). International regimes, transactions, and change: Embedded liberalism in the postwar economic order. *International Organization, 36*(2), 379–415.

Ruhrmann, H., & FitzGerald, D. (2016). 'The Externalization of Europe's Borders in the Refugee Crisis, 2015–2016. CCIS *Working Paper* 194. https://ccis.ucsd.edu/_files/wp194.pdf.

Sahlins, M. (1972). The original affluent society: A short essay. In C. Delaney (Ed.), *Investigating culture: An experiential introduction to anthropology* (pp. 110–133). Oxford: Blackwell. (2004).

Sandbu, M. (2015). *Europe's Orphan: The future of the Euro and the politics of debt*. Princeton: Princeton University Press.

Sandholtz, W., & Stone Sweet, A. (1998). *European integration and supranational governance*. Oxford: Oxford University Press.

Sassen, S. (2014). *Expulsions—Brutality and complexity in the global economy*. Cambridge ma / London: The Belknap Press of Harvard University Press.

Scharpf, F. (1997). *Games real actors play: Actor-centered. Institutionalism in Policy Research.* Westview Press.

Schäuble, W., & Lamers, K. (1994). Überlegungen zur europäischen Politik. CDU/CSU 1 September.

Schmidt, V. A. (2016). *The New EU Governance: New Intergovernmentalism, New Supranationalism, and New Parliamentarism, Instituto Affari Internazionali Working Papers* 16, 11. www.iai.it/sites/default/files/iaiwp1611.pdf.

SCP. (2017). *De sociale staat van Nederland.* The Hague: SCP.

Segers, M. (2019). Eclipsing Atlantis: Trans-Atlantic multilateralism in trade and monetary affairs as a pre-history to the genesis of social market Europe (1942–1950). *Journal of Common Market Studies*, January 2019, Special Issue.

Segers, M. (2012). Preparing Europe for the Unforeseen, 1958–63. De Gaulle, Monnet, and European integration beyond the cold war: From co-operation to discord in the matter of the future of the EEC. *The International History Review, 34*(2), 347–370.

Segers, M., & van Esch, F. (2007). Behind the veil of budgetary discipline: The political logic of budgetary rules in EMU and the SGP. *Journal of Common Market Studies, 45*(5), 1089–1109.

Social and Economic Council of the Netherlands (SER). (1992). *Advies Sociale dimensie Europa*. SER Advies 90/11.

Spaak, P. (1956). *Rapport des chefs de delegation aux Ministres des Affaires etrangeres = Report of the heads of delegation to the ministers of foreign affairs.*

Stjerno, S. (2011). The idea of solidarity in Europe. *European Journal of Social Law, 3,* 156–176.

Streeck, W. (2015). *Gekochte tijd: De uitgestelde crisis van het democratisch kapitalisme.* Amsterdam: Leesmagazijn.

Sternberg, C. (2013). *The Struggle for* EU *Legitimacy. Public Contestation 1950–2005.* Houndmills: Palgrave.

Streeck, W. (2015). *Why the Euro divides Europe*. https://newleftreview.org/II/95/wolfgang-streeck-why-the-euro-divides-europe.

Tauner, S. (2016). Asylum policy: the EU's 'crises' and the looming policy regime failure. *Journal of European Integration, 38,* 311–325.

Supiot, A. (2010). A legal perspective on the economic crisis of 2008. *International Labor Review, 149*(2), 151–162.

Thielemann, E., & Armstrong, C. (2013). Understanding European asylum cooperation under the Schengen/Dublin system: A public goods framework. *European Security, 22,* 148–164.

Tietmeyer, H. (1994). The relationship between economic, monetary and political integration. In A. F. P. Bakker, H. Boot, O. Sleijpen, & W. Vanthoor (Eds.), *Monetary stability through international co-operation*. Amsterdam: Kluwer.

Tuytschaever, F. (1999). *Differentiation in European Union law*. Oxford: Hart Publishing.

Tweede Kamer der Staten Generaal, *Burgerinitiatief Peuro: Voorlichting van de Afdeling Advisering van de Raad van State*, kamerstuk 34387/6.

Verhoef, B. A. (2003). On the (a)symmetry of shocks in EMU. *DNB Staff Reports* 106.

VerLoren van Themaat, P. (1982). Het economisch grondslagenrecht van de Europese Gemeenschappen. In Liber Amicorum (Ed.), *Mertens de Wilmars, J*. Antwerp: Kluwer.

Vooren, B. van, & Wessel, R. A. (2014). *EU external relations law: Texts, cases and materials*. Cambridge: Cambridge University Press.

Vries, S. A. de (2006). De relatie tussen de Europese interne markt en de bescherming van consumenten: tijd voor ontspanning? *Tijdschrift voor Consumentenrecht en Handelspraktijken, 6,* 183–192.

Vries, S. A. de (2016). *Grondrechten binnen de Europese interne markt: Een tragikomisch conflict tussen waarden in de 'Domus Europaea'*. Paris: Zutphen.

Weatherill, S. (2013). From economic rights to fundamental rights. In S. Vries, U. de, Bernitz, S. Weatherill (Eds.), *The protection of fundamental rights in the EU after Lisbon*. Oxford: Hart Publishing.

Weatherill, S. (2017). The several internal markets. *Forthcoming, yearbook of European Law, Oxford Legal Studies Research Paper* 64/2017. poseidon01.ssrn.com/delivery.php?ID=860065085009089102089100096002100730580160390230440671090860031110720100780070930250250310370300050380451210270030921010230021140230700690041131271210310730261250380870301070250851030010831180670730691020280951180830311050731220910680700200740810 65&EXT=pdf.

Regeringsbeleid, W. R. voor (2007). *Europa in Nederland*. Amsterdam: Amsterdam University Press.

Regeringsbeleid, W. R. voor (2010). *Aan het buitenland gehecht*. Amsterdam: Amsterdam University Press.

Witte, B. de (2012). The competence to pursue non-market aims by means of internal market legislation. In P. Syrpis (Ed.), *The judiciary, the legislature and the EU internal market*. Cambridge: Cambridge University Press.

de Witte, B. de, Ott, A., & Vos, E. (Eds.). (2017). *Between flexibility and disintegration: The trajectory of differentiation in EU law*. Cheltenham: Edward Elgar.

Witte, B. de (2018). An undivided Union? Differentiated integration in post-Brexit times. *Common Market Law Review, 55,* 227–250.

Wyplosz, C. (2017). *In-depth Analysis. A European monetary fund?* European Parliament, May 2017.

Zaiotti, R. (2011). *Cultures of border control. Schengen and the evolution of European frontiers*. Chicago: University of Chicago Press.

Zielonka, J. (2014). *Is the EU doomed?*. Cambrigde: Polity Press.

Zielonka, J. (2012). Disintegration theory: International implications of Europe's crisis. *Georgetown Journal of International Affairs, 13*(1), 51–59.

Legal Sources

Treaties

United Nations Convention relating to the Status of Refugees.

Convention for the Protection of Human Rights and Fundamental Freedoms (European Convention on Human Rights).

Treaty on the Functioning of the European Union.

Charter of Fundamental Rights of the European Union.

Treaty on European Union.

Jurisprudence

ECJ 6 September 2017, c-643/15 and C-647/15, ECLI:EU:C:2017:631 (Slovak Republic and Hungary v Council of the European Union).

ECJ 2 December 2015, C-643/15, ECLI:EU:C:2016:038/55 (Slovak Republic v Council of the European Union).

ECJ 3 December 2015, C-647/15, ECLI:EU:C:2016:038/56 (Hungary v Council of the European Union).

ECJ 22 January 2013, C-283-11, ECLI:EU:C:2013:28 (Sky Österreich GmbH v Österreichischer Rundfunk).

ECJ 6 September 2012, C-544-10, Ecli:EU:C:2012:526 (Deutsches Weintor v Land Rheinland-Pfalz).

ECJ 27 February 2012, C-131/12, ECLI:EU:C:2014:317 (Google v Spain).

ECJ 18 October 2011, C-34/10, ECLI:EU:C:2011:669 (Brüstle).

ECJ 8 March 2011, C-34/09, ECLI:EU:C:2011:124 (Ruiz Zambrano).

ECJ 15 July 2010, C-271/08, ECLI:EU:C:2007:809, recitals 186-188 (European Commission v Germany).

ECJ 18 December 2007, C-341/05, ECLI:EU:C:2007:809 (Laval).

ECJ 11 December 2007, C-438/05, ECLI:EU:C:2007:772 (Viking Line).

ECJ 7 June 2007, C-225/05, ECLI:EU:C:2007:318 (B.J. van Middendorp, then Dutch Minister of Agriculture, Nature and Food Quality).

ECJ 18 July 2006, C-519/04 P, ECLI:EU:C:2006:492 (Meca-Medina and Majcen v Commission of the European Communities).

ECJ 15 March 2005, C-209/03, ECLI:EU:C:2005:169, paragraph 60 (Bidar).

ECJ 10 March 2005, C-336/03, ECLI:EU:C:2005:150 (Easycar).

ECJ 12 June 2003, C-112/00, ECLI:EU:C:2003:333 (Schmidberger).

ECJ 19 February 2002, C-309/99, ECLI:EU:C:2002:98 (Wouters et al. v General Council of the Bar of the Netherlands).

ECJ 5 October 2000, C-376/98, ECLI:EU:C:2000:544 (Tobacco advertising).

ECJ 12 September 2000, C-180/98 to C-184/98, ECLI:EU:C:2000:428 (Pavlov).

ECJ 21 September 1999, C-115/97 to C-117/97, ECLI:EU:C:1999:434 (Brentjens).

ECJ 12 May 1998, C-85/96, ECLI:EU:C:1998:217 (Martinez Sala).

ECJ 28 April 1998, C-158/96, ECLI:EU:C:1998:171 (Kohll).

ECJ 23 April 1998, C-120/95, ECLI:EU:C:1998:167 (Decker).

ECJ 17 June 1997, C-70/95, ECLI:EU:C:1997:301, paragraph 29 (Sodemare).

ECJ 5 May 1992, C-15/18, ECLI:EU:C:1982:135 (Gaston Schul v Inspector of Import and Excise Duties).

ECJ 8 April 1976, C-43/75, ECLI:EU:C:1976:56, paragraph 10 (Defrenne II).

ECJ 11 November 1975, Opinion 1/75, ECLI:EU:C:1975:145, ECR 01355 Part B (2).

ECJ 5 February 1963, C-26/62, ECLI:EU:C:1963:1 (Van Gend en Loos v Netherlands Inland Revenue Administration).

Legal acts

Resolution 48/121 of the General Assembly of the United Nations (12 July 1993), The Vienna Declaration and Programme of Action, un Doc a/conf.157/23.

Regulation (EU) 2016/1625.

Directive (EU) 2016/0151 (COD).

Regulation (EU) 604/2013.

Regulation (EU) 473/2013.

Regulation (EU) 472/2013.

Regulation (EU) 2016/679 (general data protection regulation).

Regulation com/2012/011 (no longer in force).

Regulation (EU) COM/2010/0526 (no longer in force).

Regulation (EU) COM/2005/0155 (no longer in force).

Directive 2011/85/EU.

Regulation (EU) 1176/2011.

Regulation (EU) 1174/2011.

Regulation (EU) 1173/2011.

Regulation (EU) 492/2011.

Directive 2010/13/EU.

Directive 2008/115/EC.

Directive 2006/123/EC.

Regulation (EU) 883/2004.

Directive 2004/18/EC.

Regulation (EC) 343/2003.

Directive com/2016/0128.

Directive 96/71/EC, Article 3.

Directive 96/71/EC, Article 9.

Directive 96/71/EC, Article 88.

Directive 80/987/EEC

Directive 77/187/EEC.

Directive 75/117/EEC.

Other European Union documents

European Commission. (2017). *Establishing a European Pillar of Social Rights*. Available at eur-lex.europa.eu/legal-content/EN/TXT/PDF/?uri=CELEX:52017DC0250&from=EN(COM (2017)250).

European Commission, Staff Working Document, SWD. (2016) 51 draft, 8.3.2016 (COM(2016) 127/51).

European Commission. (1991). Proposal for a Council Directive concerning the posting of workers in the framework of the provision of services (oj 1991, C 225/05).

Memorandum of the Commission on the Action Programme of the Community for the Second Stage (OJ 1962, COM(62) 300).

www.ingramcontent.com/pod-product-compliance
Lightning Source LLC
LaVergne TN
LVHW082334200926
848481LV00012B/3341
9781013274893